The Study Abroad Handbook

Palgrave Study Guides

Authoring a PhD
Career Skills
e-Learning Skills
Effective Communication for
   Arts and Humanities Students
Effective Communication for
   Science and Technology
The Exam Skills Handbook
The Foundations of Research
The Good Supervisor
How to Manage your Arts, Humanities and
   Social Science Degree
How to Manage your Distance and
   Open Learning Course
How to Manage your Postgraduate Course
How to Manage your Science and
   Technology Degree
How to Study Foreign Languages
How to Write Better Essays
IT Skills for Successful Study
Making Sense of Statistics
The Mature Student's Guide to Writing (2nd edn)
The Palgrave Student Planner
The Postgraduate Research Handbook
Presentation Skills for Students

The Principles of Writing in Psychology
Professional Writing
Research Using IT
Skills for Success
The Student Life Handbook
The Student's Guide to Writing (2nd edn)
The Study Abroad Handbook
The Study Skills Handbook (2nd edn)
Study Skills for Speakers of English as
   a Second Language
Studying the Built Environment
Studying Economics
Studying History (2nd edn)
Studying Law
Studying Mathematics and its Applications
Studying Modern Drama (2nd edn)
Studying Physics
Studying Programming
Studying Psychology (2nd edn)
Teaching Study Skills and Supporting Learning
Work Placements – a Survival Guide for Students
Write it Right
Writing for Engineers (3rd edn)

Palgrave Study Guides: Literature
General Editors: John Peck and Martin Coyle

How to Begin Studying English Literature
   (3rd edn)
How to Study a Jane Austen Novel (2nd edn)
How to Study a Charles Dickens Novel
How to Study Chaucer (2nd edn)
How to Study an E. M. Forster Novel
How to Study James Joyce
How to Study Linguistics (2nd edn)

How to Study Modern Poetry
How to Study a Novel (2nd edn)
How to Study a Poet
How to Study a Renaissance Play
How to Study Romantic Poetry (2nd edn)
How to Study a Shakespeare Play (2nd edn)
How to Study Television
Practical Criticism

The Study Abroad Handbook

Anna Lidstone
and
Caroline Rueckert

First published 2007 by
PALGRAVE MACMILLAN
Houndmills, Basingstoke, Hampshire RG21 6XS and
175 Fifth Avenue, New York, N.Y. 10010
Companies and representatives throughout the world

PALGRAVE MACMILLAN is the global academic imprint of the Palgrave Macmillan division of St. Martin's Press, LLC and of Palgrave Macmillan Ltd. Macmillan® is a registered trademark in the United States, United Kingdom and other countries. Palgrave is a registered trademark in the European Union and other countries.

ISBN-13: 978–0–230–00761–1
ISBN-10: 0–230–00761–9

This book is printed on paper suitable for recycling and made from fully managed and sustained forest sources. Logging, pulping and manufacturing processes are expected to conform to the environmental regulations of the country of origin.

A catalogue record for this book is available from the British Library.

A catalog record for this book is available from the Library of Congress.

10   9   8   7   6   5   4   3   2   1
16   15   14   13   12   11   10   09   08   07

Printed and bound in China

Contents

Acknowledgements

We believe that nobody embarks on long, difficult trips without the help of a support team. This book is no exception. We have been incredibly fortunate to have had a strong team at the beginning, and to have added so many wonderful people to it as we went along. Especially we would like to thank the following:

Suzannah Burywood, our publisher. We could not have asked for a more supportive visionary. Each step of our journey was made manageable through her guidance.

Our publishing team, especially Karen Griffiths and Barbara Collinge, and the others who have given their skills and energy to this project. Also, Valery Rose and Jocelyn Stockley, whose focus on the detail was much appreciated. It has been great to have you all onboard.

Our international reviewers, whose feedback was invaluable. We hope we have done justice to your comments.

Tammy Kwan, of the University of Hong Kong, and Mary Ward, of the University of Queensland, for being early advocates of the project. Also Nora Chiang and Ivy Tan for their ideas and suggestions.

The hundreds of students worldwide who responded to our call and were willing to share their stories with us. We have been inspired by your experiences and awed by your courage. Also, the many student advisors and counsellors whose work has helped us on our way.

Beverley Slopen, of the Beverley Slopen Literary Agency. You are everything we could want in an agent.

Our own advisors, mentors, and supervisors in various universities who have supported our intellectual pursuits, wherever they have taken us. You know who you are. Our gratitude continues to flow across international borders unabated.

And, finally, to our inner circle of family and friends, who we carry with us everywhere. You make all things possible and all things better. If home is where the heart is, we will never be far from it.

Introduction

This book has been written in countries across the world. It has been written, quite literally, in a noodle bar in downtown Toronto (Canada); in a small library in Byron Bay, the most easterly point in Australia; in hotel rooms in Helsinki (Finland), Louisville (Kentucky, USA) and Spokane (Washington, USA); in a train station in Stuttgart (Germany), a coffee shop in Auckland (New Zealand) and an apartment overlooking the Pacific Ocean in Vancouver (Canada), as well as in several of those hard, uncomfortable seats you find in international airports when you have several hours to wait for your next connection. Our publisher is in England; we have never met her, which is slightly ironic since we have both lived – at different times – in the UK. The students we quote in this book come from all over the world, and collectively have studied on every continent.

All of this is entirely appropriate for a book on studying abroad in a century and a world in which increasing numbers of students are leaving behind the familiarity of their home universities for a few weeks, months or years in a university in another country. We have come a long way from the nineteenth-century tradition of British upper-class men going to Europe to study the classics, and women attending Swiss finishing schools. Now, the phenomenon of 'studying abroad' is one which is prevalent throughout universities worldwide, and is an accessible option for men and women from a wide diversity of backgrounds. Options for studying abroad are available in every discipline and field of study, both academic and professional or vocational.

When we were undergraduates, at the University of Queensland in Australia (Anna) and the University of Victoria in Canada (Caroline), we found it hard to access useful guidance on how to go about studying abroad. As very independent (some would say stubborn) individuals, we were unsatisfied with resources which told us simply what to do – we wanted to make our own decisions, based on our own needs. This book is, in part, a response to what we would have liked to have had available to us when we were making the kinds of decisions that perhaps you are making at the moment. You will find a strong focus here on thinking through the process, from the very first idea of studying abroad, to living abroad, to coming home again, and everything in between. Much of the discussion is focused on helping you to work out what is important to you and giving you potential things to watch out for. Since we were undergraduates, though, many things have changed. With the internet, your problem might not be too little information, but rather, too much. You could spend your entire student career online researching all your options, and never actually get on a plane to go abroad. This book will help you to focus your attention. We have offered suggestions for the kinds of questions you might need to ask, and where you might find the answers, as you need them. Much of our discussion is relevant to both undergraduate and post-graduate students; where further discussion is needed, you will find special sections for post-graduates. At the end of some chapters and sections, you will find lists of additional resources that correspond to that chapter. They are there to guide you in areas you would like to explore further; it is not our intention to inundate you with further reading. Choose one or two titles or websites that seem useful to you, and ignore the rest.

Our first chapter, 'Starting Out', will discuss why you might want to study abroad, and the potential benefits you can gain from doing so. We will help you to establish the basic building blocks that you will need to get you started on planning your studying abroad.

Chapter 2, 'Defining your Priorities', will guide you through the process of working out what you want to achieve from your study abroad, and the kinds of programmes that might best suit you. You will have ample opportunity to think through your own reactions to potential options. Chapter 3, 'Researching your Options', will help you to find out about programmes to match your needs, and how to utilize the resources you have available to you.

Chapter 4 deals with the all-important question that almost inevitably comes up for students studying abroad, throughout the process – money. 'Managing your Finances' will give you options for financing your study abroad, including applying for scholarships and bursaries, as well as make suggestions for how you can manage your money from another country.

By the time you have read to the end of Chapter 4, you will probably have made some decisions about which programmes might work for you. Chapter 5, 'The Application Process', will talk you through the various steps you might need to go through to apply to the programmes you have chosen, including how to write statements of intent or admissions essays and how to approach potential referees for support.

Once you have been admitted into a programme, there is a lot you can do before you leave to prepare yourself for what awaits you in your new country. Chapter 6, 'Preparing for Departure', talks you through the myriad practical and emotional aspects of moving to another country for a period of time, including what you need to consider in terms of immigration, academic preparation, research and packing your bags.

All of this leads up to the reason you are doing all this preparation – Chapter 7, 'Living Abroad'. From advice on what to do in your first few days to negotiating culture shock and building community, we will give you a sense of what to expect and how to deal with the potential challenges you might face, as well as how to make the most of every opportunity that comes your way. In order to do this, you will need to stay mentally, emotionally and physically healthy – Chapter 8, 'Staying Healthy', will give you some guidance on how to do this in an unfamiliar environment.

There will come a day when your programme is coming to an end and you start to think about returning home again. Chapter 9, 'A Changing Relationship to Home', will talk you through how to accommodate the growth and change you have experienced while abroad when you return home, some suggestions for negotiating reverse culture shock, and how to integrate your 'new home' into your daily life.

Chapter 10, 'Additional Challenges', discusses other potential issues that might affect your experience studying abroad, including issues of race, religion, class and LGBT (lesbian, gay, bisexual and transgendered) identities, as well as some guidance for women travelling abroad and those travelling with families. We suggest that you read this chapter even if you don't see its immediate relevance to your situation – they may be issues you find yourself having to negotiate in your new country, or you may make friends with other students who are negotiating them.

As you go through the book, you will come across 'tips', which offer you some suggestions to make your life easier; 'heads up', which give you warnings about potential difficulties and hazards you might face; and anecdotes, both from our own experiences, and from students studying as international students around the world. As you read the anecdotes, bear in mind that these reflect personal experiences and are frequently 'context specific' – your own experiences might be very different. We suggest that you initially read through the book in its entirety to give you a sense of where you are heading, before you go back and read each section. You will find a lot of detail. How you use it is up to you. Some of you will find strength in reading each detail and working through the process meticulously. Others will read for the broad brush strokes and see what jumps out at you, perhaps coming back to the detail as you need it. Try to stay true to how you best make decisions and the kind of information you need to feel confident. If you find yourself getting overwhelmed, focus on whatever stage of the process you are in at any given time, and allow the other stages to unfold when you are ready for them. The goal is that you get as much as possible from your experience of studying abroad – do whatever you need to do to achieve that goal.

For us, and for the students we have talked to, studying abroad has been an amazing experience. We have come across so many students who have described it as 'life-changing' regardless of the kinds of personal challenges they faced. It is our hope that you, too, can join the many students each year from around the world who bravely step forward, hug their loved ones goodbye, muster up their courage and sense of humour and embark on the remarkable journey which is studying abroad. Bon voyage!

ANNA LIDSTONE AND CAROLINE RUECKERT
Vancouver, Canada

1 Starting Out

Like most things in life that are worth doing, studying abroad is challenging. We will warn you from the outset that it will require a lot of work, both before you leave, while you are abroad and when you get home again. It can be stressful, exhausting, overwhelming and very, very challenging. But you will also find yourself doing things you could never imagine doing, and pushing beyond what you thought were your limits. You will find emotional and psychological resources you didn't know you had, and find reserves of stamina, endurance and determination beyond anything you could predict.

Throughout our own years of study in various countries, in our travelling, and in the course of preparing this book, we have talked to hundreds of students who have studied in a diversity of programmes across every continent. Consistently, students have told us that studying abroad was the best thing they have ever done, whether because of its challenges or despite them.

Taking the question 'Why study abroad?' as its starting point, this chapter will guide you through what you will need before you embark on the journey that is studying abroad, helping you to put into place the components that will allow you to plan confidently and make your study experience abroad the best it can be.

Why study abroad?

Some of the answers we have heard to this question are:

> To learn about another culture
> To build self-esteem and confidence
> For the adventure
> For the chance to travel
> To learn and practise a language
> To have fun
> For the career opportunities
> To study something new

1

For the cheaper tuition

For contact with experts and specialists in my field

My partner was working abroad and I wanted to take advantage of being there

I wanted my children to learn about the world

To build global citizenship and an international perspective

To learn about my family history

I needed a change of scenery

For the independence

It was the scariest option and I wanted to push myself

To make new friends

I was tired of my home town

All my friends had studied abroad and I wanted to as well

For the experience

For the job training

To learn about the roots of my religion

I wanted to challenge myself

There were more opportunities abroad than at home

I studied abroad to experience a different lifestyle, and to see more on the other side of the world. There is a Chinese saying 'to walk thousands of roads is better than to study thousands of books'. I completely agree with that. Knowledge and humanity can be gained through experiences. I also wanted a year to think about the past, and to plan my future.

Carol, an undergraduate from Hong Kong

Some enjoyed the experience immensely and couldn't wait to do it again. Others had more challenging experiences, but said they would still do it again because they learnt so much from it. Over and over, we have heard that students' study experiences abroad have been life changing and have opened up possibilities for them that they could never have predicted.

A personal journey – Why do you want to study abroad?

One of the most important factors of studying abroad is how personal the experience is. While there are consistent themes in what students gain from their time abroad, it is striking how unique and individualized each experience is. Your study abroad will be unique to you. You will make unique decisions, create unique opportunities for yourself and experience your programme differently from anyone else. Throughout this book, you will be encouraged to consider what options work for you, and how you can achieve your goals.

Even the idea of studying abroad means different things to different people. When you see the term you might immediately think of an intensive two-week summer language course in France. Or a year off from your under- graduate degree to travel. Perhaps an invigorating and exciting academic atmosphere to explore a subject not currently available to you. Some people might see 'abroad' as being the other side of the world, while for others it might just mean crossing a single border. For some, going abroad requires still being able to speak their own language. For others, 'abroad' suggests the chance to master a new one. Take a moment to consider what assump- tions and expectations you bring to the idea of studying abroad.

What does studying abroad mean to you?

It might be helpful if you write down your answers. Your priorities will prob- ably shift when you start the research process and you might forget your initial responses. If you write them down, you can come back to them later and see what has changed and what has remained consistent.

What immediately comes to mind?

Be honest. What do you visualize? Do you see yourself in an academic robe among the pillars of Oxford or Harvard? Leaving class to go down to the beach to surf? Donning a backpack on weekends to explore the Great Lakes or the Rocky Mountains? Coffees in pavement cafes in Europe? Going on archeological digs to the Egyptian pyramids? Sketching the Great Wall of China? Mastering a new language? The possibilities are infinite. Only you know what really comes to mind when you contemplate this idea.

What do you hope to get out of the experience?

Think abstractly. We'll come back to the specifics. What is it you really want to achieve? Are your immediate hopes focused on the place? On academic priorities? On personal aspirations?

What have you been taught about studying abroad?

Have you been taught by your family that either (a) you must study abroad (What do YOU think?) or (b) that would be a terrible thing to do? What are the cultural assumptions about studying abroad where you live and in your social community? Is it assumed that you will go abroad? Have you been told that this will help you to be popular/respected/liked/employable? (This may or may not be true, but it's important that you are aware that this is a factor for you.) Have you been taught which countries or which courses you SHOULD be pursuing? (Remember that those opinions are going to seem a very long way away when you are in the middle of a programme in another country.) Have you been taught by your family or community that some things are not options for you, because of your background, talents or personality? What factors are restricting your sense of the possibilities available to you? Do you agree with them?

Whose idea was it?

It's OK if someone else put the idea in your head. But if you do it for someone else, to fulfil someone else's dream, you might not be very happy with the outcomes. At some point, it will need to become *your* idea.

Your assumptions and expectations will come up over and over again as you go through the process of refining the possibilities. These are an important part of who you are. Being aware of what assumptions you are making will help you to leave yourself open to as many different options as possible. You will also have to continually reassess your expectations as you proceed.

Advantages of studying abroad

So, you probably now have some sense of what you want to achieve by studying abroad, but there might be potential benefits and advantages that you haven't really thought about. Let's look at some of them in a bit more detail.

Educational opportunities

Studying abroad can offer substantial benefits in terms of connecting what you learn in the classroom with what you can learn in wider contexts in specific disciplines. For example, if you are passionate about ancient history, imagine studying in Greece or Rome, surrounded by ancient architecture, primary sources in their original languages, and the chance to understand the geographical and historical context of what you are studying.

> *I think sharing your views on the world with other people from different backgrounds truly has the power to make you a better person…going traveling is a pause, a way to put your life on "hold" for a while and think about what you are really seeking in life. There is something great about getting thrown in an environment that you don't know and getting to know everything from scratch.*
>
> Danielle, an undergraduate studying in Montreal

Even if your interests are not so easily matched with a geographic region, studying a subject in another country can give you insight into different ways of approaching your subject, different methodologies for solving problems that arise in that subject, and an increased awareness of the kinds of knowledge that is valued in other countries.

If you work in a highly specialized academic area, especially as a postgraduate, studying abroad might give you access to experts in your field who may not be available to you in your own country or to educational opportunities that you do not have in your home country. For example, medical students may have the opportunity to treat diseases that don't even exist in their own countries.

If the programmes in your home country don't meet your needs, you will often be able to find a better fit elsewhere. You may find that programmes abroad are much better suited to your particular needs and talents because they have different values and criteria. For example, if you perform exceptionally well on exams, you might choose a programme where this is a valued skill. If you prefer to work on your own at home, you might avoid an examination-intensive programme. Once you start thinking it through, you will find all sorts of options for meeting your needs.

Language skills

If you are living in a country for an extended period of time and are immersed in a different language, you will probably learn the language more easily and more completely than if you study it from your home country. In addition, you will gain a better understanding of the social and cultural context of the language. For many students, developing a second (or third or fourth) language is one of the primary attractions of studying abroad.

Personal opportunities

Possibly one of the most advantageous aspects of studying abroad is the personal growth you will almost inevitably experience. No matter how well organized you are, there will come a time when you have to rely on your instinct and your own resources, and you will probably be surprised at what you are capable of when you are pushed. Students who have studied abroad – even just for a short time – often report that they feel more confident about their own abilities. You can expect to have your assumptions about the world challenged and to develop a new perspective on issues that you may not have considered before. You will develop new levels of independence and will be pushed to see the world in new ways.

It will open so many doors, you will make contacts from all over the world and it will really expand your mind and help (sometimes force) you to grow up and be responsible – all whilst having a great time.

Dominic, an undergraduate

Social possibilities

Studying abroad is a wonderful opportunity to meet people and make friends from all over the world. You will have to find ways of adapting to a new environment and making friends when you are outside of your comfort zone.

Even if you don't have to cope with language differences when you study abroad, you will have to negotiate cultural differences. You will have to deal with the possibility of miscommunications, and learn to communicate with people from different cultural, religious and economic backgrounds. You will have to find ways to have your needs met, and adapt to a different educational system. All of these challenges will develop your social skills.

 Studying abroad is one of the best experiences in life someone can have. It opens up your personal horizon and supplies you with a permanent stream of new impressions.

Walter, a German student who has studied abroad in countries across Europe

Career advantages

Studying abroad will often give you an edge in the employment market. There are a number of reasons for this. First, you will have had to negotiate the personal challenges of studying abroad. You are likely to have a stronger sense of your own identity and values, of who you are and what you have to offer. You may also have more confidence and maturity. Employees who are willing to take risks and push themselves personally are likely to have much to offer their workplace. In addition, the confidence in yourself you are likely to develop may help you to sell yourself to potential employers, as you will probably have a stronger sense of your own strengths and weaknesses.

Secondly, as immigration becomes more and more prevalent across the world, the workplace is becoming more culturally diverse. If you have had experience abroad, you are likely to have had to learn to negotiate cultural difference, including religious and linguistic diversity, and be familiar with how cultural assumptions affect how people interact with one another. These skills, and the openness to diversity that developing these skills represents, are often highly valued.

Finally, as economics becomes more globalized, many organizations and companies are increasingly operating within international economic markets. An understanding of how countries relate to each other economically and politically can be an invaluable asset to an employer.

International perspective

Understanding how your home country and your destination country fit into the international scene can be very enlightening. You will gain insight into your new country, seeing the way another culture approaches everyday life and its challenges. In addition, seeing your home country through the eyes of the people of your new country will give you new perceptions on such aspects of your own culture as its politics, economics, art and religion.

I think that experiencing life abroad is a really effective way to broaden your horizons and perspectives. Although travelling around the world, visiting places for days or weeks at a time is an enriching experience in and of itself, I think that when you live for more than six months in a place, you really get to experience what it's like to live there, and be a part of the culture. I would recommend the experience to anyone who is open to new opportunities.

Adrienne, in Belfast to study Irish Studies

Immigration

If you are thinking about emigrating to another country at some point in your life, studying in another country can give you a way of exploring your options and working out what is important to you. While most students who study abroad return home afterwards, it is not unusual for students to choose to stay, or to return later to live in their new country.

Reconnecting with family and ancestral roots

Although you might choose to go abroad in order to experience a *new* culture, it is also common for students to study abroad to reconnect with their family roots. If you are an immigrant, or if your family comes from a different culture from the one you have grown up in, studying abroad can be a great way to get to know the culture that influenced your parents or grandparents. You may already have the language, for example, but not really understand the culture first hand. Or you may not have had the chance to learn the language and would like the opportunity to learn more about your family roots. Sometimes, you may even have the chance to live with extended members of your family in your new country, and thus not only learn about your family origins but also get to know your extended family, while you study.

Travel

Most students studying abroad take the opportunity to do some travelling. As well as being lots of fun, travel can be very educational and give you the opportunity to learn more about your new country and the regional variations within it. It will also give you the chance to get to know other countries in the region.

Financial advantages

There can be financial advantages to studying abroad. If you live in a country where tuition fees are very expensive, for example, or where the cost of living is high, it may actually be cheaper to study abroad. If your home currency is strong against another currency, you can take advantage of this. You might have friends or family in a particular country who could help you to cut costs on accommodation. In addition, you might be able to access scholarship money that would otherwise be unavailable to you – some funding is specifically for studying abroad, and you might find that another country has more funding for post-secondary education than your home country.

I loved the incredible opportunity to live within a culture and observe it as both outsider and insider. I lived in Kenya and London for six months each. I lived with tribes in the north, herding cattle, drinking blood, climbing mountains, camping on the mouth of the Ngorongoro crater, coming face to face with a lion who had just made its kills. I had to go to the toilet in the bush, guarded by an eight-year-old Samburu boy whose mother I lived with, who carried a spear and waited for me to finish my business. In England I saw 33 plays in three months.

David, who spent twelve months studying
in several countries

Myths about studying abroad

You have already had the chance to examine some of your assumptions and expectations about studying abroad. Here are some other beliefs about study abroad which you may have come across, and which might affect your perception of what possibilities are open to you.

Only very wealthy students can afford to study abroad

Many students from less wealthy families find ways to study abroad. There are frequently scholarships and bursaries available, as well as viable student loan systems. You might be able to work while abroad, or save up before you go. See 'Managing your Finances' for more detail about your options.

Only high-achieving students study abroad

There are programmes for everyone, even if your grades are not stellar. Also, you might find that your academic 'success' increases in a system that emphasizes different values and qualities.

Only academically inclined students study abroad

There is a wide diversity of programmes you might consider to suit your talents, including artistic programmes, professional programmes, and vocational/training programmes for specific jobs. In addition, increasingly you can study abroad in almost any discipline. If you want to study abroad, chances are high that you will find a programme that is well-suited to your interests and background.

Study abroad is really just an excuse for a holiday

Some programmes will be harder work than others, but if you think that studying abroad is for tourists, you will probably be in for a shock. Many students work very hard while abroad. Studying in a new country is quite different from visiting for a short time as a tourist.

Studying abroad is only for students in certain disciplines, such as arts and humanities

There are options for students in almost all disciplines, including professional courses such as law, medicine, business or technology.

Studying abroad is only for young people/single people/undergraduates

Study abroad is becoming more and more diverse. Many older students and students with partners and families are finding options that work for them.

There are also many opportunities for post-graduate study, which often appeal to mature students or professionals.

Studying abroad is only for white/anglo students

Traditionally, there have been inequities in study opportunities abroad for marginalized ethnic and racial groups. This situation is rapidly changing, with more and more students from marginalized communities taking advantage of opportunities to study abroad.

Studying abroad is not for students who have a disability

Whether your disability is visible or non-visible, you have numerous options. In fact, many students with disabilities report that having a disability can be good preparation for the challenges of studying abroad!

Studying abroad is not for students who are LGBT

You may have unique challenges if you identity as gay, lesbian, bisexual or transgendered. But there are many ways of negotiating LGBT issues in your study abroad planning, either alone or with a partner and/or children.

Studying abroad will delay graduation

It might. But there are many programmes for which you might be able to get full credit and graduate in the same time frame as if you had stayed at home. If your graduation *is* delayed, you may find that what you learn abroad is worth the extra time.

Study abroad will be much easier academically than studying in my home country

It may be. It may not be. Some things may be easier and others harder. Don't make assumptions. It is likely to be different, that is all.

> *Go somewhere you wouldn't go anyway. Try to go somewhere far from home, so you can really feel the difference.*
>
> Sandor, a Danish student who studied in Australia

● Initial priorities

You will have the chance in the next chapter to think through in detail what your priorities are in choosing a programme of study abroad, but there are probably several things that spring to mind for you initially. This will help to get you started.

Time frame

You probably have ideas about what sort of time frame you are looking at. Are you thinking of taking six months to do an exchange programme while in your third year of an undergraduate course? Are you just finishing high school and looking to study a whole degree abroad? Are you planning a one-year master's, or a five-year (or longer) PhD? Or were you thinking more of a few weeks in the middle of your university holidays? This will obviously affect what kinds of programmes you look for.

When do you want to commence your programme?

The more you plan this in advance, the more options will be available to you. Ask yourself if this is something you want to do next summer, or after you graduate. In your third year, or after taking time off to work? Your answers will affect your options.

How long do you want to be away for?

Don't get too bogged down in detail at this stage; go with your gut instinct. If two weeks feels way too short for what you were thinking, a year might be just right. If you were thinking of a six-month exchange but the idea of doing your whole degree abroad is stirring up excitement in your belly, then you might want to think about looking into both options. This is just a guide at this stage. Let yourself dream.

Financial need

We will help you with this later, we promise. For now, you just need a general sense of what you are going to need to make this happen. If you have recently been given an inheritance or won the lottery and know that you don't have to worry about money at all, then you can proceed without concern. If, like most people, you have limits on your financial resources, being aware of them can make the process easier. Consider:

Are the options that you're currently considering already financially possible for you, or will you need help?

It is quite possible that you have been saving money for years, and know that six months abroad is well within your means. If it isn't, simply acknowledge to yourself that you will need some help.

What do you need in terms of funding/financial support?

Possible answers to this may include: 'the only way this is possible is if I get a full scholarship, and someone to pay my airfare' or 'I think that if I do some extra shifts at work, I can save up the airfare and some spending money, but I'll need help with tuition', or maybe you're fairly sure that you could get a small loan, but some financial assistance would really be useful. This exercise is just to get you thinking about where you are in the process. We will talk about money in much more detail later.

Career goals and aspirations

Studying abroad is likely to be beneficial to your future career, whatever you decide to do. Some careers, though, will require you to study abroad. We will come back to this in more detail; for now, consider the following.

What are your career aspirations? How does studying abroad fit in with these?

If studying abroad is an important part of your career, this will affect your later decisions and you will need to acknowledge that the career potential arising from your study abroad is a priority for you.

Are you doing this simply because you want to put it on your CV?

Studying abroad can be a terrific addition to your *curriculum vita*, but it takes a lot of energy, as well as time and money. Consider whether you have the motivation and willingness to make this investment. If you make a choice that 'looks good' on your CV but doesn't excite you, you may not be able to make the most of the opportunity. Try to choose an option that you will feel proud of.

> **Heads up**
>
> Sometimes studying abroad has very little to do with your career goals. If that is the case, choose a program that excites you. Do courses that interest you and make you feel alive. Being abroad might be exactly what you need to help you work it out. When you get home again, you may have to do further study to help you get where you want to. Or you may not. Either way, you've had fun and learnt a lot about yourself in the meantime.

Planning

This book will guide you through the many details you will need to consider in planning your study abroad. But we will say from the outset,

GIVE YOURSELF PLENTY OF TIME TO PLAN

It may take 12–18 months from first thinking of the idea to actually studying abroad, especially if you are going for longer than a few weeks. Your university may need at least 12 months' notice that you plan to study abroad as part of your degree requirements, and there will be many decisions you will need to make along the way. If you give yourself sufficient planning time, you are more likely to have an experience which fits what you want and need. In light of this, we suggest that you (a) don't try to rush the process, and (b) start talking to people about it as early as you can.

Creating a support team

From professional car racing to mountain bike riding to trekking in the Himalayas, nobody embarks on long, difficult trips without the help of a support team, and you shouldn't either. The earlier you get other people involved in your decision-making, the better. There are a number of reasons for this.

First, the people who love you will want to be involved in your life. This affects them too. Whether you are going for a few weeks or a few years, they are going to miss you and worry about you. They will want to be involved and feel part of the process.

Secondly, you need support. We'll talk more later about the potential obstacles to going abroad. Whether it's someone to show glossy brochures to, or to cry on when your top choice falls through, you need the people you love to be there for you.

Thirdly, other people know things. If you try to do all the work yourself, even with the help of this book, there will be things you don't think of. Other people have information, opinions, contacts and knowledge. They are invaluable to your research process.

There are many different stages of planning to study abroad. Include your team at each stage. It will be much easier for people to help you if they know what you are thinking.

In a cosmopolitical world, studying abroad should be mandatory for everybody. It is an opportunity to see how other countries structure their educational sector. On a personal level, it is a chance to meet culturally different people and encounter new ways of looking at life. And hopefully these will act as mirrors which will open one's eyes to one's own culture, one's own uniqueness: the lines which keep us apart, culturally, but also, more important, the lines which connect us.

Scott, studying English literature in Scotland

Kinds of support

There are a number of different kinds of support you will need. Take advantage of the different kinds of support offered to you, to help you to negotiate the academic, practical and emotional aspects of your planning.

Talk to your teachers, advisors, career resource centres and peers

These are invaluable sources of information. They will often know what options might be available to you in your area, and may have contacts in other countries. They may also have other students who have done what you are planning to do, who can give you some great advice and encouragement. Later in the process, you may also need references and letters of support, so getting your teachers on side at the beginning, and allowing them to be part of the process, will benefit both of you. If you don't really have teachers who seem supportive, pick a few that you like and admire, and get to know them a bit better. Tell them what you're doing and see who seems encouraging (teachers are often very happy to be allowed to be useful). Advisors include anyone who is currently involved in your academic or career planning.

Talk to your friends

They may have 'heard' about good programmes and may have other friends or family members who have studied abroad. They also know you and what you like to do so they can get excited with you. They might be planning their own trips, too, so you can plan together.

Make contact with other people who can support you

You could also take this opportunity to make contact with some other people who can help you to achieve your goals. Look around in your local area or on the internet. There might be groups of people who are also thinking about studying abroad or just travelling who will understand some of your excitement. Contact your career resource centre, or the international student centre at your university or college or in your local area – there may be information sessions you can attend where you might meet some new people.

We'll talk you through some of the details of support teams later. For now, you just need to start mentioning your ideas to a few people close to you, so that you're ready for the next stage.

Negotiating resistance from family and friends

The more time family and friends have to get used to the idea, the more supportive they are likely to be. However, it is not unusual for family and friends to be resistant to the idea at first. In these cases, it's worth making a little bit of effort to try to work out why they might have their reservations. If you tell your closest friend that you're leaving for a year, she might be caught between wanting to wish you well but really wishing you weren't going. Parents' reactions are also frequently mixed. Parents often worry about their children's safety (and we mean 'children' in the broadest possible sense). They may be worried about feeling obliged to help you financially when they might not have the money. They might be worried about your degree and your grades. They might also hate the idea of being without you for any length of time. If you have particular responsibilities within your family, such as working in the family business or looking after children or elderly family members, consider what impact your absence may have on the family and see if you can find viable solutions. Try to be patient and let them know what it means to you to go abroad.

• • •

You've thought about some of your big-picture goals, you've given yourself plenty of time to plan and you have started to assemble your support team. The next chapter will help you to think about some of the details as you go about defining your priorities.

2   Defining your Priorities

You may already have a clear sense of where you want to go and what you want to do. You may even have a particular programme already in mind. Or perhaps you have nothing more than a vague sense of what's important to you when you study abroad. Either way, take some time to think about what your priorities are. There are many different factors that will make up your experience abroad, and many more options than you can probably imagine. Remember that whatever decision you end up making is one that you actually have to live with, for a few weeks or a few years. This chapter will help to guide you through some of the decisions you may need to make in the planning stages. Working out what your priorities are will help you to do focused research and, ultimately, to create the best opportunities for yourself. We have offered some advantages and disadvantages of various options; you will probably find that you have your own considerations to add to these.

In brief

How you go about making decisions will depend on what is most important to you. For example, consider the following scenarios:

Top Priority: You want to learn or practise a language (and you have a particular language in mind).

Influencing Factors:
- Which countries speak this language?
- Which region would you prefer to live in?
- Which programs will give you the best chance of learning the language and/or help you to get a language credential?

Top Priority: You want to study with specialists in your field.

Influencing factors:
- Where is this work being done?
- Which universities and programmes have the best reputation in your field?

17

● Which programmes have specific faculty who you would like to
work with?

As you can see, your starting point will affect how you go about choosing
appropriate options. In the first example, your choice of country is likely to
be an important consideration. In the second example, where you go might
be much less significant to your goal of studying your specialist field. How
you go about narrowing your options will depend on what you identify as
your priorities.

In depth

The following section will help you to define your priorities more specifically. Depending on how you like to make decisions, you might go through
each question in detail, or you may just read through the options and
consider what jumps out at you. The categories are listed in no particular
order; how you negotiate them will depend on your own priorities. Each
section highlights some of the issues you might consider and then a chart
gives you the chance to identify where your priorities currently lie. Your
final decision(s) will usually be made up of a balance of a variety of different
factors.

> **TIP**   If you are not sure of the answers to the questions, talk to your support
> team, take time to think about it, or go on instinct. Often, if you leave
> some answers blank, they will answer themselves as a result of your other
> decisions. Try to think of this activity holistically – individual questions may
> not be as important as the big picture that emerges.

● Academic priorities

Consider how important the academic aspects of your study abroad are to
you. Think about such questions as:

How academically challenged do you want to be?
Some programmes of study abroad are designed to be easier academically so
you can focus on learning about the culture, travel and social activities.

Do you want to be at a highly ranked prestigious academic institution?
How important is the 'name' to you? Highly prestigious universities may
have a competitive academic environment. This can be a great motivator,
but a lot of students prefer an environment which is a little less intense,
where they get the kind of support they need. Bear in mind that a top-

ranking research university does not necessarily have top-ranking student support systems.

Do you need to be able to get very high grades while abroad?

What will you need in order to be successful academically? Consider the language of instruction, as this might make a difference to whether you are academically successful. Are you willing to make sacrifices (travel, free time, socializing) in order to achieve these goals?

Is it important to work with highly regarded specialists in your field?

This will affect your options as to which universities are a potential choice for you. Bear in mind that universities with well-known specialists often have high costs as well. You may find that these programmes are also competitive, both when you apply and while you are there.

How specialized or general do you want your programme to be?

This will be affected by how far you are into your degree. If you are planning to complete an entire degree abroad, how do you want this to fit into your wider plans? What will it be important for you to have studied when you get back home? It may be important to find a programme which is compatible with the kind of programme you might have done at home. If you plan to go on to do post-graduate work, you might have to develop highly specialized knowledge.

Before going: Spend your energy choosing the right academic programme. That is going to be the core of your experience. But at the same time, don't be too proud to change your classes while abroad, if something turns out to be dramatically different from your expectations.

Kolina, studying in Vancouver

Are you planning to be a part-time or a full-time student?

Full-time can be a lot of work. Are you expecting to hold down a full-time job, look after children, do extensive travelling, or work on other projects as well as studying? Be clear about what you want to do. Also, be aware that if you do less than a full-time load, you might not be eligible for some kinds of funding, student visas, access to resources and many other considerations. It is usual for international students to be full-time.

TIP If the reason you want to study part-time is because of a disability, health concern or family responsibility (looking after children, or an elderly or sick member of your family), there may be ways around the usual regulations. You may be able to do a reduced course load but still maintain full-time status. Bear this in mind if you have particular circumstances which might warrant a lower course load.

	Yes	No	Not sure
Are academic aspects of your study abroad a priority for you?			
Do you want to work with specialists in your field?			
Do you need a highly specialized programme?			
Is the prestige of the university important to you?			
Is it important to excel academically while abroad?			
Do you do your best work in a highly competitive environment?			
Do you expect to be a full-time student?			

Academic priorities for post-graduate students

Do you want to do a coursework programme or a thesis or a combination?

Some universities offer master's degrees which are done entirely by course-work. In others, a master's is a research degree and fulfilled by a thesis. Sometimes you can do a combination. PhDs might be thesis only or a combination (and take different lengths of time). Doing one rather than the other might limit your future opportunities. For example, if you want to do a PhD in a country which values research, it might be a limitation to have done a coursework master's. Students from cultures where PhDs routinely include coursework might not be competitive on the job market if they have done a thesis only.

What components do you want in your programme?

Do you want to sit specialist exams, fulfil a language requirement, do course-work, write a thesis, have the opportunity to undertake a practical compo-nent, do field work? Programs vary enormously in terms of what they are made up of.

Do you plan to do further post-graduate work, or even just keep your options open?

Some universities offer 'terminal master's' programmes, which can't be used for entrance into a PhD programme or equivalent. Some professional degrees cannot be used to open doors for future study. If you are sure that you don't want to go on, these can be very good, but can be limiting if you don't know what you are getting yourself into. You will need to find out what credentials you will need in order to go on, if this is an important considera-tion for you.

What kind of supervision do you expect and need, to perform well?

Some universities offer intense supervision where your supervisor will have only a few students and have a lot of time for you. Others are much more 'hands-off'. Some place considerable emphasis on preparing you for the job market, while others do not. There is often no correlation between the pres-tige of a university and the amount of attention you can expect.

What library and other resources will you need to have access to?

There is no point in choosing a university with an excellent reputation in some fields if it doesn't have the basic resources you will need to complete your research.

Undergraduate credit and enrolment options

One of the aspects you will need to consider is whether you want your study abroad to fit in with a programme in your home country and whether you want your study abroad to count towards programme requirements in your home university. Many students study abroad while an undergraduate in their home university, while others study abroad between high school and university, after their undergraduate programme, or while on study leave from their job. There are a variety of possibilities.

Full credit

If you want to get full credit for all the courses you do abroad, you will need to make sure that your university approves your programme. It will often be specified what kinds of courses you must do, how many you must do and what grades you must achieve. You will have to get prior authorization from your university for any credits you do abroad.

Advantages	Disadvantages
You can usually still complete your programme in the original time frame, without having to take extra credits when you return home.	Your options will be limited to universities and programmes which are compatible with your home university, and to courses authorized by your home university.
You will have some structure and guidelines to help you make your academic choices.	You will have pressure to take on a full course load abroad, which might limit travel, social opportunities and work opportunities.
You may be able to take financial assistance that you receive from your home university with you to your new university, as well as being eligible to apply for other sources of funding.	Your grades from abroad will affect your transcript at home – remember that you won't be able to predict your performance, not only because you will be learning within a different academic system, but also because you will be dealing with the added stress of being in an unfamiliar environment.
You will not need to pay extra tuition fees because the length of your programme will be the same as at home.	

Partial credit

Often, you will be able to get partial credit for your work abroad. This means that you get credit for some of your courses but not all of them or only partial credit for each course instead of the full weight. Often, you will be able to have the courses count towards your program requirements, but may not be able to have the exact grades count towards your Grade Point Average (GPA).

Advantages	Disadvantages
You can try new things, and take courses that are different from what you would do at home.	You will probably take longer to complete your programme than if you stayed at home, and will have to do extra courses once you return.
You will still make progress towards your home degree.	It may end up costing you more, because you will have to pay for the extra courses you will need to complete your programme.
You will still have some structure and some guidelines to guide you.	You may still be limited in your options because they will need to be approved by your university.
You may be able to take financial assistance with you.	
You can probably afford to have your grades drop (as they sometimes will when you study abroad) without your home GPA being overly affected.	

I didn't have to worry about my grades as much as at my home uni. So I could dig into the subject I liked the most, and pay less attention to the ones I liked less. Another thing was the fact that I got to experience a new way of teaching. Wanting to be a teacher, it was great for me to see how other countries educate their youth.

Gregory, in Glasgow on the Erasmus programme

No credit

There are opportunities for study abroad where you get no credit for a home programme. If you are already a student, you might be able to take a leave of absence to take advantage of these opportunities.

Advantages	Disadvantages
You can take advantage of diverse possibilities that give you very different experiences from your home programme and try things that are completely different from anything you might do at home.	You don't make the same kind of progress towards a home programme, and so may graduate later than others of your age/level.
You can learn an entirely new set of skills.	You may not be able to access some kinds of financial assistance.
You have a lot of control over what you do because you are not bound by the standards and policies of your home university.	You will not have guidelines and structures to guide you in your decision-making, or the same kind of help to achieve your goals.
You will probably have less pressure to achieve certain grades.	You will probably not be regarded as enrolled in your home university while abroad, which may affect your status as a student (for the purposes of taxation, debt repayments and so on) and may prevent you from accessing your home university resources.
You don't have to worry about getting approval from your home university or finding compatible courses and programmes.	

Full degree

If you do a full degree as an international student, you commit to spending much longer abroad. In this scenario, you fulfill the credits required of your program in your new country.

Advantages	Disadvantages
You can truly immerse yourself in your new country for an extended period of time.	You will have to be away from family and friends for an extended period of time.
You may have access to academic opportunities you would not normally have.	You will have to adapt sufficiently to your new culture to be successful in completing a full degree.
You don't have to worry about getting approval from a home university, and finding compatible courses, so you have more options.	You may not be able to access financial resources from your home country.
You can go wherever you want, without restrictions from a home university.	You may not have the necessary prerequisites or knowledge base that are expected of students in your new country.
You will have time to get to know your new education system, and watch your improvement over an extended period of time.	You may have to negotiate legal ramifications surrounding residency and international student status which are different from those required for shorter-term programmes.
Your degree will be from your new country, rather than from a university in your home country, which can have benefits for future study or for employment.	Your degree may not be compatible with the requirements of your home country, thus affecting opportunities for future study or for employment.

Many students will wait until they are pursuing post-graduate work to do a full degree in another country, when it is more common to complete an entire programme abroad and it is often easier to access financial resources.

	Yes	No	Not sure
Do you want to earn full credit for your study abroad, at your home university?			
Can you afford (in terms of both time and money) to do some courses abroad for which you don't get credit?			
Do you need your study abroad to count towards your GPA and/or towards requirements for graduating?			
Is studying abroad what you really want (or are you really after a break from school and university to do something different, such as working abroad or travelling)?			

Whether you get credit or not may very well depend on what kind of programme structure you choose. Generally speaking, your study options abroad will probably fit into the following categories.

University-sponsored programmes

University-sponsored programmes are those where your institution has an agreement with an institution abroad. They may make some arrangements on your behalf, although the extent of these will change depending on the university. Your home university will generally have already worked out the details of what courses you can take, how long the programme should be and how much credit you will get. You will probably have access to other students who have been to the same places as you are considering, who can provide valuable information. There may be limited options, because your choice will depend on which other universities your own university has an agreement with. On the other hand, your university will do a lot of the work for you, and there will be established procedures and protocols for you to follow.

 I grew up in a big city which has mostly new buildings. When I went to Europe for two semesters, I ended up in a small town living next door to a castle. Most of the buildings were hundreds of years old. I bought my produce from the local market that

looked just like all the pictures I saw of the 'olden days'. I loved the connection to the history of the place. Of course, everyone was talking on their mobile phones, which didn't happen in the pictures.

Margaret, a third-year engineeering student in Italy

Provider

A private organization submits all application materials on your behalf and organizes most aspects of your study abroad. This may include the courses you enrol in, the kind of housing you stay in, and the travel you do at weekends or holidays. They will often do much of the organizing for you, freeing you from having to work out all the details. On the negative side, they are often expensive and may limit your options. You will generally find that several providers vie for your business, so shop around and compare them (more about that later).

Government programmes

These are programmes that are not directly organized and sponsored by your particular university, but are established programmes for students in your geographical region. You will often have some flexibility with where you go, although the countries and programmes on offer are likely to be those with which your government is trying to foster relationships.

Direct enrolment

In this form of study abroad, you enrol directly in an overseas institution, without any help from a service provider or your home university. This can take a lot of organization on your part, and will demand a high level of independence. You will generally arrange each aspect of your study abroad yourself. If you want to complete a full degree abroad, or if you are taking time off from your university, this might be the only option open to you. If you enrol directly in an overseas university, you might still be able to get some kind of credit at your home university, but will have to apply for formal approval. You may also be able to use the credit you gain to offset requirements for a future programme (often referred to as 'prior study'). There are likely to be financial implications for direct enrolment, but you will have almost limitless possibilities available to you, and more freedom with your choices in terms of places, universities and courses. You will have to be organized and highly motivated to make this work for you, but it is likely to be very rewarding as well.

TIP Researching, planning and organizing can take up a lot of time, but can also be exciting and be a great way of motivating yourself. You can also learn a lot from the planning stages, which you might miss out on if someone arranges the whole trip for you.

	Yes	No	Not sure
Do you want to be entirely independent, and make all of your decisions on your own?			
If so, do you have the time and energy to make this happen?			
Do you want some aspects of your study abroad program organized and decided for you?			
Would you like to be able to pay someone to organize the whole thing, leaving you free to just enjoy your trip?			

Many of my friends study abroad and I also felt the urge to travel. In my field of studies I find it rather important to know how the world looks from other people's point of view, and the experience of being somewhere else than normally helps, widening the perspectives. I most enjoyed the networking and the fact that there was no stress – I did not have to think about everyday worries because everything was taken care of before I arrived and I only had to enjoy my stay. I least liked the semester before leaving, since I had to use huge amounts of time on administration.

Rachel, in Rome to study theology

Duration and timing

Your choices will also be determined by how long you want to go away for. Study abroad ranges from only a few weeks to several years. You will probably want to work out your other priorities and then find programmes which work for what you need (including academic goals, language-acquisition goals, finances and so on). If, however, the length of time you can afford to be away is very specific, or you must leave at a particular time, this will obviously affect your options.

When do you want to leave?

When you are thinking about when to go and how long for, bear in mind that school years vary from place to place. For example, the academic year in North America usually starts in August or September, while in Australia, the school year generally starts in February or March. Professional or highly specialized programmes might have completely different school years.

Also, different universities use a different semester system. Some have two semesters each year, sometimes divided into four terms. Others use a three-semester system. Some universities run summer schools (don't forget that your summer may be someone else's winter). If you are trying to fit your programme into an existing degree structure, you will need to find a programme which has timing compatible with your own. If you are doing a stand-alone course, you may have to work or take time off before starting the degree.

Do you need a break before you start?

This may not be an option if you are doing a student exchange as part of your existing degree, but if you are a high school student or just finishing one degree, think seriously about some time off before you start. This can be beneficial in terms of giving you time to work out what you want, as well as to save some money.

Heads up

Before you embark on post-graduate study, seriously consider whether you need some time off. Studying at the post-graduate level is very challenging, and if you have been pushing yourself through exams and papers for years, sometimes post-graduate school can tip you over the edge. It is common for post-graduate students to burn out, whatever their background and no matter how good a student they are. See the chapter on 'Staying Healthy' for more on burn-out. For now, consider whether you might need to take some time off to get a job or have a break before you apply for post-graduate study.

How long do you want the programme to take?

Obviously, the kind of programme you do will affect how long it will take. But even the same kinds of programmes can take different lengths of time. The same undergraduate programme could take three years in some places and four or five in another. Some will include an honours year and others will be a basic degree. A one-year post-graduate course in one place might be a four-year undergraduate degree elsewhere. Specialist diplomas can be very short or very long. Some programmes require periods of time for internships or practicums, which can add extra time to a course. Others have long completion periods, but minimal residency requirements, meaning that you only have to be on campus for a short period of time (maybe a year or so) and can then finish the programme from elsewhere.

Heads up

Increasingly, universities are offering special programmes to international students where a three-year degree can be completed in two years or less. If you choose this option, don't expect to get any time off to work, travel or have a summer holiday – these programmes are very intense.

Will studying abroad make your degree longer? Will you need to do further study on your return?

You may not know the answers to these questions yet, but if you are determined to finish your degree at a particular time, you will need to find a programme that will allow that to happen.

If you are an undergraduate, are there exams you are hoping to sit after you graduate?

These might include exams for law school, medical programmes, post-graduate programmes, professional accreditations and so on. Will your time abroad interfere with preparation time for these? How will you minimize the interruption? For example, you could go abroad a year earlier or later, postpone the exams or find a way to sit your exams while abroad.

Will time abroad get in the way of applications for jobs or post-degree opportunities?

Consider how you will balance these commitments with your study abroad.

	Yes	No	Not sure
Do you already know how long you can afford to be away for?			
Do you want to be abroad for a full year?			
Do you need your programme to start and end at a particular time?			
Are there other factors which limit how long you can be away for, when you can leave and when you need to return?			
Do you need a break before you start?			

● Different kinds of universities

When you start researching your options in depth, it is worth knowing a little about the different kinds of universities you might encounter. The names for these different kinds of universities vary from country to country, but the trends are quite consistent across a diversity of countries and cultures. The following are not discrete categories – some universities might have characteristics from a variety of them, since universities are often hard to categorize. The kind of university you choose will be determined by what you want to achieve from your experience studying abroad.

Traditional universities

While the specific histories of these universities vary, these are generally universities that are older and were established as research institutions. The focus is frequently on academic skills, and faculty usually have PhDs or equivalent and are 'career academics' who may or may not have practical experience of their subject area, and will usually be engaged in research as well as teaching. The disciplines available are generally well-established areas of study, although traditional universities are increasingly broadening their offerings to 'new' areas of study. They can be competitive to get into, with the criteria for entry generally being academic. Traditional universities will almost always be PhD-granting institutions (or equivalent) teaching both undergraduates and post-graduates, and having well-established traditions.

New universities

These are universities that have emerged in the past half-century or so. Although they used to have reputations for not being as good academically, increasingly they are ranking alongside the traditional universities (although perhaps not having the same 'prestige'). They are usually PhD-granting institutions, although the faculty may not be predominantly 'career academics'; faculty are likely to have experience in industry and other areas before they work for the university. There is often a higher focus on professional and vocational skills than in traditional universities, and they will typically offer a range of subject areas which will cater to non-traditional disciplines. Entrance criteria may take into account non-academic skills as well as your academic background, and programmes may offer a range of non-traditional subject areas.

Universities of technology

These are universities which are either new universities or formerly technical institutes which have become universities. While most teach a broad range of subjects, the focus may be on areas associated with technology, including engineering and sciences. They often emphasize connections between the classroom and the wider world, and faculty will frequently have practical experience in industry and commerce. Research will often focus more on the practical rather than on the theoretical. They may or may not be PhD-granting institutions.

Online universities

Some universities have reinvented themselves in light of the increasing prevalence of the internet. They range from offering some component of online learning (which is more and more prominent in universities worldwide) through to universities which have only a limited physical presence and where students fulfil *all* requirements online. An increasingly common model is for students to complete a large proportion of their programme requirements online and then physically attend classes for an intensive summer school or equivalent. The use of online teaching methods has opened up a variety of education options to students who otherwise might not be able to attend university (including those with young children, people with disabilities or those in geographically remote locations), as well as options for students to study abroad. Online learning is often used in conjunction with correspondence universities, where students receive their course material via mail and complete requirements in their own time – these students may never meet their teachers in person.

Technical and vocational institutes

Often called colleges, these are vocation-based institutes for training in particular fields. The emphasis is usually on training for particular jobs. These days they are often highly specialized and programmes might cover anything from computer programming to specialist gardening to dental-assistant training. Courses are generally shorter than traditional academic degrees and may lead to qualifications such as a diploma or certificate, among others. They range from evening classes for part-time students to intensive, full-time programmes. Entrance criteria might be quite broad or may require specialized skills, depending on the level of training. The costs are likewise very diverse.

Art colleges/academies

These may be discrete institutions in their own right or may be part of larger universities. The courses offered range from short programmes to full degrees or higher degrees, and their focus is on the practical components of creative and artistic pursuits, although longer programmes will often include an academic component. Faculty will generally be practising artists and entrance criteria will often require some kind of portfolio or demonstration of artistic ability, sometimes in conjunction with an academic background.

Language institutes

These may be part of a larger institution or may be discrete private institutions designed specifically for international students to learn a particular language. They may include some courses in cultural education as well. Faculty might be qualified language teachers, but may not be. The quality, costs, entrance requirements and other features of these colleges vary enormously from college to college.

	Yes	No	Not sure
Are you interested in a university with a strong academic orientation?			
Are you attracted to non-traditional areas of study?			
Are you interested in vocational/professional training?			
Are you interested in intensive language/cultural training?			

Remember that the reputation of an institution is often discipline-specific. Some universities are regarded as prestigious by people outside of the field, but may not have the same respect within the disciplinary community. Other institutions are known to be highly reputable within a particular field but non-specialists may never have heard of them. Basing your decisions just on perceived prestige can be problematic – remember that you have to live with your decisions.

One of my professors mentioned some programmes to me, after I talked about my emerging interests in post-colonial studies. I ended up at one of the leading universities in the world for post-colonial studies, in a specialized programme that was a perfect match for my interests and goals. If I had applied only to universities I personally knew about, I would have ended up at a university which wasn't so well matched to my interests.

Author insight: Caroline

Language integration

If you are planning to go to another country to practise a second language, you are likely to have options about how you integrate your language learning into your academic work. The choices you make will depend on your objectives in studying abroad, your academic goals, language competence and what options are available to you. The following are some of the options you may come across.

Courses taught in your new language

In these courses, your discipline/area of study will be conducted entirely in your second language. These courses require a very high level of proficiency and you will be expected to speak, write and think in that language while working with complex, often specialized, material. You will need to understand the language and its complexities in order to survive in lectures, tutorials, discussions, written papers and examinations, and there will probably be little consideration in the grading and assessment for the fact that it is your second language.

> *Having classes in German was the greatest and best challenge (part of what I came for). It was unique as it has given me the belief that I can learn German again if I need to for work or some other reason.*
>
> Sean, in Vienna

Courses designed for international students in your new language

In some universities, you will be able to study your discipline in your second language, but courses will be designed specifically for international students, so some consideration and allowance will be made for the fact that it is your second language. You will need to be fluent in your second language and be able to understand the language at a specialized level. Occasionally, you will find programmes where you are taught in one language, but have the option of writing papers and exams in your native language.

Courses taught in your native language

If your native language is very widely used, you may be able to access opportunities to be immersed in a second language, but study university courses in your native language. This is particularly true of countries which have a colonial history, where the language of the colonizers has become integrated into the education system. For example, many universities will teach classes in English or French (especially to international students) but give you the opportunity to learn a local language as well. If you pursue this kind of programme, you may need a less advanced grasp of the local language and can focus on conversational skills, which may give you more academic freedom.

Language immersion programmes

These are programmes designed specifically for students to learn the language and culture of a given country. The teaching focus is generally not on the content of a particular discipline, but on developing and practising language skills. Whether you can get credit for these kinds of courses towards your degree will probably depend on your field of specialization.

Heads up

If you want to practise a second language, don't just think of the obvious countries. For example, you could study French in Quebec (French-speaking Canada), African countries (such as Chad), Haiti or Martinique, or New Caledonia. You could study Spanish in a country in Central or South America or Portuguese in Brazil.

	Yes	No	Not sure
Are you fluent enough in your second language to understand lectures, write papers, be successful in exams and engage in discussion?			
If you have second-language skills that would enable you to understand lectures and discussion, would you prefer to be able to do your own work in your native language?			
Would you prefer to be completely immersed in a second language?			
Would you prefer to work entirely in your native language?			
Do you mind which second language you work in?			
Do you find operating in a second language fun and exciting?			
Do you find operating in a second language exhausting and stressful?			

Credentials and qualifications

Consider how important it is to receive a particular credential or qualification. This might be academic, based on your language skills, or relevant to a particular job or profession. Some programmes are internationally recognized while others are only acknowledged locally. This may have implications for your future options. Find out what credentials and qualifications you might need for your future study goals or career plans. If this is a priority for you, you will have to make decisions that will give you the appropriate qualification.

Heads up

There is a lot of misinformation around, about what is and is not good for your future career. If studying abroad is an important part of your career goal, find out what aspect of studying abroad is valued in your field. Is it studying in a particular locale or institution? The contacts you make abroad? The language skills? Will your experience still be valued in your field if you do poorly academically? If you can, talk to people in the area, both in your home country and internationally. Find out specifically what it is that employers in your field value about studying abroad. If it is a particular credential or body of knowledge, make sure that the decisions you make will meet these needs. Remember that you can never be sure how you will perform in a study programme abroad until you do it.

	Yes	No	Not sure
Is it a priority for you to receive a credential or qualification from your study abroad (even if you don't really mind what it is)?			
Is it a priority for you to receive a *particular* credential or qualification from your study abroad?			

● **Different kinds of campuses**

The kind of campus you are on will also have a significant impact on your experience abroad, especially in terms of the amount and kind of social contact you have. You probably will not find campuses describing themselves in precisely these terms, but the broad categories will give you a sense of what to look for.

Central campus/satellite campus

Many universities will have a central campus which has most of the facilities, including social hubs. Beyond this, they will have what are sometimes called satellite campuses, which are often in the suburbs or in a more rural area and have fewer facilities and resources. These are often specialized campuses, catering to particular disciplines (medicine, for example) or for particular demographics of students. You might think you are heading for a lively, active, sociable campus only to find that you are actually at a satellite campus, which may not be what you want.

Commuter campuses

These may or may not be satellite campuses. On these campuses, there are few or no students living on campus, and the campus is in a non-centralized location. Students and faculty, therefore, have to commute to get to campus. There may or may not be good public transport – students might be expected to own cars. This scenario is likely to be more prevalent in cultural contexts where the average student lives at home with parents and goes to university locally. In these situations, if you do find yourself living on campus, you might find yourself isolated. If you enrol at a commuter campus, you will also need to make sure that you have appropriate transport. In contexts where students go away to university, you are more likely to find students living in and near campus.

I lived quite far from university which was really annoying sometimes, because I had to go home early or spend the night at another student's house. That was a bit difficult in the beginning when I didn't know people that well.

Sara, studying in London

Rural campuses and city campuses

Universities in rural areas might be the focus of an entire town or city, and so many of the resources you will need will be on campus. They have the advantage of giving you access to particular environments, such as agricultural regions or wild habitat areas. Rural campuses often have self-contained facilities, with the majority of students living on or near campus, which can create a community. You may need a car, though, to go beyond the campus and see the local area, as public transport might be limited. City campuses, on the other hand, often have resources off campus, which can offer greater variety. The wider community is often more diverse and travel might be easier. The university will generally be less of a focus, and you will have access to other resources and social networks. Transport is often convenient and cheap.

College-based universities/collegiate universities

Many universities are based on a college model, whereby each student is a member of a college which forms a micro-community within the wider university. In some cases, students live in residential colleges and these form the nucleus of the social activity on campus; in others, they also play a crucial role in the academic structures of the university, and in still others, college membership is optional and less crucial. Understanding how this system works might be very important in helping you to find good options for yourself. For example, if everyone else lives on campus in a college, you might find yourself isolated or having difficulty making friends if you live elsewhere.

Faith-based institutions

Many universities are associated with particular religious groups. Often, individual colleges will also have various religious allegiances. In some cases, this association is mostly historical and ceremonial, while in others, the religious basis plays an important role in the everyday life of the students. Consider how this may affect your comfort levels and make decisions accordingly.

Same-sex or mixed-gender institutions

Some institutions or colleges are single sex only, for example a men's college or a women's college. Some will cater to both genders but will have separate floors or wings for men and women, while others are completely mixed. Consider the kind of environment where you will feel most comfortable.

	Yes	No	Not sure
Would you like to be at a large city campus?			
Would you like to be on a rural campus?			
Is living on campus with other students a priority for you?			
Are your choices of campus likely to be limited by your discipline (for example, if you study medicine, you may have to be on a satellite campus)?			
Would you prefer a university or college with a particular faith orientation?			
Would you be willing to be in a college/ university which worships within a different religious faith from your own?			
Would you be comfortable commuting onto campus each day?			
Would you like to be in an all-male or all-female environment?			
Would you like to live in a college?			

Lifestyle priorities

It can be easy to get caught up in the academic decisions around studying abroad and forget that there are other aspects of your identity that need to be taken into account. Often, the most important things in your life are those you take for granted, and you might not even consider the possibility of being without them when you go abroad.

Location

For many students, the country they go to is a top priority. Are there particular countries you have always wanted to go to? Do you find yourself particularly drawn to certain countries and cultures? There is nothing wrong with going somewhere you have wanted to visit since you were a child. There may also be particular regions within a particular country that you are drawn to – you could start your research in these regions.

While students of many study abroad programmes spend their entire study period in one country (with perhaps a little travelling to other countries on breaks), there are also options for spending time in more than one place. These are often theme-based. For example, if you are interested in studying ancient civilizations you could join a programme where you spend time in Greece, Italy and China, or you could learn about Native cultures of Mexico, Canada and Australia. You can even go on a study abroad cruise, where you stop off at a number of different ports and receive instruction from both local instructors and resident teachers. If you can't find anyone who does the kind of programme you would like, you could try to organize it yourself.

Environment

When you think about location, consider also what kind of environment you like to be in. Would you prefer to live in a big city or in a rural area? By the sea? Are mountains important? Whatever you are used to, it is easy to assume that it will be the same wherever you go; consider what you can live without. If you love to hike in the mountains, would you consider going somewhere without mountains?

Climate/weather

Also, consider what kind of climate and weather you like/need. This is not as trivial as it sounds. If you have a sensitivity to heat, hot climates might be the last thing you want to cope with. If you are used to a lot of sun, you may find overcast and rainy climates unbearable. The long winters of Northern countries can be very difficult to handle if you are used to the short and balmy winters of parts of Australia. On the other hand, weather might be something that you don't really care about. Just make sure that this is a decision and not just something you ignore. And if you think weather might matter, make sure you take the time to try to match the place with your needs or consider how you might compensate.

I enjoyed travelling, getting to know new people, and my courses were interesting. What I enjoyed least was the weather; it was very cold for a person from the Middle East. Living alone for such a long time was also a big challenge - to be by myself in a society where I didn't speak the language. Always remember it's a trip that will end sooner or later so enjoy each single moment there regardless of any difficulties that you may face.

Amir, from Jordan, living in northern Europe

Extracurricular interests

What are your hobbies and interests outside of academia?

Again, we tend to take what we have for granted and assume that it will always be available. If you are an excellent cricketer, and get a lot of your exercise and self-esteem from being a great bowler, you might be shocked to meet people who don't know what a cricket bat is. On the other hand, if you have always wanted to learn to ski, this could be your chance to live near a snow-covered mountain.

What community resources are important to you? What sustains you and gives you support?

These might include religious or spiritual communities, ethnic or cultural groups, linguistic resources, or other kinds of communities. If you are part of a faith-group, for example, and expect that you will be able to continue to practise elements of worship when you are studying abroad, make sure that you acknowledge that to yourself now, so that you can research it later. Often, certain kinds of communities are crucial to our sense of identity and well-being, and without them we might be very unhappy. They are so much part of the world as we know it, it can be very easy to assume that they will be there wherever we go. This is not always the case.

Distance

How far away from home do you want to be?

Remember that your final choice has implications for how often you will see your family and friends. If you are going somewhere for just a few months, it may not matter. For longer programmes, it may be crucial. Do you assume that you will fly home for major family events or holidays? Is this feasible – given the costs, the amount of time and the potential conflict with study commitments? Are you OK with missing out on these important events?

(Don't forget the alternative, though – would you even enjoy these events if you had given up the opportunity to study abroad so that you could spend time with your family, or would you just resent the lost opportunities?) There are, of course, also financial implications, as well as the problems of what happens in an emergency (we'll come back to this later).

> *I haven't lived in Australia with my family for about seven years. Although I have seen my family during this time, I have missed Christmas – an important family occasion – every year except one. I miss out on my niece's and nephew's important occasions, which makes me very sad. This is a consequence of the decisions I have made, but one I am not entirely happy with. Sometimes, I wish there was a middle way, but Australia is so far from Canada that I don't really have the option.*
>
> **Author insight**: Anna

We are not at all suggesting that you only go to places that replicate what you already have at home. This is very limiting, as well as unrealistic. But be aware of your assumptions, and if there are aspects of your life which are too important to disregard, then make that a priority and find a programme that can accommodate you. There is almost always a solution if you are aware of the issues that are facing you. Being abroad can be very stressful – sometimes it makes more sense to make sure that you have the one or two things that keep you sane than to try to do it all without. There is beauty everywhere; just be aware of what you need in the world to help you function at your best.

Financial priorities

We will discuss money in considerable detail further on, but for now, consider what your general attitudes are to money.

Do you find that stress about money makes you unable to focus on studying, makes you grumpy and impossible to live with? Do you find that money is fairly flexible for you, and that you generally find that your budget works well? Can you live with very little money? Do you have the need to feel totally in control of money or are you a little more relaxed? Can you conceive of possibilities without knowing where the money is coming from, or is money the first thing you need to even start imagining what you might do? Do you have the option of going into debt if there are no other options? How would you feel about that?

These are important questions because it gives you a sense of your priorities. If money is a huge stressor for you, you may feel that you have to solve that problem before you conceptualize the rest of your plans. If you are less inclined to worry about money, you might be willing to pursue a line of investigation and apply for some funding and see what happens. Once you are at your destination, you might not have a lot of fun if you are constantly worried about spending money. On the other hand, if you are the kind of person who routinely overspends and then has to borrow money from friends or family, you could get yourself into a lot of trouble when you're abroad and away from your usual support networks. This is not to say that you can't change bad habits around money – sometimes being put in a different situation can bring out responsibility you never dreamed you had – but you may as well be honest with yourself now about the potential challenges for you. And only you know how you relate to money or the absence of it.

Bear in mind that some universities have a culture of students being in debt, while others assume that you have entirely your own financial resources.

	Yes	No	Not sure
Do financial matters cause you great anxiety?			
Do you feel comfortable going into debt to fund your study abroad?			
Can you imagine starting to make plans without knowing where the money will come from?			

● Refining your priorities

Having worked your way through the previous questions, you should have a better sense of what your priorities are. Take the time to write them down, so that you remember them and so you can trace how your ideas shift once you start doing detailed research. Write down the categories that are most important to you, and list your top five priorities overall.

Category	Very Important	Somewhat Important	Not at all Important
Academic			
Getting credit			
Independence/control			
Duration and timing			
Type of university			
Language considerations			
Campus/housing			
Lifestyle/environment			
Financial considerations			

Top five priorities

1. _____

2. _____

3. _____

4. _____

5. _____

• • •

Now that you have worked out what your priorities are, you will find it easier to begin researching your options. You might find that your priorities shift as you find specific options that excite or interest you, but try to remember what it was you wanted to achieve when you started out. You may want to come back to this chapter after you have begun your research, to see how your priorities have shifted and to remind yourself of what initially seemed important.

3 Researching your Options

By now, you should have a better sense of what your priorities are when you study abroad. This chapter will help you to research your options and narrow down the many diverse possibilities available to you. As you work your way through this chapter, keep in mind the answers you came up with to the questions in the previous chapter, but don't be surprised if some of your priorities shift a little as you find out what your options are. Most importantly, let yourself enjoy thinking of all the different possibilities – eventually, you will make a choice but in the meantime, enjoy dreaming! And you can learn a lot about yourself just from the kinds of opportunities that excite you. If you are a post-graduate, your process might be different – read through the following, but make sure you also read the section for post-graduates.

Using your resources

In trying to work out your options, don't try to do it alone. There are a number of resources that can help you to figure out what possibilities are open to you.

Study abroad advisor

If you are currently studying, you will probably find that your university or college has information about options. See if you can find a study abroad advisor, who may be affiliated with student services or the international student centre. Career counsellors or guidance officers may also have useful information. Your campus may have a study abroad library or resource centre. Previous students might have completed surveys about their own experiences studying abroad, which can be invaluable sources of information. You may find that these resources are comprehensive and extensive enough for you to do a large part of your research there, or you may have to look further afield. Take the time to browse through the information and see what possibilities excite you.

Bear in mind that universities will often have information about organized programmes, or exchange programmes between your university and an overseas university. There may be many other opportunities which would be equally good or better for you, so don't assume that what your university has to offer are the only options. On the other hand, these programmes are often a good choice – your university generally will help you to organize your trip and may have funding available to you.

Brochures and books

The study abroad library will probably have books and brochures enticing you to study abroad. Some of these will be reasonably objective, while others will be advertising for specific programmes. Bear in mind that many books and brochures will be designed as promotional material and are full of smiling students saying that they had a terrific time. While these resources generally do not lie as such, they are designed to look as appealing as possible and to portray a very positive image. Take them with a grain of salt, and make sure that you do further research to check the information in them. Also, check how recent the information is – it can go out-of-date very quickly.

University catalogues

The study abroad library or the main campus library might have access to the catalogues of other universities. If there are particular universities you are interested in, you could go to these catalogues to learn more about them, or just browse.

Many countries or regions have a 'good universities' guide, a resource put out by a private organization ranking different universities according to a set of criteria. They will not only give you information about universities you might not know about, but will also give you invaluable insights into how the student experience has been rated, what students and critics have thought of the university and what the university prides itself on. They may also alert you to potential issues that you should know about. The ratings will vary depending on the criteria used; these are less important than the other information the guides contain.

Information sessions or study abroad fairs

On campus, or in your community, you might come across information sessions telling you about study options abroad. These may be put on by study abroad advisors and give you a range of options, often including presentations from students who have returned from an overseas institution,

Heads up

> There are many, many more universities in the world than you have probably heard of or even imagined. The fact that you have not heard of a university does not mean that it would not be an excellent choice for you, so leave your options open.

or they may be put on by a particular organization or company that wants you to buy their product. Sometimes, you may have to go to several different sessions to learn about different countries. It can be worth going to them even if they are offering different opportunities from those you are really interested in; you will probably meet other students who are considering their options, as well as speakers and presenters who might be able to head you in the right direction. It can be fun to learn about possibilities even if you don't end up choosing them. You may have the chance to add your name to mailing or email lists, which can be a valuable way of hearing about opportunities.

Bear in mind that some study abroad providers at fairs or information sessions might be actively trying to recruit you to their programmes. As with all purchases, don't make snap decisions and don't sign up for programmes without having time to do further research and discuss it with your support team. If it is a reputable organization, you will be given time to think about it.

 Make sure that the university and programme you are thinking of offers the right level of academic challenge for you. Spend some extra money on a phone call to the chosen university, write many emails and read whatever material there already is . . . The academic part of our stay – which was our main motivation – didn't live up to the social part at all . . .

Mariah and Pieter, a couple studying in the Netherlands

 It does not matter where in the world you go or what university you choose. You're going to have fun! But, as much as possible, make sure that all your courses are more or less at your level. It is not fun sitting in a class where you do not understand anything, nor when you have learned it all before.

Anders, in Canada

Talk to people

Ask around among your peers, teachers, advisors and friends. Do you know anyone who has studied abroad? Are there people in your department who are international students or who have spent time overseas? Ask them about their experiences, including how they found out about their own opportunities. You may be amazed at how many people have something useful to offer to your search.

It is perfectly legitimate to contact potential destination universities, departments or programmes to ask to be put in contact with other students who have studied there. Remember, though, that most of the time, they will recommend that you contact someone who is known to have enjoyed the programme and who will cast it in a positive light. You may have to ask specific questions to get the information you want, and ask a number of students to get a variety of opinions.

Just go for it...unless it's going to be very expensive. In that case, try to choose somewhere else that is cheaper. But wherever you go, you won't regret it. The experiences, the new things you could see...they're priceless!

Palvai, a Singaporean student on exchange in Europe

Internet

If you have access to the internet, this can be a great resource for finding out about opportunities. The information you find might be more up-to-date than books, and you can access information that might not be otherwise available to you. The internet is particularly useful when you have some information, and want to find out more. However, you should not rely entirely on the internet.

Some difficulties with internet research

- You may find yourself getting very overwhelmed if you do general searches on opportunities for study abroad. You could spend years wading through the options and getting no closer to your goals. (We have included a list of useful websites at the end of this chapter to help you.) Alternatively, use specific search terms to narrow down your options. If you have some idea of the country you want to go to, you might find the internet a useful way of finding out about universities in that country.

- Many of the websites you find are likely to be designed for students from countries other than your own, and so may be of limited use.
- The information might be out-dated, so check when the website was updated last.
- Remember that almost anyone can create a website and offer advice and opinions – check whether you are accessing a credible source and then double check the information you are getting against other sources rather than taking it at face value.
- If you find websites owned by providers or study abroad companies, bear in mind that they will be trying to sell you their products and so might lack objectivity. As you browse, ask yourself who made the website and why?
- If you do decide to do general searches, remember that the options that come up first on a search engine are not the only options. There might be excellent programmes that are not immediate 'hits'.
- Remember that 'key word' searches do not take into account variations in terminology from country to country. For example, if you search for courses in the 'arts', you may miss options from 'humanities' departments.
- Remember that search engines are owned by companies from particular countries and so the options you find will reflect this cultural bias. For example, using a US search engine will mean that many of the options you find will be American.

Heads up

A university website can be very telling about the kind of experience you might have as an international student. For example, is information for international students easy to find on the website (many will have a link from the home page)? Does it include substantial well-written advice for international students? Does the university have programmes for language learning, or cultural exchange? Does it have an international student centre? Does it offer any funding for international students? Does it employ staff to advise international students? Is information about applying as an international student easy to access and understand? All of these components indicate an openness to international students and that there are systems that will help you in your new home. This is not to say that studying at a university without these aspects on their website might not be a fantastic experience, but there may be less support.

Organizing your research

When you first start researching, you might enjoy just browsing and seeing what appeals to you. Once you start to have a firmer idea about what you want, though, it will help if you create a system to keep a track of what you are learning, to avoid forgetting things or getting different options mixed up in your head. You will probably need to combine a variety of different resources to get a full picture. For example, a brochure might give you some initial information, a website might teach you more, and you might have to phone the organization or send them an email with specific questions.

Come up with a system which you can use consistently for each programme or university you research. It should be easy to read, and remind you of the important elements of each, so that you can compare them. Keep a track of websites and other identifying information, to save you time if you want to go back to it later. Keep a note of questions you need to ask or information you need to research.

Questions to ask

As you research your options, there are specific questions you should ask, so that you can compare different programmes accurately.

Organized programmes

If you are researching organized programmes, the kind of information you need to find out includes:

- How long is the programme? (do you have any choices here or is it set?)
- What aspects of studying abroad are organized for you by the company?
- What would you have to organize for yourself?
- How much does it cost to participate in the programme?
- What is included in the cost? (More about money in a later chapter; for now, write down what the resource specifically mentions as being included, and make a note of anything that is not included.)
- When does the programme begin? (If you have no choice over the start date, this may affect whether it is viable for your personal circumstances.)
- Are there scholarships available?

Heads up

Many programmes will offer a choice of how long you can go for and may even allow you to choose aspects of the package. As you do your research, make sure that you are clear about what options you are researching. If you think that you are researching a four-month programme, for example, you might get a shock if you realize that the prices you are looking at are only for one month.

- What are the eligibility requirements for students to apply to the programme?
  - Do you have to be a particular nationality to apply?
  - Do you have to be a particular age?
  - What university or college or programme or major or discipline must you be enrolled in to apply?
  - Are there any prerequisites? (Some programmes will only accept students who have fulfilled a certain proportion of their degree requirements.)
- How do you apply?
- When are applications due?

As you proceed, you may find that there are other questions which prove to be important to you and your personal circumstances.

Accreditation

There have been a number of media reports in the past few years in many different countries about study abroad providers which have turned out to be fraudulent or lack appropriate accreditation. Students have embarked on a programme in a language college or programme abroad only to find out that the school does not meet minimum standards, leaving students without the credentials or experiences they were hoping for. There is no sure-fire way to guard against such future contingencies, but there are a few things you can do to protect yourself. Ask:

Is the company (or college) accredited?

If it is a company operating in your home country, it will probably have to conform to some kind of local or national accreditation. Alternatively, it might be accredited in the country of destination. Legitimate programmes will usually go out of their way to display their accreditation on their brochures or websites, and you can then follow through with the governing body to check its legitimacy. The internet can also be an excellent way of searching to see if there has been any controversy around the college or programme. If your programme is recommended by a study abroad advisor on your campus, it is unlikely that you will have this problem, but if you are researching your own options, be vigilant. Trust your instinct, as well, and ask your team for advice if anything seems to be a little odd.

What credential do you receive on successful completion of the programme?
Will the credential be recognized in your home country and elsewhere?

Language programmes often give you a language qualification, which you might need in order to apply for future language programmes, to fulfill language requirements for your programme or future study, and to prove your skills to employers. It is very important that you find out not only whether the organization is accredited but what the accreditation is. It might be entirely reputable but not recognized – or widely used – in your home country. To prevent problems later, find out whether the credential will be recognized in the contexts where you will need it to be.

I had to adapt to the place; first I had to adapt to my labmates, and then to my flatmates. During this time I felt confused, and sometimes lost. Sometimes I just wanted to go home. But the friends I have made from around the world have made the Erasmus period one of the best experiences of my life. I would like to recommend that university students join an exchange programme. It's a way to learn about people and to have new experiences, but it's also a way to develop self-esteem and to grow as a person.

Alonso, a chemistry major on the Erasmus programme

Universities

If you are researching specific universities, go back to the questions we asked in the chapter on 'Defining Your Priorities'. Taking your top priorities, find out how each university matches up to them. You may find that you add some questions to the list as you go, as you refine what is important to you.

Narrowing your choices

If you use all the resources we have suggested, and record what you find as you go, you will get to the point where you have found a number of different options that seem viable for you. Finding that you are no longer uncovering new options but coming across the same ones repeatedly from different sources is a good sign that your research has been comprehensive. Look back over your research and compare the different programmes. If there is anything missing that you think is important, go back and check the answers to your questions before you go on. Ask yourself whether you think that you have found some good options. You may need to go away and do some more reading to find some other options if you are not happy with the ones you have.

Once you have found a number of good options, you will need to narrow your choices down. If you are applying for a programme which is not competitive, for which you satisfy all the eligibility criteria, and you are sure you can afford it and it is exactly what you want, you can narrow your choices down to just one option. In most cases, though, the goal is to narrow your options down to a few options. It is possible that you might not get into your first choice, or might not finish the prerequisite courses or might not have the money you thought you would have, or you may just want to have a few definite options – choosing to apply for more than one will reduce the possibility of not being able to do what you want and having to try again in a year's time.

To make your final decision(s), go back to your original responses in 'Starting Out' and 'Defining Your Priorities'. Which options best match the dream you originally had? Which options best fulfill your needs and wants? You may find some conflicts here, where one option will help you to fulfil one desire but not another. Your decision should ideally balance:

- Pragmatic concerns (Are you eligible? Does the programme have what you want?)
- Academic concerns (What credit will you get, if any? What credentials will you gain? What course options are available?)
- Financial concerns (Can you afford it? Is it within your financial reach?)
- Emotional concerns (Do your options meet your emotional needs, including any lifestyle components you identified as priorities?)

Talk to your team, which by now might include a study abroad advisor. Your teachers and advisors might have suggestions or opinions about the courses, or might know people who have had positive or negative experi-

Heads up

Consider your 'adventure quotient'. Some people are happy when they are in situations which are incredibly challenging and push them to their limits. Others find these stressful and would be much happier in a less challenging environment. Consider what your needs are; challenge yourself but also be realistic about what you can cope with.

ences with the options you are considering. And finally, check in with your instinct. How are you reacting to the options you are considering. You should feel excited and energized when you think about the options (although you may also be nervous – that's normal). If you are feeling lukewarm about the opportunities available to you, it is likely that you just haven't found the right fit for you yet.

TIP   If the options you are considering are viable except for finances, read the chapter on 'Managing Your Finances' for funding options before you abandon the idea of applying.

The parties were really the best. I was living in a corridor of 20 international students . . . 18 out of 20 were always ready to party . . . I've never seen such a concentration of great peoples, we were really like a family, every time someone was going away for more than 3 days, everyone missed him. I don't think I will ever see something like that again. . . . For most of the people in the corridor, this period was the best time of their life.

Armelle, a French student enjoying the freedoms of an undergraduate exchange programme in Sweden

For many undergraduates, detail about the academic reputation of the university and the exact courses available are less important than the wider experience of studying abroad. If you are planning to study abroad for a whole degree, or if the academic opportunities that studying abroad will open up for you are of particular importance, read the following section for post-graduates for advice on how to gauge your academic 'fit'.

● Post-graduates

You will probably be affected by many of the same concerns as undergraduates in thinking through your options for study abroad. However, it is also likely that there will be an increased emphasis on the academic components of a programme. You will need to know not only whether your academic background is likely to gain you entry into the programme, but also whether the programme will suit your academic needs. You might need to know, for example, whether your research can be supported by the expertise of the current faculty, what the library resources are like, and whether the courses you would take will give you the skills and credentials you want or need in your field in the future. Even apparently simply questions such as "How long is the programme?' might have complex answers – it is not unusual in post-graduate work for a number of factors to influence completion rates. In order to get answers to these questions, you will probably need to use a number of different research methods, and will need to go about it in a fairly systematic and organized way in order to get an appropriate balance in your final selection(s).

Before you begin, you will need to have some idea of the discipline you want to work in. In some cases, this may be simple – you will continue whatever you studied as an undergraduate. But it is also common for post-graduate students to shift in new directions – a music student might decide to move into music education or music therapy; a biology student might have to decide whether they would prefer to focus on genetics or marine biology. Post-graduate programmes range from the quite broad to the highly specialized, so consider carefully the questions we posed in 'Defining Your Priorities'.

Researching post-graduate programmes

There are a number of steps you can take to find out about which universities and programmes might be an option for you.

Follow the leads in your bibliographies. If you have cited specialists from your field in your papers, find out if they are still writing and where they are based. It is quite likely that they are teaching at a university and working with graduate students. You could be one of them.

Take some time to look through the leading journals and books in your field. Which ones excite you the most? Are there particular contributors who speak to you? Who is on the editorial board? Follow up the names to find out if you could potentially work with them.

Using the internet or printed conference proceedings, look through the programmes of some recent conferences in your field. Again, follow up on the names of anyone whose paper seems interesting or exciting to you.

TIP If you are unsure what you want to work on (which is very common for students considering post-graduate work), the process of looking through journals and conference programmes, as well as talking to your teachers, can be an excellent way of identifying and honing your interests. Keep a note as you go of ideas and subjects that particularly jump out at you, as well as the academics who are working on them.

If you have some idea of the country you want to go to (which might be partly defined by your field of interest), check the 'universities guide' for that country or region. Does the university have a strong track record of post-graduate teaching and supervision? What is its reputation as a research institution? In which discipline does it have the best reputation (as marked by its capacity to attract research funding, its publication and citation record and so on).

I wanted to live in Japan, study Japanese and continue my research, which concerns Japan...The thing I like the most is being in a city I love, having new experiences, meeting new people. I find it hard having to work out a new system of administration and working in a different language. Also, I miss having access to English-speaking libraries. There are tough times and sometimes I am lonely but I would whole-heartedly recommend it.

James, from Glasgow,
in Japan as a master's degree student

Heads up

Make sure you check data in your particular field of interest. Remember that a university might have an exceptionally strong track record in one discipline, but might be relatively weak in another. Often, a university will get a good reputation based on a small area of expertise, but this may not translate into a strong programme in your field.

When you have narrowed down your options to a manageable selection, you will probably want to make contact with specific universities. Ask for copies of post-graduate brochures in the department(s) you are interested in.

Heads up

> Some universities refer to their 'post-graduate' programmes, while others will use the term 'graduate' instead. Try both search terms if your searches are unsuccessful.

Many universities will have a school or department devoted to post-graduate studies, and these often offer extensive information on the internet.

At this stage, you will probably also want to make contact with someone in each of the departments you are interested in. This does not have to be your future supervisor (although it may very well be). You might contact the chair of graduate studies or equivalent for recommendations, or you could find a particular academic with whom you share research interests. Many university websites will list details of their faculty to help you to do this. Find out what kinds of work they have published and worked on in the past, and what their current research interests are. Do they have a strong track record? What kind of 'vibe' do you get from their work? Although it may seem over-whelming at first, it will become clear fairly quickly that there will be some academics who seem to be a good fit for you and others who are not. Making contact with members of the department is often an important part of a post-graduate application.

Your email or letter to them should introduce yourself and outline briefly what you are interested in working on. Depending on what stage of your thinking you are at, this might be quite broad and vague or might be quite specific and detailed. This is not a formal statement of interest (see 'The Application Process') but it should nonetheless be well written and well thought out, well articulated and well edited! This is your first contact with the department, and first impressions are very important. You might also use this method to find out more information about coursework that you might undertake, if the programme includes coursework. It is perfectly legitimate to contact the teacher of a post-graduate course and ask for a more detailed reading list or information about what would be taught in the course.

From the replies to your emails, you will probably start to get a sense of which universities and individual academics might be viable options for you. Some people are likely to respond to you with warmth and helpful sugges-tions. Others might ignore your emails altogether. Some might tell you that they are not taking on any more students, or are close to retirement, or might suggest reasons why the university might not be the best option for you (sometimes these reasons will be financial).

Heads up

> The emails will probably tell you a lot, but take them with a grain of salt. An academic who sends very short, unfriendly emails may be a terrific supervisor in person. Someone who is very approachable might not have the expertise you need to guide you through your post-graduate work

You will also probably want to get a sense of the university and departmental culture. Are the post-graduate students happy? Why? Why not? In order to get answers to these questions, you might need to use a little imagination. The chair of the department or the chair of graduate studies may be able to give you some information about the challenges facing students in the department, but might not be able (or willing) to go into much detail. Many individual academics will only be able to speak about their own students, and might not know of some of the wider concerns (and will often be unaware of practical issues such as funding or the kinds of bureaucratic obstacles students face). You are more likely to get the low-down from other students. Try to make contact with the association for graduate students in your department. Many departments will have these student-run advocacy groups and most have list-servs for contact between students. All departments have their issues, but if several of the post-graduates you have talked to are very unhappy with their programmes, you might be better of elsewhere.

Other concerns for post-graduates

Post-graduate programmes will often specify clearly what prerequisites you will need to get into the programme. Mostly, you will need to be able to demonstrate that you have these prerequisites in order to be eligible to apply. These may include examinations, language qualifications, or professional accreditations or experience.

However, sometimes there is some flexibility to these prerequisites, especially for international students. For example, if your language skills are not at the level they are expected to be, you might be able to do a language course before the start of your programme. If you are interested in a particular programme but do not have all (but most) of the prerequisites, it is worth finding out whether you might still be eligible. You may have to offer some ways of demonstrating your background, or fulfilling the prerequisite at a later time. But don't give up on an otherwise exciting programme without checking whether there is any flexibility.

Heads up

If you do need to check for flexibility, it is best to do so with the chair of graduate studies. Individual academics might not know about entrance requirements and might mislead you with comments such as 'I don't see that it would be a problem' (when the entrance committee might think otherwise). If you are given special consideration, keep copies of your correspondence in case you need to refer to it later. Also, remember that nothing is definite until you have a formal offer with all the accompanying paperwork after you formally apply, no matter what is agreed on in the informal contact you have with the university before you apply.

Qualifications and credentials

Make sure you research exactly what the qualification is that you will receive. Will it allow you to pursue further post-graduate work if you want to, either in your home country or elsewhere. Is the credential acknowledged in your home country? Will it give you the access you need to professional organizations or associations and, if not, what would you need to do to get this membership? Is the qualification recognized by employers in your field?

Holding onto your needs

As you find out about more and more options, it is easy to get overwhelmed. Hold onto your priorities. Some of your priorities may shift and some of your needs may change. This is entirely normal as you go through the process of narrowing your options. Revisit the questions in the first two chapters to remind you of what is most important to you.

You will learn something from whatever programme you finally decide on. Don't let yourself get paralysed by choice – keep your vision in mind and work towards it. Don't spend so much time thinking about your options that you never actually make a decision. It is more important that you make *something* happen for yourself than that you make perfect choices. Make a decision, and then move on to the next step, thinking through your financial options, and putting together your applications.

Further resources

- UKCOSA: The Council for International Education.
www.UKCOSA.org.uk
- Intended for UK students studying abroad, or students wanting to study in the UK. It includes some detailed advice on financial concerns, and funding opportunities, as well as a list of potentially useful links.
- The Education and Training Branch of the European Commission.
ec.europa.eu/education/index_en.html
    This is the organization that organizes the Erasmus programme, a source of support for European students in higher education to study elsewhere in Europe. From the main page, click on 'Programmes & Actions' and then on the Erasmus link.
- Commonwealth Universities Database Online Service.
www.acu.ac.uk/cudos
    Sponsored by the Association of Commonwealth Universities, this site offers a detailed search engine of opportunities within Commonwealth countries. A very impressive resource, but you will need to be a student or staff member of a member university to receive a password to access the site.
- Institute of International Education.
www.iie.org
    A US-based organization primarily for US students studying abroad or other students interested in studying in the US. It offers information on programmes and funding opportunities. It puts out an excellent series of brochures and information packs on a variety of topics relating to studying abroad.
- Language Course Finder.
www.language-learning.net/
    A comprehensive resource for finding language schools and language courses. It boasts 10,000 language schools in 88 languages and 115 countries.
- *IIEPassport: Academic Year Abroad* and *IIEPassport: Short-Term Study Abroad.*
    Put out by the Institute of International Education (US), these publications are published annually, and contain comprehensive lists of opportunities worldwide for study abroad opportunities.
- *World List of Universities and Other Institutions of Higher Education* and *The International Handbook of Universities.*
    Produced by the International Association of Universities and

published by Palgrave, this resource is published every two years and lists 17,500 universities worldwide. You will be able to find information such as the university structure, departments, courses of study and so on. Check whether your university library has copies of these resources.

- Transitions Abroad.
www.transitionsabroad.com

  This is an extensive website which covers numerous aspects of study abroad and travel. The list of affiliated universities is by no means definitive, but the site includes useful links to study-abroad databases, as well as online articles on a broad range of topics.

- www.studyabroad.com

  A site which offers suggestions of study abroad programmes, as well as a list of useful organizations who offer scholarships. It has a strong US bias, but offers an eclectic list of options for study abroad, which might help you to get your imagination going. Searching according to your subject area might elicit more interesting matches than by city or country.

- www.goabroad.com

  Another US-biased resource, but its database of study opportunities abroad is quite detailed and useful if you have a sense of what country or city you are interested in. It also has a useful database of opportunities for language certification.

- www.worldwide.edu

  This 'Consortium for International Education & Multicultural Studies' is useful in that it can be searched according to your subject area as well as country. You will have the opportunity to request further information about programmes that interest you.

4 Managing your Finances

Money is likely to be an important consideration as you start to think about studying abroad. Ideally, you should take financial considerations into account at every stage of the process. Start to think about finances when you are at the initial stage of exploring your options and then revisit money questions frequently as you go through the planning process. You may have to reread this chapter several times at different stages of the process, as you find yourself with more detail.

> **TIP** Try not to dismiss options on financial grounds until you have thoroughly explored your options; there may be funding opportunities you are not yet aware of.

Make sure you think about the finances well in advance of putting in applications to study abroad, so that you can take advantage of any potential funding opportunities that may come your way. There will often be strict deadlines, so make sure you are organized and prepared.

Assessing costs

 Money. You always need more than you think.

Ingemar, a Scandinavian student in the US

In order to make the dream of studying abroad a reality, you will need to take the time to assess the costs involved. This means looking at the detail of what is involved financially and being realistic about what you can and cannot afford. Some of the costs involved will be similar to what you would pay within your own country, but there will also be some differences and some hidden costs.

Heads up

> Deadlines for funding applications may not be the same as for admissions, so plan accordingly. They might be earlier!

The cost of your study abroad will depend on a number of factors, including what choices you make. For example, the location of your study abroad, your programme choice and the university you go to are all likely to affect what you will have to pay. You will probably remember to budget for the obvious costs, but frequently we find that students underestimate the 'hidden' costs, which can add up and make a substantial difference to your finances.

 TIP Make sure you do your research; don't assume that the costs you incur at home will necessarily be comparable to what you can expect while abroad.

Costs to consider

University/college tuition fees

Be clear what your status would be with regards to tuition fees. Tuition fees can vary according to academic considerations such as the discipline of study, the length of study, whether you enrol in academic-year or summer courses, and the qualification you receive. In some countries, tuition fees may be standardized and therefore comparable across different universities; in other places, tuition fees are set by individual universities or colleges – in

Heads up

> If you plan to study in a country of which you are a citizen but where you have not been residing, don't assume that you will be eligible for domestic student status – many countries require that you have been living in the country for a minimum period (often several years) to claim domestic status. In addition, this period of residency must often be directly prior to the period of study. This means that even if you were born in the country and have citizenship, or lived there previously and now want to return to study, you might be regarded as an international student.

these circumstances, 'prestigious' universities may be significantly more expensive than less well known ones (although this is not always true).

Tuition fees are also affected by such things as your nationality/citizenship status, your country of residence, your home university (if applicable), and whether you are regarded as an international or a domestic student.

Some tuition fees will be set for a term or year, while others will vary depending on how many credits you take.

Incidental/auxilliary fees

In addition to tuition fees, you will probably have to pay incidental/auxiliary fees. These cover such things as student service and student union fees. Find out what is included. Will you have to pay extra to join campus clubs and activities? To use sports/athletics facilities? If you are travelling with family, how much will it cost to give them access to facilities?

These fees are affected by such things as whether you are a full-time or part-time student, which campus you are on (where there are multiple campuses of the same university), and sometimes which programme you are in.

Travel

This includes the cost of your airfare, and other travel to get you to your destination and home again. In addition, you will need to take into consideration whether your programme has a travel component to it, whether you want to travel independently before or after your programme, and whether you intend to make it home for holidays (especially if you are planning to stay abroad for longer periods of time). Post-graduate and professional students might also need to consider whether research and conference travel will be an important component of their professional development.

If you want to travel before or after your programme or during holidays, this will be an additional expense. Bear in mind that travelling is often much more expensive than staying at home, because you have the additional costs of accommodation such as youth hostels or hotels, you tend to spend more on food because you eat out more, and may spend money on attractions and souvenirs, as well as the costs of transport.

My most expensive cost was the travelling I did, but I knew I wouldn't come back so I wanted to make the most of it. And buying clothing appropriate for the different climate was extremely expensive. If retailers realize you are an international student they take advantage of it!

Megan, on exchange for six months in New Zealand

Housing costs

Depending on your choice of housing, you will probably have to pay rent or board or perhaps college fees. Find out what the rent includes. Will you have to pay more for electricity/gas, phone, internet, water, heating? If you are paying for a food plan through a residential college or boarding house, which meals are included? Which meals are not? Furniture, bedding and kitchen equipment might also constitute additional amounts.

In addition, you may have to pay extra for deposits to get electricity and phone connected, to pay for laundry costs, and contents/tenant's insurance (to protect you against theft or fire and so on). You may have to pay extra for housing during holidays, as well as additional food costs in many cases, if you choose to stay during these times.

Health costs

These include vaccinations, medical/travel insurance and costs associated with accessing local health care (often extra for international students). See the chapter on 'Staying Healthy' for further details.

Application costs

The application process itself can be expensive. Make sure you take into account such things as application fees, processing fees, transcript costs, postage, photographs, printing/photocopying costs, housing application fees, and college application fees.

Immigration costs

These include application fees, international student visas/work visas, passports, and passport photos. Sometimes, you may be asked to pay for medical costs associated with medical check-ups prior to your visa being authorized, although this is unlikely for short-term students abroad. If you have to organize documents such as a birth certificate or citizenship paperwork, there will be additional fees.

Study costs

These include textbooks, laboratory equipment, stationery, photocopying, printing, library fees (overdue fees, inter-library loans and so on). Don't forget to include tools of your trade (anything from a camera to a spade to an electric drill to specialized computer software to canvases).

Taxes

When you are doing your calculations, find out what taxes are payable. For example, is there a goods and services tax payable on food, clothes, rent, and public transport? Many countries include this in the price tag but some don't. If you don't anticipate it, your budget could be wrong by up to 15%!

Many scholarships and bursaries are regarded as 'taxable income', which means you have to pay tax on them. Depending on your programme, you might have to pay taxes in your home country while abroad, or to your new country, or both. Bear in mind that this is not just on your living stipend – you may also have to pay tax on scholarships or bursaries that pay for your tuition. This could leave you with less money than you anticipated.

Many airports charge an airport tax, sometimes called an airport improvement tax or an airport security tax. Sometimes you will pay this when you buy your ticket, but sometimes you have to pay at the airport before you are allowed to leave the country.

> **Heads up**
>
> The flip side of having to pay tax on scholarships and bursaries is that you may be able to claim tax back through 'tuition credits'. Many countries will give you a tax credit if you are a student, and you may be able to claim taxable income back according to your course load. It is well worth taking the time to find out what arrangements are available in both your home country and your destination country.

Climate/environment-related costs

Costs associated with your new climate and environment might include additional clothing to protect you from extreme heat or cold, clothes which allow you to be more culturally sensitive, particular kinds of footwear, as well as such things as insect repellent, snow treads for your car, a mosquito net, water purifier, warm duvet or anything else that will help you to negotiate the environmental conditions of your new home.

Emergency funding

You should have some back-up money that is not included in your daily budget but which you can access in case of unexpected expenses or emergencies such as health problems, family crisis, theft and so on.

Money-exchange fees

Each time you exchange money, you are likely to be charged a fee. Each time you use a bank account (withdrawals, deposits, charges) you are likely to be charged a fee. There may be account-keeping fees. And if you have to cash a foreign cheque, you will have to pay for the privilege each time. Money orders also cost money. All this adds up.

Tips and gratuities

You will need to take into account how much it is standard to tip in your destination country, as well as who you tip and when.

> *I grew up in Australia where tipping is not common and where GST is included in the price of things. When I moved to Toronto, I had to add 15% to everything I bought for GST and PST, and then a further 15% for tips in restaurants, taxis and so on. My budgeting was sometimes out by as much as 30%! Now, when I go back to Australia, I regularly over-tip, because the habit is now ingrained in reverse.*

Author insight: Anna

Prior debt

If you have prior debt that you need to continue paying off, don't forget to take your monthly payments into account when you are working out your costs. (You will also need a plan for how to make payments from abroad – more about that later.)

Late fees

If you pay any of your student fees late, you might be subject to a late fee or be charged interest. In most cases, this is unnecessary. If you suspect you might have to pay late, contact the student accounts or equivalent office and ask if there is any flexibility.

> *Be open to the culture and the people of the country you are travelling to. Be openminded about their traditions and habits – even when they seem strange. If you are openminded, you get the most out of your stay. Other advice – of a more practical nature – bring lots of money. . . . If you want the most out of your stay, it will cost some money.*

Susan, studying in Spain

● Exploring your funding possibilities

There are several ways you might fund your study abroad. For most people, it will be a combination of several methods:

Personal savings
Support from family
Loans
Scholarships/bursaries
University/government aid
Sponsorship
Working abroad

Personal savings

If you plan in advance, you will often be able to save up some money before you go abroad. This may not be enough to cover all your expenses but can certainly make a difference to the experience. If you plan to do this, it might affect the timeline you choose as you might need enough time before you go to save up the money. Some students, for example, take a year off from studying to save up the money to study abroad, or take on extra hours at work for the few months before they leave.

> **Heads up**
>
> We have repeatedly heard from students that the work they had to put in to save up the money for study abroad and travel made it all the more worthwhile, even though they sometimes wished that someone else would just pay for it all.

Support from family

Obviously, this is a more viable option for some students than others and depends enormously on the financial situation of your family and whether you feel comfortable asking for help. Don't make assumptions about what is available to you without talking to the family members involved and offering a budget of how you would spend the money. Be respectful, too, that someone else is probably working hard for that money. We've seen a number of families become frustrated with family members for failing to budget effectively while studying abroad and then asking for more money. If you phone your family from abroad and ask for more money, you potentially put them in an awkward position – concerned for your well-being, safety and happiness, they might not feel that they have much choice, even when they can't really afford it. Planning beforehand can mitigate this problem and make sure that everyone is aware of what is possible.

> **TIP**   While many students study abroad with the help of their families, there are many others who do it on their own, so if your family is not in a position to help, don't give up on the idea. Remember, too, that support comes in many forms, and your family may have other things to offer, such as emotional support, good ideas or contacts.

Loans and credit

Sometimes the only feasible way to study abroad (or to study at all) is to go into debt. There are different kinds of loans that may be useful to you, each with their own advantages and disadvantages.

Government-subsidized loans

Many countries offer government student loans, whereby the government helps you to subsidize your education. Usually, you will be expected to pay the money back after you graduate, or as a percentage of your income when you get a job. You might already have this kind of loan.

Advantages	Disadvantages
You may be able to take an existing loan abroad with you.	Because they are so common, it can be easy to forget that they are still debt.
They are designed especially for students and so are often cheap and flexible.	Being in debt has repercussions for future financial planning.
Repayments are often not due until after you finish studying.	The amount you get might not be enough to cover your study expenses abroad and you may need to supplement it.
They are relatively easy to access, if you are eligible.	You may not be eligible.

Heads up

Organize your loan before you leave; it is rare that you will be able to access credit in your new country until you build up a credit rating or become a citizen or permanent resident.

TIP Check whether your home country has government student loans specifically for studying abroad. It is also worth checking to see if your destination country has similar programmes for which you might apply, although in most cases you probably will not be eligible.

Bank loans

Many banks, building societies or other financial institutions offer loans.

Advantages	Disadvantages
If you cannot get a government student loan, you may still be eligible for a bank loan.	You will need a good credit rating, collateral and/or a guarantor (who will take responsibility for your loan if you cannot pay it).
Often available in higher amounts than government student loans.	Interest rates and fees can be very high.
Can be approved very quickly, saving you from lengthy application processes.	Repayment is likely to start while you are still abroad.
Counts towards building a credit rating, which can be useful in the future.	Loan conditions might not be in your favour.

Student Line of Credit

These are special forms of credit for students from banks or equivalent organizations. You will usually need a guarantor to secure the loan and then you will get approved for a particular amount of money. You can then pay it back and borrow it again as you need to.

Advantages	Disadvantages
Interest rates often start quite low.	You may need a guarantor.
Repayments usually don't start until you have finished being a student.	The amount you are approved for might be insufficient to cover your expenses abroad.
You can access the money only as you need it, making it a good 'back-up' plan.	Interest rates go up rapidly after you stop being a student.
It can be approved quite quickly, saving you from lengthy waiting periods.	You will have to begin repayments after you graduate regardless of your income.

Heads up

If you already have some kind of student debt, make sure that your eligibility as a student continues while you are abroad, or you might have to start paying it back. This will depend on what kind of programme you undertake – if you do an exchange from your home university, you will likely still be regarded as a student. If you take time off from your home university and directly enroll abroad, you might not be. Make sure you check.

Credit cards

These are of course another form of bank loan.

Advantages	Disadvantages
Widely used internationally.	Interest rates can be very high.
Very convenient and easy to use.	You will have to make regular payments onto the card, even while you are studying.
They allow you to spend money you don't have.	You will have to pay back the full amount of credit, plus interest.
Limits on maximum credit can prevent you from overspending.	It can be easy to spend more than you can afford.
Often you can keep track of them online, avoiding the need for expensive phone calls or face-to-face contact.	You may not be approved for credit without a guarantor or assets.

Heads up

If you have had a credit card for a while, and have reliably paid it off, your credit card company might increase your credit limit. This can give you more flexibility, but also increases temptation, because it is so easy to spend more money. In addition, you might not even be aware that your limit has been increased, so you might find yourself spending much more than you anticipated, and then have to pay back more than you can afford. Credit cards can take a lot of discipline, because they are so easy and convenient.

Private loans

Family or friends might be able to offer you a loan to help you to study abroad. Make sure that you are both clear about how much the loan is for, when it will be payed back and how (e.g. weekly instalments, lump sum, and so on). Will you pay interest? Remember that money that they are lending to you is not earning interest in the bank, so paying some interest can help to compensate for this. Make sure you are both comfortable with the arrangement. Take these loans just as seriously as a bank loan; you can harm your relationships very quickly if you don't pay them back on time, or renege on your part of the bargain, as well as leave your family or friends in a difficult financial situation themselves.

Tips about debt

Shop around for the best rates and conditions. Make it clear that you are using it for educational purposes, since there may be plans designed specifically to help students. Make sure you are familiar with the terms and conditions. Will you be expected to make payments while you are abroad? How much interest will you have to pay? What time limitations are there on when you have to begin to pay it back? Are there any provisions for payments if you fall ill or can't work (you might need to purchase credit protection)? Is there any way of accessing more money if you find yourself in financial difficulty?

Work out how much you can afford in your debt. How will you pay it back? How long is it likely to take? Remember that working to pay back a loan after you have had the fun is much harder than when you can anticipate your upcoming trip. How will the debt affect your future opportunities (such as future study, buying property, future income expectations)? Are you being realistic about your capacity to repay it?

Do detailed calculations to ensure that you get a loan of an appropriate amount. You don't want to find that you have too little and end up with financial problems while abroad. If your loan is too large, you might spend a lot more money than you were planning while abroad, which can affect your options later on, as well as increasing the interest you pay.

Heads up

If you default on a loan or cannot keep up with the payments, your credit rating will be affected, which can in turn limit your future financial freedom. Do your research before you take out a loan, to make sure that you can avoid this situation.

Make sure you work out an effective way of accessing your loan money from your new country, to avoid problems down the line.

University/government subsidies

Depending on where you are currently studying (if you are), you may receive financial aid from your government or university to help you with your studies. Sometimes, this financial aid is transferable to a university abroad. Find out if this applies to you by talking to your financial aid office or study abroad office. Make sure you are clear about the details: many universities will only allow you to use part of your financial aid for this, and there may be very particular eligibility conditions. Bear in mind, too, that the amount of financial aid you receive at your home university may have a different 'value' abroad, and may need to be supplemented. You may find that your options are determined by which destinations would be included in your financial aid.

Scholarships and bursaries

It is possible that, if you plan ahead and do some research, you might be able to get a scholarship or bursary to study abroad. Scholarships are generally merit-based (academic, sporting, cultural and so on), whereas bursaries are often based on financial need (and you will need to show evidence of your financial status).

TIP Scholarships and bursaries may also be known as 'fellowships', 'awards' and 'prizes'.

There are many different kinds of scholarships and bursaries and they can be given for a variety of reasons. Criteria might include:

Financial need
Academic achievement
Achievement in another area (community service, sports, cultural
    activities and so on)
Potential
Membership of and contribution to a particular group (ethnic, racial,
    social, minority and so on)
A combination of these.

They can be given to support a number of different aspects of your study abroad. Types of awards include:

Fees scholarship   The scholarship might cover all or part of your fees. International students often benefit from scholarships which reduce international fees to those of a domestic student, leaving you responsible only for the difference. They will usually only cover tuition fees; you will still be responsible for incidental and auxiliary fees.

Living stipend   Money that you are given to cover daily expenses. You will be free to spend it as you choose.

Research scholarships   Often available for post-gradate students, these will help to pay for travel to a conference or for research purposes, or to fund a particular project. You will generally have to request a specific amount of money, which is then allocated to particular expenses. You will usually be asked to produce receipts and perhaps write a report on the expenditure.

Housing/college scholarships   These cover part or all of your board and meals, often by way of reducing the final fees payable.

Text book allowance   To help you to buy books and equipment needed for your study. You will generally have to buy them on campus, or show receipts for your purchases.

Travel scholarship   This may pay for part or all of your airfare or other travel expenses to study abroad. For longer programmes, especially at the post-graduate level, there are some competitive scholarships that will pay for an airfare home periodically to visit family as well.

Provider scholarships   If you are using an external provider for your study abroad, you may be able to get a scholarship which reduces the amount you have to pay to the provider.

Many scholarships will be a combination of the above: for example, paying your fees and a small living stipend, or a textbook allowance and a reduction in the costs of boarding.

Some scholarships will be available to a wide diversity of students; others will specify eligibility criteria for members of particular community groups, ethnicities, communities or interest groups. It is not unusual to find scholarships with highly specific criteria for eligibility – if you match the description, you have a good chance of being successful.

Accessing scholarships and bursaries

Some scholarships you will stumble across on your university's notice board; others you might have to search for and research. Main sources include:

Your home university   Scholarships might be available for exactly what you want to do (or the possibility of a scholarship might inspire you). Ask your department, your faculty, the financial aid office, the office dealing with scholarships and admissions, and the international student centre, as well as the study-abroad office if there is one.

Your destination university   The university's website will probably list a number of scholarships, some of which may apply to international students. It is also worth asking individual programmes and departments to find out what the main sources of support are for students, especially international students, and to find out if there are other sources they can recommend.

Your provider   Many organizations that provide study abroad have scholarships and bursaries available.

Government departments, in both your home country and your destination country   Many countries offer scholarships to particular countries that they are trying to increase contact with, which will help you to study in that country. Some have reciprocal arrangements which you can become involved in, and may offer other sources of funding for your programme. Often, these are post-graduate scholarships (see section below).

Local and community organizations   Organizations that target students and young people may have funding available to help you. There may be organizations in your community that are specifically designed to help you to study abroad. (Rotary International, for example, offers opportunities for study abroad in return for your agreeing to be a cultural ambassador for your town or country.)

Organizations that you are involved in   These may include youth organizations, churches, cultural groups, sports groups and so on. They may have an organized system for support, or may be willing to do some fundraising for you. It is worth asking around.

Employers   In some cases, especially when you have a reasonably senior position in an organization that you have been involved in for a while, your employer might be willing to support a study opportunity abroad, especially if you can show how it would benefit your employer in the long term.

To find out about these scholarships, contact the organizations, search online, and make some phone calls or send letters until you have a strong sense of what is available. Don't forget to ask your teachers and other students you know who have studied abroad, and find out how they did it. It is also worth checking your local bookshop or library for resource guides on scholarships. Bear in mind that many of the resources you might find will be for students of other countries, and you might not be eligible for them. Before you spend the money (or time) on them, check that they are actually useful to you and your circumstances. The US market is particularly saturated with resources, most of which have limited applicability to students from elsewhere.

Heads up

If you get some kind of scholarship or bursary, find out when you will receive the first instalment, and how you will get it. It is very common that your first instalment might not be processed until several weeks into your programme, so you will need funds to tide you over. Bear in mind that if you then receive a cheque, it could take a further five business days for the bank to clear it. Also, make sure you know where it will be sent to. We have both had scholarship cheques sent to the other side of the world, or waited patiently for our money only to find that we were supposed to have picked it up ourselves.

Applying for scholarships

Some scholarships and forms of funding for study abroad are easy to apply for, and require completing a simple form. Often, though, they will be more complicated, and may require evidence of your education and grades, employment, and financial situation. Some may involve statements of intent, explaining why you want the scholarship and what you hope to gain from it. Take the scholarship process seriously. It needs to represent you at your best and requires care, careful writing and strong editing.

Review this chapter in conjunction with the chapter on 'The Application Process'. Many of the suggestions we make about your university application will also be true of scholarship applications. In addition, consider the following tips.

Tips for scholarship applications

Do your research

What is the scholarship for? What values is it setting out to reward? Who/what kind of student has won the scholarship in the past?

Find out a bit about the history of the scholarship

Who was it named after? Why was it established?

Take the scholarship application seriously

It needs to represent you at your best and requires care, careful writing and strong editing. Get help with your scholarship applications from your advisors.

If you are applying to more than one, tailor each application to suit the scholarship you are applying for

Highlight the necessary criteria. Be specific about why you would be a good fit for the particular scholarship you are applying for. Try to focus less on how good the scholarship would be for you, and more on why you would be good for the scholarship

Be disciplined about conforming to word limits

This is an important part of the 'art' of writing applications.

Answer all of the questions put to you

If there are no specific questions, address each criterion and explain how it applies to you.

Check and double check your scholarship applications

Make sure you have not inadvertently left the name of another scholarship on your application.

Be selective

Some scholarship applications deliberately give you little room to list your accomplishments. Instead of listing them all, you will need to select those you see as most important. You might need to get some help from your teachers and advisors to work out what to leave in and what to take out.

Be precise

Some scholarships will ask you to specify what you plan to spend the money on, and ask you to include a budget. Do your research thoroughly. Don't make up answers. Take the time to create an accurate budget which includes each aspect of your financial planning. Be precise about the amounts. Make sure your submission is neat and easy to follow. Don't forget to take currency exchange into account.

Complete all documentation accurately and carefully

If you are asked to produce evidence of financial need, complete all documentation accurately and carefully. Explain any anomalies in your financial-need circumstances (for example, family responsibilities, accommodation needs for disability). If you are asked to include paperwork to verify your financial status (tax returns, bank statements and so on), make sure you include everything you are asked, to avoid delays in processing. You might include a list of documents that you have included in your application to make it easier to follow.

Never lie or even exaggerate on a scholarship application

If you are found to have misled the committee, you might be asked to pay back the funding, even if you have already spent it. If your circumstances change, check that you are still eligible for it, and inform the committee of your new circumstances.

Heads up

> Even if the criteria for the bursary are only financial needs, you will still be judged on your professionalism, your ability to follow instructions and the way you present your application. Take the time to do it well.

Communicate with your referees

Make sure your referees are aware of the criteria for each scholarship you are applying to – it gives them a chance to tailor their response to highlight particular skills or talents you might have which would make you a good fit for the scholarship.

Be organized

Respect all deadlines and be organized and thorough in your own application and in dealing with the other people involved in the process.

TIP   The bigger the scholarship, the stronger the competition, but there are also often smaller amounts of funding available. If you are eligible for a scholarship, it is worth putting in an application. We have both seen situations where students don't apply for a scholarship because they assume that they won't be competitive, while the scholarship committee laments the low numbers of applicants and ends up giving the scholarship to a less worthy candidate, simply because others did not apply.

Working abroad

The other option for funding your study abroad is to work in your new country. This can help you financially, as well as give you invaluable insight into your new culture. Often, students do not plan to get a job, but then find that they need extra money. In fact, the story we hear most often from students who have studied abroad is that they underbudgeted or mismanaged their money and so ran out of funds and had to find ways of supporting themselves. The most common solutions are to beg for more money from family members and to get part-time work.

Heads up

Job opportunities while abroad are usually contingent on your immigration status. There will probably be restrictions about whether you are allowed to work, the kinds of jobs you can hold and the number of hours you can do. Often, immigration laws differentiate between working on campus and working off campus. Make sure you check your status and know the restrictions that apply to you before you consider working.

We have a few words of caution about planning to work as part of your financial planning for study abroad:

- Studying abroad is generally more stressful than studying at home (see our chapter on 'Staying Healthy'); consider whether taking on a job will be too much for your time, energy and stress levels.
- Many programmes have limits on how many hours you are allowed to work outside of the programme. Find out what these limits are.

- Consider what you will do if you can't find a job. It is very difficult to apply for most jobs before you arrive and you may not know if your skills are transferable. This could leave you with a financial problem after you arrive, if the job market is significantly different from what you are used to.
- Bear in mind that many jobs will require good local-language skills.
- Having a job may limit your opportunities to socialize and travel in your new country, so you might miss some good opportunities. Think about how you can find a balance.

Heads up

Before you leave, research whether it is common for students in your new university to have a part-time job, and whether there are many options available. Some universities will have many opportunities because it is part of the university culture, while at others it will be quite rare. Find out what you are likely to be able to find, rather than make assumptions.

TIP   In your new country, try to attend workshops (often through student services) on writing job applications to make sure you are competitive. Take the time to adapt your application materials (cover letter, curriculum vitae and so on) to local needs and expectations.

Kinds of jobs

On-campus jobs

There are a variety of on-campus jobs which can be held by students. Possibilities include working in campus eateries, libraries or student services, guiding visitors on tours of the campus, or doing research for one of your teachers, among many others.

Advantages	Disadvantages
Usually sympathetic to students' needs, allowing you flexible scheduling and hours which are compatible with your study goals.	Positions can be competitive because a lot of students want them.
Job security.	Positions may not be in your area of interest or expertise.
Pay is often reasonably good.	You will have to spend even more time on campus than you otherwise might.
You may be protected by a union.	It can take time to get seniority (so other students might get the hours or the tasks you would like).
Often easy to access and find out about, even before you arrive in the country.	Positions might be available only during term time, leaving you without a job during holiday periods.

Heads up

If you do work in your new country, make sure you find out what your taxation status is – this will probably depend on whether you are deemed a resident of your home country or your new country. As well as taking taxes into account in your budgeting, make sure you complete all the paperwork you need in order to be legally protected in your new country.

Off-campus jobs

Off-campus jobs can include anything you might be employed to do, from casual baby-sitting to working in your field of expertise.

Work-study jobs

Some countries offer the opportunity for students to have 'work study' positions. These are positions that a university creates for eligible students which

Advantages	Disadvantages
More choice about what you do than on-campus jobs.	You will probably need to have a working visa for off-campus positions.
You may find something better and more suited to your skills.	Possible lack of flexibility in scheduling – may be difficult to combine with study commitments.
Chance to practise language skills in a wider context.	Commuting may be time consuming (and expensive).
Chance to have deeper immersion in cultural and social aspects of your new country than from university alone.	It may be difficult to find out about job opportunities until you arrive at your new campus.
Chance to meet a diversity of local people, and you may have the opportunity for networking in your field.	Your background and credentials might not be recognized in your new country.
Position is likely to continue through university holidays.	Depending on the job, you may not have job security and workers' rights; and the pay may not be good.

Heads up

Make sure you know how many hours you can expect each week. Many student jobs work by calling you in when you are needed, which means some weeks you work a lot and other weeks you work very little. This can be great because it offers flexibility, but can wreak havoc on your capacity to plan your studies, have a social life and organize your finances. Find a job that will suit your needs.

allow you to combine your study with the chance to earn some more money. They may or may not be in the field of your expertise, but can offer you some valuable and interesting work experience, as well as the security of a job to fund your studying. If your destination university has this kind of programme, find out what the eligibility requirements are and whether international students can apply. You might have to apply ahead of time, so research this before you leave if it is something you are interested in.

Finding a job

> **TIP** Find out what the words are for the different kinds of positions you might hold. Learn how job advertisements are presented in your new country and what the abbreviations and terminology means.

> ### Heads up
>
> You might come across jobs in your new country that are 'unofficial', meaning you can do them without a working visa and you are paid in cash. We urge you to be vigilant in these circumstances. Not only can you get into trouble with the police and with immigration for working illegally, but you are vulnerable to exploitation because there is no workers' protection. Be very cautious about the situation you are getting yourself into, even if you are concerned about money.

Your destination university will probably have some kind of student employment service. This may range from a single bulletin board listing opportunities, to a full resource centre with advice, counsellors, books and databases. You may be able to sign up for online access to job listings (which you can start to check out before you even leave) or email lists. Ask where else you can look for jobs. In addition to the student job services, some options might include:

- University email lists and bulletin boards – in your department, other related departments, colleges, student services, athletics facilities bulletin boards, and central eating places. All of these places may list opportunities.
- Wider community resources – community bulletin boards, internet job databases, recruitment agencies, newspaper advertisements, employment publications and shop window advertisements.

TIP Don't forget to investigate job opportunities related to your hobbies. For example, if you love plays and movies, you could work at a cinema or sell tickets to theatres. If you play a sport, you might be able to assist at the local sports club.

Money management

Once you have sorted out the source of your funding, you will need to consider how you will manage your money. This includes not only how to budget and make your money last, but also the practicalities surrounding accessing your money while abroad and how to negotiate payment options.

> *My funding was in my own currency, which decreased in value with every grant cheque, so that I was always having to take on more additional paid work. Studying abroad can be a great risk (personally, academically, and financially) if you don't have much sense of what you're getting yourself into.*
>
> Catherine, a post-graduate in the UK

Payment options and accessing your money

Find out what the options are for accessing money in your new country, and how transactions are usually conducted. You may be surprised how different it is from your home country (or how similar!).

> *When I went to the UK, I decided not to open a local bank account, but to access money from my Canadian banks. While in the UK, I needed to apply for a special entry visa back to Canada and I had to pay for it using a Canadian bank draft. I found that to organize this, I needed to have a local bank account.*
>
> *When I did open a local bank account, I got a savings account, rather than a chequing account, so I didn't have a cheque book. But I soon discovered that electricity bills and phone bills were paid for by cheque – nobody would accept my credit cards. I had money, but no way of paying my bills. I could have saved time and energy if I had known this earlier.*
>
> Caroline

Heads up

Find out if you will be able to open a bank account – sometimes you can only open one in advance, other times you need to be there in person. Some places will not allow international students to open a local bank account.

Maintaining a home bank account

If your money is in your bank at home, you will need to work out how to access it. (If you need to get money from your new country to your home account, you might use similar methods.) Options include:

- Directly taking it out of your home bank account whenever you need it; or
- Transferring it to a local bank account and then drawing it out from there.

The following will give you a sense of some of your options, and their advantages and disadvantages.

Heads up

Increasingly, banks give the impression of being multinational. You might find a bank in your new country that has exactly the same name as one in your home country. Don't assume, though, that you will be able to access your home account from the new country, or that being a member of the bank in your home country gives you any advantage in the new one. Many banks run independently, sometimes not even connecting to others of the same name in the same country. Make sure you check.

Cash

Advantages	Disadvantages
Widely accepted.	Can easily be stolen and is non-replaceable.
No need for cards, technology, banks and so on.	Carrying large amounts of cash is a significant security risk.
You won't overspend, or spend money you don't have.	Most countries have limits on how much cash you can take in and out of the country, so carrying it with you may not be an option.

In order to access your cash, you might be able to use a debit card or get cash advances through your credit card. This will rely on you having easy access to an electronic bank machine or to a bank. If you use a bank, you will need your passport with you. You will have to pay a fee each time you get a cash advance. There may be a daily limit on how much cash you can withdraw.

Debit Cards

If you are traveling to a country close to your own, you may be able to use your debit card from your bank at home for purchases such as groceries, getting cash out and so on.

Advantages	Disadvantages
Prevents need for cash.	Often only recognized locally – you may not be able to use it in other country's bank machines.
You can only spend money you have in your account (preventing spending beyond your means).	You may need authorization beforehand to use it in another country, where possible. You may have to organize this several weeks before you leave.
Convenient and sometimes widely used within particular geographic areas.	You may be restricted to a daily limit.

TIP   Ask your bank if there is any way to reduce the fees payable on your debit cards while you are abroad; they may be able to offer you options that are not advertised.

Heads up

Have a back-up plan. What will you do if the machine is out of order, or if your card gets stolen? Even a seemingly small problem, like the security strip on your card getting scratched, can prevent you from accessing your money. Leave a copy of all your credit cards, bank cards, traveller's cheques and travel documents with someone at home; this will save you time if you need to replace them.

Credit cards

Check whether credit cards are widely used in your destination country. What are they used for? In some places, credit cards can be used to pay for everything; in others, they are used only for very expensive items or in particular places, and in others not at all.

Advantages	Disadvantages
Widely used and accepted in a variety of contexts.	Can be stolen or damaged, leaving you with no access to money.
Can be cancelled quickly if stolen.	Credit card numbers can be misused, leaving your money vulnerable to theft, or the possibility of identity theft.
Can sometimes be used to access cash.	Replacement can take time (so have a back up).

Heads up

Find out about security in relation to credit cards in your new country. What efforts are in place to ensure that your number is not misused? Bear in mind that the more you use your credit card, the more likely it is that the number will be compromised. How will your bank support you if your credit details are stolen?

Traveler's cheques

You can buy these at foreign-exchange agencies and banks. You exchange them for cash at an exchange bureau. Sometimes, you can use them directly for payment.

Advantages	Disadvantages
Prevents need for cash.	You pay a fee for each cheque.
Replaceable if lost or stolen (keep a record of the serial numbers).	You will need to be close to an exchange bureau or bank during opening hours in order to get money (consider what you will do on a public holiday for example).
They are used widely in some countries.	You are at the mercy of the daily exchange rate, which can fluctuate.
	In many countries they are hardly used.

TIP Find out what currency you should get your traveller's cheques in. Some currencies are more reliable than others, making them a safer option, and some currencies are more widely used than others and so easier to exchange. Also, find out which companies' travellers cheques will be recognized in your new country. You need them to be widely recognized for them to be useful.

International money orders

You can transfer money from one country to another using international money orders, which you can get at a bank.

Advantages	Disadvantages
Can be used instead of cash, especially if you have to send money through the mail.	There is a fee for this service.
You can transfer money internationally (to others or to yourself).	You will need a bank account in your new country to cash the money order (you can't use it directly as a form of payment).
	You will need to ask for the money order from your home bank, which can be costly and inconvenient.
	The money order might not be accepted in your new country (find out first).
	It is not a viable way of accessing your money on a daily basis.

TIP Find out when the local public holidays are, and remember that banks will be closed. Also, find out the opening hours for banks. Are they open in the evenings? Do they close at 3 every day? Do they close for several hours every afternoon? Plan accordingly.

Maintaining a local bank account

If you can transfer your money to a new local bank account, which can then look after your finances on a daily basis, this has significant advantages.

Advantages	Disadvantages
You will be able to access money – including cash – as the locals do, which is often more efficient and less problematic.	It can be very difficult to open a bank account as a foreigner.
You won't have to pay international exchange fees each time you access your money.	The local currency might be unstable, leaving the value of your money constantly changing.
You won't be at the mercy of rapidly changing exchange rates, potentially saving you money and making it easier to budget.	You will have to have access to the bank (consider proximity, opening hours and so on).
You can pay what you earn from your job into your account, where it will be relatively secure.	Fees might be high.

TIP   Compare different options to find one that gives you what you need. There might be a student account available, which will lower fees.

Heads up

To get a job locally, you may HAVE to have a local bank account, so that your pay can be directly deposited, or where you can pay in pay cheques.

Other options

Money transfers

There are agencies that operate internationally where you can 'wire' money from one country to another. You will need there to be a local agency in your home country for the depositing of the money, and a local agency in your new country where you pick up the money.

Advantages	Disadvantages
They are quick and usually very efficient.	They are very expensive.
Excellent in some emergency cases.	Access to agencies can be inconvenient, depending on location and time of day.
	They involve someone at the other end to deposit the money (and who has access to the money in the first place).
	Not widely used in some places.

Money transfers can be excellent in an emergency if you have someone at home who is willing to send money to you, but are not a sustainable way of accessing your money on a day-to-day basis.

TIP Before you leave, consider giving a family member or friend signature rights on your home bank account, so that you can enlist their help if you need it.

Combinations

The most effective way of negotiating money while abroad is to use a combination of different methods, so that if one fails you still have others to fall back on. Check the local conditions as well, to ensure that you are making choices which are viable for the place you are going to – remember that anything that involves complex technology is useless if you cannot rely on electricity supplies and computer connections working. If a method of payment is not widely used in your new country, you might find yourself stuck. Find out how the local economy works and make decisions that fit in.

Heads up

Many students report facing seemingly impossible bureaucratic tangles, where, for example, you can't open a bank account without a stable address, but can't rent a flat unless you can give your local bank account details. Or you can't get a job without an account, but the bank wants the details of your employer. If you find that you are getting nowhere, enlist the help of an advisor at the university – not only will there be people who can offer 'local knowledge' but a letter or phone call explaining that you are an international student and that the university will vouch for you can be all you need to break the cycle.

University finances

If you are studying through a programme affiliated with your home university, make sure you are clear about how the finances work. Do you pay fees to both? Do you just continue to pay your usual fees to your home university while you are abroad? Do you only pay the destination university? The arrangements may differ for tuition fees and for incidental fees, so be clear about who is paying what to whom and by when. Follow up to make sure that the appropriate fees have been received – mistakes happen all the time, so be vigilant to make sure that all relevant student accounts are paid and up-to-date.

TIP   If a mistake occurs, it can be tempting just to pay the money and then sort it out later. Try to avoid this if you can; it is much harder to get money back once it is paid than to resolve a problem before you pay it.

Effective budgeting

To make your money last, as well as to keep track of how it is being spent, you will need to utilize effective budgeting. You should start to do this when you initially begin thinking about studying abroad, and then revise and update your budget as you accumulate more detail.

Tips for budgeting

- Plan ahead.

- Budget generously.
- Research the cost of things online. The international student centre at your destination university might be able to give you information about what you can expect. Guidebooks may give you an indication too, but check how old the information is. Remember that the costs you research may have gone up, sometimes significantly.
- Leave yourself flexibility for fun and for the unexpected.
- Take into account such events as your scholarship cheque getting delayed in the post, or your financial aid getting tied up with a bureaucratic glitch, your credit card getting stolen, or finding that you have unexpected costs you couldn't predict.
- Your costs in the first month are likely to be higher than in subsequent months. Make sure you have the funds to be able to accommodate this.
- As you are working out your expenses, be overly generous. If there are two options, always write down the higher option. Round up, not down.
- Talk to other students who have studied in the place you are going. You might need to contact your destination university to make contact with people. Ask about unexpected costs.
- When you are listing your sources of income, don't forget to take into account currency exchanges (which fluctuate). Include all of your pre-departure expenses, as well as what you expect to spend while abroad.
- When you have a final figure for everything you can think of under expenses, add a further 15%.

Budget, budget, budget! Consider price differences and think about what kind of life you would like to lead while studying abroad. Being a student is not about living like a queen or king, but you might want to consider whether you have enough money to get you to the pub or clothes shopping once in a while.

Angela, studying African Studies and Chinese development in London (she decided not to finish her degree there because of the expense)

Emergency financing

You may find yourself in the position of needing more money than you anticipated. This might just be a shortage of 'fun' money and you might solve it by getting a part-time job. Or it might be as a result of an emergency, such as having your money stolen or facing unexpected medical expenses. Plan for this in advance and have back-up plans.

Consider:

- Do you have assets you could liquidate (including investment plans, items you could sell and so on)?
- Do you have family or friends who would be willing to transfer money to you?
- What kind of support can you get from your travel insurance?
- Can you get emergency credit from your bank?

Tips

If viable, start by contacting the financial-aid office at your new university. They might have emergency funding you can access, or advice on where to go for help. You might be able to defer your fees for a period of time to give you a chance to sort your financial affairs out.

If the emergency is related to a crime or a medical difficulty, your travel insurance might be able to help.

Make sure that you have alternative ways of accessing your money, in case your credit card gets scratched or you forget to clear your pockets before doing a load of laundry (leaving you with clumps of wet paper instead of cash or traveller's cheques – it happens more than you might think).

I got a scholarship to study in the UK, but I didn't know that it wouldn't be enough to buy winter clothes and to have some fun with friends. I also got really homesick and wanted to visit my sister in New York for Christmas. I don't know what I would have done if I didn't have a work visa for the UK. I was lucky because I got a part-time job, and that made me much happier. And I spent Christmas with my sister.

Ama, a student from Kenya, in the UK for a year
to complete her master's.

Heads up

> In major emergencies, there will often be people and systems to help you. It is generally the smaller emergencies that cause the most problems and the most stress, especially if they are the result of a mistake on your part.

Try to avoid emergency loans through organizations you don't normally deal with. There are places which will give you loans rapidly and with no need for a guarantor but they are often very expensive and the conditions are often very unfavourable or even dangerous. Beware that in an emergency you can be vulnerable to exploitation, and make sure you make sensible decisions that you can live with in the long term.

Don't rely entirely on family or friends for emergency funds. While this can work, consider what will happen if the people you are relying on are away when you need them. It is quite surprising how many students report that the only time when they had some kind of emergency corresponded with the one weekend that their family or friends had gone away or were otherwise unavailable, and they had to find other ways of solving the problem.

Post-graduate scholarships

Post-graduate scholarships are much more widespread than undergraduate funding opportunities, and so it is likely that you will be able to get at least some funding. In addition to the sources listed above for undergraduates, make sure you get in touch with organizations devoted to your disciplinary field. Many post-graduate scholarships are highly discipline-specific and may not be advertised widely. Often, you will be asking for funding for at least a year or more, and it is important to look at the big picture and work out what your needs are.

Many post-graduate scholarships are incredibly competitive, and may take several months to prepare. You will often have to have a clear idea of your research at the post-graduate level, and there may be several stages to the process. Many post-graduate scholarship applications have very specific requirements – make sure you get advice from your advisors about the precise genre you are expected to use and any idiosyncrasies of your field. Make sure you know who your audience is – for example, are you writing to an audience of peers within your field, or to a more general audience? Often, it will be a combination of both, which means you will have to balance the specialist content with a more accessible style.

> ### Heads up
>
> Many scholarships for post-graduates are conditional upon you returning to your home country after your study and working in a particular context for a period of time (sometimes several years). This is especially true of scholarships offered by government organizations. While this may be exactly what you want, take the time to think through the implications of this. It is not unusual that international post-graduate students, particularly at the PhD level, might want to stay in their new country and apply for residency/citizenship. If you do want to stay, it might be very difficult to do so if you have a scholarship conditional on your return home. This is something worth considering before you begin the arduous process of applying; there might be a better scholarship for your circumstances.

Scholarship offers for post-graduate students

Post-graduate scholarships are often worth a lot of money and are designed to help you over the course of several years. Over this time, both your circumstances and the circumstances of the scholarship can shift, and you need to protect yourself against these changes at the beginning. This includes protecting yourself legally. While it would be nice to think that your scholarship will be honoured, we have come across several examples of a department reneging on original scholarship agreements and students have had to go to arbitration or through the legal system, with varied results. It is worth, then, clarifying the conditions of the scholarship before you accept. Get everything in writing.

Negotiation/clarification

In some universities, it is common to negotiate scholarship offers much as one might negotiate the terms of a new job. In other universities, this is not common. Find out what flexibility there is. Even if negotiation is not possible, make sure you still clarify the terms.

From a legal viewpoint, it may be important to distinguish between a letter from your department offering a scholarship and the official letter of offer, which might come from the school or faculty of graduate studies. Make sure you are clear which is the legally binding document, in case you do ever have to contest an injustice. This will often be confusing. Persist.

On the official letter of offer, clarify the exact phrasing of the offer. How much money are you being offered? For how long? Is this the full length of your programme? What happens for the remainder of the programme?

There may be phrases such as 'renewable three times subject to satisfactory progress'. Find out what these phrases mean, exactly. (The answer will often be given as a grade point average.) What will you do if you are unable to satisfy the requirements? Will you be expected to pay the scholarship back? How are these conditions determined? Will your funding definitely be renewed or is this just a possibility?

If your scholarship covers 'Fees' find out which fees. Usually this includes tuition, but ancillary/incidental fees will be your responsibility. Will you be covered if tuition fees increase? (If you will receive an exact amount, there might be a difference payable.)

Consider the impact of inflation. What may seem like a manageable living stipend this year might not be much in four years' time if it does not increase with inflation.

How much are you expected to pay from your own pocket? Check the hidden costs involved – your scholarship might not cover health insurance, student services, sports facilities and so on – you need to know this before you go.

What happens to your scholarship if your immigration status changes (for example, if you become a resident or citizen; if you get married, and so on)?

As a graduate student, you will probably need to attend conferences or symposia, submit articles for publication and engage in other scholarly activities. Is there funding available for this? Will you have to apply separately? Will you even be eligible for this funding, as an international student, and on your particular scholarship?

What are the conditions associated with the scholarship. Are these realistic and reasonable? Are they fixed, or can they change from year to year?

Heads up

When you ask questions about applying for other forms of funding, you might receive comments that casually suggest that you will be successful. 'Don't worry; you'll be fine' might be very reassuring at the time, but is useless in the event that things do not go as planned.

Other post-graduate funding options

Many post-graduate students teach, work as a research assistant or do other departmental work in order to fund their way through their degree. Often, some employment is a component of your scholarship.

Heads up

We know numerous post-graduate students who accepted scholarships which included some teaching or research, but which didn't specify how many hours were included. A few years later, the students find themselves having to work more and more hours, without extra pay, to claim their scholarships because the conditions have shifted. This is unethical, of course, but it happens all the time. Clarifying the detail at the beginning may not ultimately protect you, but is a good way to start.

Questions to ask about this include:

- Is this work part of the scholarship?
- How many hours are included in the 'funding package'? Is this fixed or can it change? How much do you get paid for work over and above what is included in the scholarship? Does having this scholarship make you ineligible to apply for extra work or opportunities? If the salary rate for teachers/research assistants goes up during your programme, will your rate go up as well?
- Are student teachers/researchers protected by a union?
- In subsequent years, do you have the option of working more or fewer hours if you need to? How would you be compensated?

It is tempting to ask these questions and to accept casual answers. Make sure that everything you ask is answered IN WRITING and that you keep all of this correspondence. Clarify anything you don't understand. Chances are that you won't have any problems, but it is worth taking the time before you accept the scholarship to clarify the terms.

It is not unusual that you might be offered an entrance scholarship for the first year of your study and then be asked to compete for additional scholarships once you are a member of the department. This can work well, but make sure you check the following.

- Are you eligible for these other scholarships? Many scholarships are not available to international students, or you have a very low chance of getting them; you need to know this in order to make good decisions.
- What happens if, for some reason, you DON'T get another scholarship? Will you have to leave the department?

> **Heads up**
>
> Many scholarships are regarded as taxable income. Be clear about how much tax you will have to pay or you may find that your scholarship is significantly less than you had budgeted for.

Don't assume that, once you are in, money will be found. This is sometimes true, but it is very risky for an international student to begin a programme without assurances of financial support after the first year. This is also true if you are offered funding for less than the full term of your course – three years of funding for a five-year course, for example; it is easy to ignore the implications of this but you need to consider seriously how you will fund these final years.

 All problems are augmented when you are away from home especially financial ones so you should think carefully before you go.

Erin, studying in Berlin

> **Heads up**
>
> Students may be expected to hold jobs outside of the university in order to 'make ends meet'. Bear in mind that you might not be permitted to do so, if your student visa does not permit it. Be clear about these restrictions *before* you go, and have alternative arrangements in place. The fact that other students are able to make it work does not mean that you, as an international student, will have the same opportunities.

If you are not ready to think through the minutiae of your finances, focus your attention on the big picture. As you narrow down your options, revisit this chapter and continue to revisit your finances as your planning gets more detailed. Many students have told us that they wished they had been more realistic about their budgeting and financial needs before they left. Have a financial plan and be willing to change it as you need to.

● **Further resources**

- UNESCO scholarships database.
  www.unesco.org/ed_sa/cgi-bin/search/index.cgi
    This is a comprehensive database of scholarships available across the world, and is searchable by subject area or country. The list of universities in each country is very extensive, and the information is accurate.
- The Association of Commonwealth Universities.
  www.acu.ac.uk
    Click on 'ENTER' and then on 'Funding your studies or work abroad' for a list of scholarships available at universities in the Commonwealth.
- Student Money.
  www.scholarship-search.org.uk
    Primarily for British students, this has a search engine of funding opportunities, as well as other information about money matters, such as budgeting and financial planning. You can search for scholarships specifically for part-time students, mature students and students with a disability.
- Gail A. Schlachter and R. David Weber, *Financial Aid for Study and Training Abroad, 2006–2008* and *Financial Aid for Research and Creative Activities Abroad 2006–2008* (Reference Service Press, 2006).
  www.rspfunding.com
    These resources provide extensive opportunities for accessing funding for study, research and artistic study worldwide. It is worth looking at Reference Service Press's other titles as well, as some of the books discuss funding opportunities for specific disciplines. Some of the titles are available in e-book format.

- Jean-Marc Hachey, *The Big Guide to Living and Working Overseas* (International Systems/Systèmes interculturels).
  www.workingoverseas.com
  > This book is intended to offer 'international career advice for young professionals', and is useful for students who want to work abroad or who want to use their international experience to build their career. Available online as well as in print.
- Institute for International Education Study Abroad Funding.
  http://studyabroadfunding.org
  > A searchable database of scholarships for study abroad around the world. Although it is designed primarily for US students, there are a number of opportunities which are not nationality-specific. Many of the opportunities are replicated in the print resource *Financial Resources for International Study*.
- The British Council.
  www.educationuk.org/
  > Primarily for UK students or others wishing to study in the UK. Also offers options for foreign students to study for a UK qualification from their own home.
- *Financial Resources for International Students*: Peterson's Guide.
  > A print resource which is regularly updated. US-biased, but can be useful for students of other nationalities as well.
- International Education Financial Aid
  www.iefa.org
  > Mostly focused on funding for US students, but has an interesting list of links about funding options in other countries as well.
- Rotary International
  www.rotary.org
  > Rotary International – often provides scholarships and awards for students to study abroad as 'cultural ambassadors'.
- Susan Griffith, *Work Your Way Around the World* (Vacation Work Publications, 2003).
  > Not targeted specifically at students, but many of the tips for travelling and working are potentially useful.

5 The Application Process

So you've narrowed your options, started to think about your finances, and chosen one or more programmes to which you would like to apply. The application process might be very simple, involving a single application form, or might be quite involved. Either way, it can be lots of fun. This is your chance to work out how you want to represent yourself. Your application is a testament not only to what you have already done but also to your goals and potential. It can be a great way to reflect on how far you have come, and to imagine where you want to go in the future.

Keeping your options open

Some programmes – especially short language and cultural exchanges – assign places until the programme is filled. In these cases, you will probably just have to fill out an application form and pay a fee and you will be assured a spot. However, if the programmes you are interested in are competitive, or if there are limited places, you might choose to submit applications to a number of different ones. If you are applying for longer programmes, especially as a post-graduate student, you will almost certainly be in competition with other students, and we strongly recommend that you put out more than one application to avoid disappointment. Make sure, though, that you don't submit so many applications that you don't have the time and energy to do each one well.

Heads up

As soon as you decide which programmes you are applying to, find out whether you need to submit an application, or be put on a waiting list, for housing, if you are hoping to live on campus. Housing is often in high demand and requires early application.

Aspects of the application process

Some applications will involve several different parts. For some programmes, you might have to submit different applications to different parts of the university: for example, a departmental application to gain entry into the programme you want to do and then another application for an individual college or for housing. Scholarship applications might also be separate, with different deadlines. In addition, the application process can be a lengthy one, sometimes taking several months or more. Obviously, the more involved each application is, and the more applications you are preparing, the more work you will have to do.

Organization

When you put together your application(s), you will probably be doing it while you juggle other commitments, and the people on your team are also likely to be busy. Maintaining a high level of organization as you go through this process then, is crucial. Being organized will ensure that:

- You can make the best decisions – if you are rushed, you might not make decisions that are right for you.
- You have the thinking time you need to do your best work.
- You have the time to get the appropriate feedback from people who can help you – including your teachers, family, or study abroad/career counsellors.
- You meet all your deadlines (universities and educational programmes are under no obligation to consider applications that arrive late).
- You have as many options open to you as possible – for example, you won't miss an opportunity for an orientation session about studying abroad, or might have the chance to talk to other people who have been to your destination country.
- You can sit any examinations you may need to sit.
- You have time to deal with unexpected difficulties.
- Your referees' time and energy is respected (more about referees later).
- You are more likely to be able to take advantage of funding and housing opportunities. For example, a scholarship deadline might be *earlier* than an academic deadline, and campus housing might be competitive and require early application.
- You can keep costs down (the later you leave the application process, the more likely it is you will have to pay late fees, expen-

sive courier charges or extra fees for express transcript services).

- You are less at the mercy of technological problems, for example faulty internet connections, computer problems and so on, and you will have more time to find alternatives if you do encounter technological difficulties (imagine waiting until the last possible minute to submit an online application, only to find that the server is too busy to process your submission!).

In order to meet deadlines, make sure you keep a clear record of when different applications, and different parts of an application, are due. Make sure you are also very clear about what is expected of you, so you don't inadvertently forget part of an application.

TIP When you are recording the deadlines for various parts of the application, double check whether the dates are when you have to put things in the mail (often designated by 'post-marked') or when they have to arrive. Leave plenty of time for international mail delivery, remembering that times of the year around significant holidays, in either your home or destination country, can often delay mail significantly.

Effective contact with universities

Throughout the processes of working out your options and applying to universities, it is likely that you will have contact with a number of different people both at your home university and at your destination university. Keep the following tips in mind as you communicate with them:

Be polite and respectful

Use a formal email address which includes your name

Having an email address such as i_really_want_to_get_in@hotmail.com is a bad idea. So are confusing email addresses which do not include your name.

Always include a descriptive subject line in an email

Universities often have sophisticated 'anti-spam' software, and badly labelled emails may be rejected by the system, or end up in a 'junk-mail' box.

Be strategic about who you contact

If you send the same email to ten different people, they are all likely to assume that someone else has contacted you. As a result, you might not get any replies.

Be patient

It will take time for people to get back to you. If you have not received a response to a query within a reasonable time, it is fine to send a follow-up checking that your email was received, but remember that these are busy people and are trying to help many other students at the same time as helping you.

Do your research

Check the university's website for answers to your questions before you send an email asking someone for help.

Be reasonable in your expectations

For example, a university is unlikely to return an international phone call. Staff and faculty may not always be available to help you immediately, and there may be limits to what they can do to help.

Be aware that the people you are contacting have numerous responsibilities and so may not remember everything about your particular case

Politely remind the receiver of who you are and what your query was, rather than assuming that they remember. Don't force them to check their files or go through old emails if they don't have to.

Be intelligent about your questions

Different people have expertise in different areas. For example, don't ask the chair of the department about whether the university has a ballroom dancing club, or a student services official about specialists in the department. If you're not sure who to ask, politely raise your query and ask for guidance in getting in touch with the right person.

Use formal language in all your correspondence

This will often be the university's first impression of you, so avoid slang, colloquial language, and email chat language. If you are communicating in a second language, have a native speaker check over your correspondence.

Check attachments for viruses

Infecting someone's computer is not a good way of making a good first impression.

Don't add the people you are communicating with to your personal contacts list.

We both regularly get emails from former students inviting us to read their online blogs. Consider how this might affect how professional you are perceived to be.

Be conscious of using appropriate forms of address

Use official titles (Dr, Ms, Mr), and check that you are using them correctly. You can usually find these on the university's website or in its documentation. If you are unsure of the gender of the person you are contacting, refer to them using their full name, for example 'Dear Caroline Rueckert.' If you receive a reply which uses a personal name (e.g. 'Regards, Caroline'), it is reasonable to use this first name in future correspondence, but you should revert to their title in formal situations. Once you are enrolled as a student, some of these rules may change, but it is best to maintain formalities during the application process.

Treat everyone with respect, regardless of 'rank'

We have both experienced colleagues who treat administrative staff badly; this is not only offensive but also very bad judgement.

Application costs

There are a number of aspects of the application process which can get costly, and you will need to take this into consideration when you decide how many applications to submit. Costs can include:

- Application fees – for example, university application fees, study-abroad programme fees, or the fees involved with housing applications
- Costs of transcripts (many universities charge high amounts for copies of your transcript)
- International phone calls (less of a problem with the advent of email, but sometimes still an issue)
- Postage
- Late fees – costs are sometimes higher if you miss early deadlines

Grades and transcripts

For many exchange programmes or language programmes, your transcript might not be relevant to the application process. Often, though, you will be asked to include a transcript, indicating what courses you have taken and what grades you were given.

Heads up

One of the popular misconceptions that we have come across is that you have to be an outstanding student to consider studying abroad as a post-graduate student. This is not necessarily true, although grades do often play an important role. In fact, changing countries can make you a more competitive candidate. We know several people who have been 'average' students (according to grades) within one country's education system who have moved elsewhere and found that they were regarded as exceptional students in their new environment because different skill and talents were valued. Having said this, grades are an important part of an application in most cases, and transcripts will almost always form a part of a post-graduate application.

If you do have to include a transcript with your application, even if you are concerned that your grades are not good enough, there are a number of reasons why your application might still be successful:

- Universities are interested not only in what you have done, but in your potential. This means that poor grades can be compensated for by, for example, strong references and a good statement of intent.
- Universities usually understand that it may have taken you a while to find your feet intellectually. Many students struggle during the early stages of their university or college education, and then find that they excel later. Committees are very sympathetic, and will usually care more about your recent grades, especially if you can explain how you have developed, in your statement of intent.
- Transcripts not only offer grades, but also valuable information about the courses you have taken. These might be important to assess whether you have the necessary prerequisites for your study. They are also used to assess your interests and what other courses you have done, to evaluate how you might fit in with the new programme. In this context, grades are less important than your commitment to the courses you have taken.

Tips about transcripts

Bear in mind the costs of transcripts when you decide how many applications to submit.

Check the expectations of your destination university or exchange programme. Are transcripts expected to be laminated and to include an official seal? Should they arrive in specially sealed envelopes? Almost inevitably, the university you are going to will have a different system from your home university, and you will have to negotiate the differences. This may involve including a note in your application explaining, for example, that your university does not put its transcripts in an envelope to ensure authenticity, or that you have been unable to include a transcript with your application because your university only sends them directly to other organizations.

Make sure you are clear whether the application process requires transcripts to be sent directly to the university or if they are to be included in the application.

Leave plenty of time to order your transcripts, and for postal times.

Make sure that your transcripts are up-to-date. For this reason, unless you have graduated, don't order too many transcripts, since they will go out of date quickly.

When you order transcripts to be sent to your application university, double check the addresses they are to be sent to.

If you are lucky, the university might accept certified copies of your transcripts. Unfortunately, though, most ask for originals, which can be challenging for your budget. It is highly unlikely that you will get them back.

Equivalence qualifications

The ways that students are rated differs from country to country and from university to university. If, for example, you have been rated on a scale of 1–7, your grades may seem meaningless (or inaccurate) in a system which uses a 1–4 scale, or a 1–9 scale. Some universities are sensitive to this problem, but most are unlikely to do the mathematics to convert grades, which can disadvantage international students. You may consider including a brief explanation of your grades, even if an explanation appears on your transcript, to make sure that the university is aware of what they mean. This is especially a problem when the scales appear to be the same, but mean very different things. For example, a grade of 70% is a 'distinction' in some university systems, while in others a distinction might be a grade of 90%. If these differences are not explained clearly, a student from either system might be inadvertently penalized in the selection process.

Universities may also be unsure whether the courses you have taken are equivalent to what they offer, in terms of the demands, content, assessment and time commitment. One of the ways of demonstrating equivalency is through a detailed list of all the subjects you have studied at university and the requirements for each. Some universities routinely offer this with your transcript, but many do not. If your home university does not, you might consider creating one yourself, especially if you are unsure whether a foreign university will accept your degree or programme as being equivalent to their own programmes. You could do this by going back to descriptions in the course handbook for each relevant year, or by summarizing the information on your course syllabuses.

TIP Even if you do an entire degree in another country, you may still need to ask questions about equivalency. Will your degree be recognized in your home country by employers and universities? If you later want to go on to do further study, will you have the prerequisites that you will need? Much more is possible than it may seem, but you do need to think ahead and know what questions to ask, so that you don't find yourself frustrated later. This is especially true of professional degrees – for example, getting a law/teaching/medical degree in one country does not necessarily mean that your credentials will be recognized by professional associations in your home country, so you may not be able to practise your profession without further accreditation.

Language and translation

If you are applying to a university that teaches in a language other than your own, you may have to take this into account in the application process. In some programmes, it will be fine for you to submit your application in your own language – especially if it is an exchange programme with your own university. In other cases, though, you will need to write an application that demonstrates command over your new language. Make sure you are very clear about the expectations in this regard.

If your official documents, including transcripts, are in a language other than the one you will be using, you will need to have them translated. It is worth investing in an official translator, not only to ensure accuracy but also to offer credibility. You may need to get them 'notarized' as being an authentic translation of the originals. Bear in mind the costs involved with translation when you decide how many programmes to apply for.

● Tailoring applications for different cultural expectations

The question of 'translation' is more complex, though, than just working in different languages. Different universities and countries will have different expectations about what it appropriate in your application. These expectations are often implicit and understood by students working within a given system, but may take some negotiation from those coming from outside.

Some tips for 'cultural translation':

If you have to include a curriculum vitae (CV) with your application, try to find out what is expected in your new country. There may be aspects that you will need to include that you might not usually have to, or aspects which you should leave out. For example, in some places, it will be standard to include your birth-date and marital status on your CV, while in other places, this would be deemed inappropriate or just unnecessary.

Make sure you read instructions carefully; the expectations will often be implicit in the language that is being used. For example, a personal statement and a research proposal are asking for different things. (More about that later.)

The appropriate tone of your application will vary from place to place. In some cultures, students are taught to downplay their credentials and there

---

Heads up

If the programme you want to undertake is a specialized programme of some sort, for example an applied arts course, you may have to include a folio of work or other specialized form of application. Interviews or samples of work may make up a significant component of your application process, and it may be especially difficult to work out credit transfer. Make sure you ask a lot of questions and check exactly what is required of you. Bear in mind, too, that folios, videos, music samples and so on are also culturally specific so be clear about what is expected. In addition, if your application makes use of technology (for example, audio, video or digital technologies) bear in mind that specifications vary from country to country; check that the formatting you use will be able to be accessed by the selection committee.

may be an emphasis on sub-text, or reading between the lines. In other university cultures, students are taught to be quite explicit about their achievements and may come across as boastful. If you are unsure what is expected, find someone who has experience of that country. Many academics have experience overseas, so it may be quite easy to find someone to advise you. Check with your study abroad office or international student centre. The internet may have samples you can look at (although make sure they are relevant for the country you are going to). And if you are still unsure, contact the international student centre at the university you are applying to and ask for some guidance.

> **TIP** Many universities run workshops for their students on how to write a curriculum vitae, letters of interest, job applications and so on, and information on these topics is increasingly being posted online. You can use the information offered by your destination university to give you a better sense of the implicit assumptions and expectations of the university to which you are applying, in order to find the appropriate tone and content of your own application.

Transferring credits

If you are a student going abroad for part of your degree, and hope to get credit from your home university, you will need to ensure that this will happen ahead of time. If your study abroad is part of an exchange programme organized through your university, this will probably be a very simple process, but if you are organizing it yourself, it might get more complex. You have probably already researched credit as you were exploring your options; now, though, you will have to check what you must do in your application to ensure that you get the credit you need.

The people you need to speak to about how to get credit may include a study-abroad counsellor/advisor if your university has one. Alternatively, your registrar, dean or admissions officer may be able to help. If in doubt, ask your departmental secretary (holder of all wisdom) for advice about who to approach. Most universities will have some kind of official policy to guide you – this policy may or may not work in your favour. Depending on the programme you chose, credit transfer might be a very simple process, or may require some imagination and negotiation. You may need to include additional documentation in your application to set this process in motion.

Heads up

> Make sure you organize credit transfer BEFORE YOU LEAVE. It is usually much harder to claim it when you return if it has not been pre-approved. Get all approvals in writing.

Some questions to ask

What documentation do I need from my study-abroad programme to claim credit?

Sometimes you will just need the course or programme description from the handbook/calendar. Sometimes you may need to provide a lot more information such as the number of hours of study, information about the teaching faculty, course format, mode of assessment, grading system and criteria, and reading lists. Some universities will also ask you to keep copies of all the assessment you do while abroad and ask you to submit it for approval before granting you credit.

What accreditation does my programme need to have to be approved?

If your study abroad is through an organized programme, there may be certain kinds of accreditation required in your home country in order for it to be able to count toward your degree.

What can I earn credit for?

Check whether your proposed programme of study will count towards your major or only your minor or both, and, if applicable, whether language courses count. You might also want to check whether you can get credit for volunteer work, independent study, internships or job placement programmes, depending on what you want to do abroad. Also, if you plan to write an undergraduate dissertation while abroad, check what you need to do to have this recognized by your home institution.

Will the credits I gain overseas be regarded as fulfilling the necessary prerequisites for other courses I want to complete?

Many upper-year courses rely on you having particular prerequisites. Check whether you will fulfil these in your study abroad, or if you will have to take extra credits when you return (which could make your time to degree longer).

> **TIP** While you are studying abroad, you will probably want to take advantage of opportunities to travel, explore your new country, socialize and so on. To make this possible, try to avoid taking more courses than your university regards as a normal load while abroad, even if you can get credit for them. Bear in mind that it is harder to be a student in an unfamiliar environment, and you will have additional stresses anyway, without extra work.

Will my grades while abroad count towards my Grade Point Average (GPA), and towards having enough credit to graduate?

Your grades from studying abroad might not count towards your GPA – this can affect future opportunities (such as post-graduate work). In addition, there may be no system for recognizing your credits in working out when you are eligible to graduate. This can postpone your graduation, and therefore be disappointing if you are not prepared for it.

> **TIP** Bear in mind that there is sometimes a difference between being able to use credits earned abroad as prerequisite requirements for other courses and being able to use those credits towards your degree. You might find that you can do the former, but not be allowed to graduate. With a little planning, you might be able to avoid this scenario.

What grades do I need to maintain while abroad in order to claim credit?

Many schools will specify that you need to maintain a minimum grade in order for it to count. Make sure you are aware of this. Also, check whether pass/fail courses can be counted.

How is transfer credit calculated?

Bear in mind that different universities calculate credit according to different criteria with regards to semesters, terms, year, course hours and so on. Be clear about how the differences in these systems might affect how your credit is calculated.

How will my grades from abroad appear on my transcript?

Sometimes grades will be translated and incorporated onto your transcript at your home university, and sometimes your study abroad will be noted without grades on your transcript. This may also influence your GPA.

References

In many applications for study abroad, you will be asked to provide at least one reference from someone who knows you. Many universities will ask for two or three references, attesting to different aspects of your background and potential. For scholarships or graduate programmes, you may be asked to provide several references from a variety of referees. You will need to take some time to consider who you would like to ask to be your referees.

There are a variety of different kinds of references:

Character reference   this comes from someone who knows you at a personal level and can write about your character. The best person to choose for this kind of reference is someone who has known you for a long time and is a leader in your community. This person may be a sports coach, extracurricular activity leader, teacher, religious leader, or family friend, for example.

Professional reference   This comes from someone who has worked with you in a professional capacity, which may include paid work or volunteer work. S/he will usually be your immediate supervisor, manager or leader; someone who has worked with you and knows what you have done and what you are capable of doing but who is not a peer.

Academic reference   Most university applications will place an emphasis on academic references. An academic reference is written by a teacher, professor or lecturer to attest to your academic credentials. As an under-graduate, this may be one of the teachers for one of your courses who can comment on your work; as a post-graduate student, this will include detailed discussion of your research, publications, conference presentations and so on. Many academic referees may also address your character or your other activities, if this is relevant.

Make sure you are clear about what kind of reference is being asked for. Sometimes, it will not be specified and you will have to make a judgement based on the kind of application you are submitting, and the level that you are at.

Most of the time, universities ask for written references, but occasionally you might simply be asked for the names of your referees. The university will then phone or email them, often with specific questions. It is also standard practice that anyone who writes you a written reference might also be contacted for further information, if necessary.

The importance of referees

Your choice of referee is an important one. These are the people who will be testifying not only to your current abilities but to your potential. Selection committees at all levels tend to take references quite seriously, so they can have a huge influence on whether you are successful in getting into the programme you want.

Bear in mind, too, that your relationship with your referee will often go beyond a single application. Sometimes, your relationship might last for years, and you might continue to use your reference for many different applications throughout your career. It is not unusual for post-graduate students to still be in contact with the people who supported them when they were undergraduates. Referees can also be a wonderful source of emotional support; having someone who believes in you and sees your potential can help you through some of the doubt, anxiety and disappointment that you might experience on the way, as well as being someone to celebrate with you when you achieve your goals. If you are applying to do post-graduate-level work, your family and friends might not have the specialized knowledge to understand your research or your ideas. In this case, your referees might be the only people with whom you can really discuss your ideas and who see the potential in what you want to do.

Choosing a referee

Occasionally, someone will offer to help you without your having to ask, but most of the time you will have to initiate a conversation by asking someone to be a referee for you. Sometimes, your choice of referee will be obvious – there will often be one or two people who have been very supportive of you, having given you various forms of encouragement, such as good grades and/or supportive feedback on your work. But if your choice is not so obvious, there are a few things to consider.

Professor Famous vs personal contact

You might be tempted to approach a faculty member who is famous and very well known in their field. Think through this carefully. Does this faculty member know you and your work? Can they write enthusiastically and in depth about your achievements? If the answer is yes, great. But if there is another faculty member who is less well-known, but knows you personally and has worked with you for longer and knows your work better, choose him/her. It is important that your referee knows you as an individual, and can write with confidence and detail. Having said that, rank and seniority can make a difference, so don't dismiss this consideration entirely.

Heads up

Never choose someone as your referee who doesn't really know you. If the university does contact your referee and he/she barely remembers your name, this does not bode well for you, even if the written reference is strong. In some cases, your teachers might not know you personally, especially if you have very large classes. They may still be willing to be a referee, and will probably ask you for some additional information, and might consult your tutors or teaching assistants or others who have had more personalized contact with you.

Recent contact

Choose someone who has worked with you recently. The person who taught you piano when you were eight might write you a glowing reference but it won't have much sway with a committee now. Try to choose someone who can write about who you are now, and what your potential is. If you have the option of someone who knows you well now, but can also write about your development because they have known you for a while, that can also be a good choice.

Pick up cues

It is completely acceptable to approach a potential referee and to let them know what you are planning and to ask 'Do you think you would be able to write me a strong reference?' (Don't just ask for a reference; you need to know that this person supports you and will write a *strong* reference.) Few people will say no, though, so you may need to pick up verbal cues. If they say something like 'I would love to' or 'It would be my pleasure', they will probably be supportive. Hesitancy, on the other hand, might reflect that you can do better. Listen for phrases like 'Well, I suppose I could but I have a very bad memory' or 'Well, I'm very busy at the moment. Could you ask Dr X?' – your referee is telling you that s/he doesn't really want to write you a reference, and it is in your best interests to hear these cues rather than pushing; if s/he is not supportive, the reference will probably also be lukewarm.

Balance

If you have been asked for more than one reference, consider the total package they will create. If you have two referees who know you in exactly the same context and will write very similar things about you, you might be better choosing someone who can highlight your other strengths. If one of your referees is a young, less experienced member of faculty, you might choose to balance this with a more senior faculty member. Think about how you will be represented to the selection committee and proactively balance the referees you choose. If you continue with university education as a post-graduate student and beyond, you will probably end up with a small team of referees, and will choose which ones are the most appropriate for a particular grant, job opportunity or application.

Reliability

Some referees might be very supportive of you in terms of what they think of you, but might not be able to be relied on. If you have experience of one of your referees forgetting what they have promised to do, or of finding that a crucial reference was never put in the mail, or if that person won't respond to phone calls or emails and so on, you may have to cut your losses and choose someone else. An occasional error is to be expected, and it is OK to send your referees a reminder, but if you find that you don't fundamentally trust your referee to come through for you, it might be worth finding someone else.

Intuition

Your intuition is very likely to bea good guide as to who you should ask for support. If your gut instinct is that a faculty member is not supportive of you, trust that instinct, even if you don't really have any tangible reason for thinking so. At the very least, you will feel happier and more confident if you trust that your referee is on your side.

Experience abroad

When you are applying to study abroad, it can frequently be useful to have a referee, or at least a mentor, who has had experience in the country you are planning to go to. They will have a better sense of what is expected than others might. Utilize whatever help they offer you.

Treating your referees with respect

It is probably part of your teachers' jobs to write references, but at the same time they are under no obligation to help you in this way. Most faculty do so because they are genuinely supportive and want to help you to achieve your goals. There are a number of ways in which you can respect them and help them to help you.

Give them plenty of time

You want them to be able to think about your reference, to write it well and to have the time to review your work. Also, bear in mind that your teachers may go on study leave, and not be contactable for extensive periods. Email is making this less of an issue, but don't assume that because your teacher is in email contact, s/he is necessarily available to help you.

Include them as part of the process

Your referees can be a strong source of support throughout the entire process. Talk to them about your options before the applications are due. Listen to their input. By the time you ask them to be a referee, they will be expecting it, and will have a strong idea of your goals.

Never list someone as a referee who has not agreed to it

If you are using the same referee repeatedly, drop them a line to let them know that you are applying for a new opportunity and re-ask permission to list them as a referee. Keep your referees updated on your latest achievements.

Prepare a package for them

Your referee will remember you, but may not remember details. For example, they may remember you as being intelligent, committed and enthusiastic but may not have a clue what topic you chose for your final essay. Don't tell them what to write, but do give them the information they need, to be able to write about you in detail. The package should include:

- Examples of your work, especially work that they graded. Guide them in remembering that they wrote 'Brilliant' in purple ink on every page.
- Your academic transcript. Your references will be stronger if your referees can comment on your overall academic achievement, as well as their own impressions of you.
- A curriculum vitae. Sometimes your referees will care what else you have done, and sometimes they won't. Give them the option of taking into account all of your achievements.
- Your statement of intent or personal essay (if applicable). It is easier for them to support your goals if they are clear about what your objectives are and how you have represented yourself.
- Relevant information about the university, scholarship, and so on. Don't just offer them a website – this takes time for them to look at. If the programme you are applying for wants to know about

your academic achievements, your success as a musician, and your character, you are not being fair to your referees if you don't give them this information. Make sure they are aware of the 'buzz words' in the criteria of whatever you are applying for.

- Other relevant information. If you have 'gaps' in your transcript – time off from university due to sickness or military service, for example, or had a semester when your grades dropped significantly because of personal or family issues, let your referees know about them. They can then choose to include this information in their reference, thus offsetting any questions the committee might have about why these gaps appear.

- Clear details about when the application is due, and where it should be sent. Also make it clear whether there is a special form to be filled in (many programmes ask for referees' reports to be sent using official departmental forms). If you are applying for multiple programmes, make it very clear when *each* of them is due, so your referee doesn't get confused, have to spend extra time working it out, or worse, miss crucial deadlines.

Send your referees follow-up emails, thanking them for their help and letting them know how your application turned out. This is not just for your benefit (remember you may want to use them as a referee in the future) but also because they have taken the time to care about you and they also have an investment in the outcome. They want you to be successful.

> **TIP** Remember that international academic communities can be surprisingly close-knit, and academics regularly meet at conferences and exchange notes with each other. Treat everyone, whether they are your referees or not, with respect; people have surprisingly long memories for students who are rude or disrespectful.

Examinations

Some programmes will ask you to sit an examination to demonstrate your language proficiency. Many of these are internationally recognized. Check which examination you are being asked to sit, but if you have already sat a language examination through a different organization, find out if this can be recognized instead.

In addition, some programmes require students to sit either general proficiency or discipline-specific exams. For example, if you want to study in the U.S. you may have to sit the SATs (Scholastic Assessment Test) for undergraduate work, and the GREs (Graduate Record Examination) for graduate work.

If your programme requires exams, you will need to plan for these up to a year in advance of your application date, and you may have to spend considerable energy studying for them.

In some cases, you will be able to sit the exams in your home country. You may have to travel to a capital city to do so, and some exams will have one session once a year. Others will have sessions frequently throughout the year in a variety of venues. Make sure you are clear about what exams you have to sit, what results you need, and how the university wants to receive the scores.

Many exams will have specialized resources to help you to prepare. You may have to order these from other countries, which can be expensive. Make sure you leave plenty of time for these to arrive if this is the case.

If you don't get the results you were hoping for, don't give up. Some universities see the examinations as a formality and may still accept you. You may have the chance to take a course during your first term in your new programme to make up for it. In some cases, you may need to sit the examination again, in which case you will probably have a better sense of what is expected of you from your 'practice' run. We know several students who have been extremely despondent after such exams, and believed that their dreams of studying abroad were over, but who found ways of moving forwards and reaching their goals. It is worth realizing, too, that some exams are far more culturally biased than they admit, which can make it tough for international students.

● Undergraduate statements of intent and personal essays

The statement of intent or personal essay is one of the most common aspects of an application. The university may ask for one essay or statement, or for several. Sometimes, you may be guided in writing your statement(s) by specific questions, such as:

What do you have to offer x university?
Describe a time when you have demonstrated leadership.
Where do you see yourself in five years?
Describe why you want to study x? or
Why do you want to study abroad?

Sometimes, you won't be given any guidance at all, and you will have to formulate your own statement.

Whether you are given guidance or not, the personal statement is intended to be your chance to show that you are a human being. You are more than numbers on a transcript, more than exam grades and more than your referee's opinions. Think of it as a personal narrative, which discusses who you have been, who you are now, and who you want to be, specifically showing how this application is going to help you become who you want to be. This is true whether the question is about your academic work, your extra curricular activities, your work experience or your leadership.

Heads up

There are many websites that go into considerable detail about how to write statements of intent and personal essays. Bear in mind that universities have different expectations and these are often discipline-specific. Use the examples you read as guidelines, but don't try to copy them, and check with your advisors to make sure you are on the right track. Personal statements are very diverse – don't buy into the belief that there is a perfect way to write one.

Heads up

The vast majority of examples of personal statements on the internet are heavily biased towards certain kinds of US models, even when they seem to claim to be 'universal'. This model might not be appropriate for where you are going.

Process

Give yourself the time to be able to respect the process involved in any good writing. If you sit down to a blank white page and expect to produce a brilliant personal statement you are likely to find yourself facing major writer's block, with all of the panic and anxiety that goes along with it. Allow yourself to go through the writing process:

- Brainstorm (all ideas are useful; don't worry about detail).
- Select viable ideas (cut ideas which are not relevant or which don't fit into what you want to say).

- Create an outline (organize your thoughts and plan each paragraph).
- Draft (no need for writer's block because you have already decided what you want to say).
- Edit for content (don't worry about language).
- Edit for spelling, grammar and language (by now the content should be strong).
- Re-edit and revise.

Following this process will help you to organize your ideas and the final result is likely to be stronger.

Keep in mind that you are writing an essay about yourself, so there is very little research needed. There are no right or wrong answers. You are unique, so your statement will also be unique.

If you find it hard to write your statement, go back to why you want to study abroad and how it fits in with your future goals. If you need to, ask some people you trust what makes you unique and why they like/respect you. Tune into that voice inside you that *knows* why you should get into the programme you are applying to.

Tips for personal statements/statements of intent:

Think of this as your academic story. Don't repeat information that is available on your transcripts or application form. Use it as a chance to explain how you got to where you are and where you intend to go from here.

- Be specific. Use specific experiences and examples to demonstrate who you are.
- Avoid clichés.
- Try to 'show' rather than 'tell'. Rather than make your statement a shopping-list of your achievements, use your experiences to demonstrate what you have learnt. Explain why your experiences are important, and how they have affected you. Relate these experiences back to the goals of the programme you are applying to, and why your background would lead to your success in the programme. Show that you have thought about who you are and what you have to offer.
- Use facts and be specific. Avoid arrogant statements about how terrific you are and how much you have to offer; let your examples show that you are great. Give them the facts of what you have to offer, and let the committee decide.

- Be respectful of length requirements.
- Explain any gaps in your application, for example time off due to sickness, bad grades for a term, work experience, family duties and so on (make sure your referees are also aware of them, so that they can back you up).
- Be specific about your past experiences and projects and let your reader know whether you are building on these or moving in a new direction. Use personal detail, rather than vague generalizations.
- Be concise. Every word should be carefully chosen. Don't use ten words if you can use five, but make sure you explain your ideas.
- Use your own voice. Don't use a thesaurus to find words that will make you sound 'smart/knowledgeable/erudite/intellectual. . . .'
- Share your statement with people who might be able to help you.

Heads up

If you are applying to several universities, it can be easy to forget to change the name of the university in your application. Make sure you check repeatedly that you have edited your application each time you submit it. Also, check the spelling of the names of any faculty members you mention.

- Edit and re-edit. And then edit again. This is crucial.
- Be cautious about using irony, parody, humour or sarcasm – these are highly culturally specific and often to do not 'translate'.
- Be cautious of phrases and turns of speech that might not be understood in another country.

Statements of intent will usually be read by a committee, and it is strange sometimes what people will remember. We have both been in the position of meeting faculty members a long time after our application process and having them remember the oddest aspects of our applications. 'Oh – you're the one who . . .'.

TIP Keep copies of your personal statements. You never know when you might want to revise them for a new opportunity. It is also a great way of tracing your own intellectual development.

● Post-graduate applications

If you are applying to a graduate/post-graduate programme, your statement of intent will be a little different from the undergraduate model. There is usually very little emphasis on personal anecdotes or your experiences. It is more the narrative of your thinking than your personality. You will often not be given any guidance, so it is important to tailor your statement to the particular discipline and context. Generally speaking, use the statement of intent to discuss what you have done intellectually, how that has affected your thinking and where you intend to take your ideas in the future. In addition, you should specifically explain why the university you are applying to would fit in with your research interests and how its resources would be a good fit for you. To this end, your statement will generally contain mention of specific faculty members (who you have already contacted and with whom you have been in dialogue) and how their research coincides with your own. Make sure you show clearly how your current goals fit in with the choices you have made previously. If this is a shift for you, explain how that shift evolved. You should also use your statement of intent to explain any 'gaps' in your application, for example any inconsistent grades, or time off.

There is generally less emphasis on extracurricular and community involvement at the post-graduate level than at the undergraduate level, although some scholarships are looking for more than just academic skills. However, bear in mind that your volunteer work or your professional experience may well be very important to your programme. For example, we have come across students who, in applying to a Masters of Education programme, have neglected to mention that they have twenty years' teaching experience. Think of your application as a holistic entity – strong professional experience or professional development work might offset some less-than-stellar grades, and clear potential in a new direction might mitigate a lukewarm reference. So think carefully about whether your hobbies, volunteer work or employment history are linked to your area of application and make sure you include anything that is relevant.

The post-graduate research proposal

At post-graduate level, the statement of intent may or may not include a research proposal – sometimes these are separate documents and sometimes they are not. If you are asked for your research plans, or proposal, you are being asked to talk specifically about your area. You may have to do considerable research to be able to produce an articulate, clear proposal in your field, and you may be asked to include a bibliography.

If you have a clear sense of the research you want to do, make sure this comes through in your application. Often, though, you will find that you have a set of ideas and research interests. It is perfectly reasonable to discuss these interests without having a very detailed proposal in mind. The university may ask you to provide more detail later. If you are applying to a programme which is composed only of the thesis, you may need to have more detail than if you are applying to a programme which includes coursework and other requirements before you begin the thesis. In either case, it is understood that your ideas are likely to change, so don't worry too much about tying yourself in to your project. But it should include a level of detail appropriate to your area, bearing in mind that it will probably be read by both specialists and non-specialists in your area. By this stage, try to avoid statements such as 'I want to study history because I have a passion for the subject' – you wouldn't be applying if you didn't love your subject, so get on with explaining your ideas and why you want to do the research you are proposing.

Heads up

Many disciplines will have very specific expectations for the research proposal, and you will need to show mastery of the genre in order to be taken seriously.

Different universities will often ask for a different level of detail in research proposals. So you may find yourself preparing a 20-page document with detailed annotated bibliography for one university, and a 500-word abstract for another. If you have both documents you will have to make a decision. You should not submit documents that are longer than the length you are asked for. Some people advise that you should never submit extra documents with your application. We have both found, though, that if you have a much longer, more detailed proposal than the one you are officially submitting, it is worth including it in your application, especially as an international student. It may not always be photocopied and distributed to the selection committee, but it will usually be kept in your file. In addition, if you have made contact with a particular faculty member, you should make sure that s/he has seen the detailed proposal as well.

TIP If you have written a detailed proposal as well as a shorter (official) version, mention in the shorter version that a longer version exists. This means that, if committee members have not been given a copy of it, they are alerted to the fact that it exists – they may then ask to see it.

Putting your application together

When you put all the different parts of your application together, label things carefully, organize the package and make it clear what is enclosed and what is being sent later. Keep it neat and organized and make sure that the receiver of the package (usually a secretary or member of the administration support team) is aware of any unusual aspects of your application.

Consider the reactions of the committee members who have to read so many applications. To this end:

- Make sure your application is easy to read.
- Respect length requirements.
- Use reasonable font sizes and legible font types. (If you are asked for a one-page document, this is not your chance to show how many words you can fit on a single page by using a 4-point font.)
- Avoid coloured fonts or illustrations, unless you are applying for a programme where this is expected. You want to stand out for the right reasons, not because you use 'gimmicks'.
- Respect page margins.
- Label each section clearly.
- Try to leave some white space on the page; this is easier on the eye than dense text passages.
- Label each section carefully.
- Include a check list of contents for more complex applications.

Online applications

Increasingly, you can submit applications online (although often you still need to send in hard copies of documents such as transcripts or references). If you submit online, consider the following suggestions:

- Print off your draft application and edit it on paper; it is easier to detect errors on page than on the screen.
- Ensure that no errors are introduced into the document as you 'cut and paste'.
- If you have to edit your work to fit into a designated number of characters, lines or pages, be careful that you do not introduce new errors – reread and edit your work thoroughly.

- Give yourself plenty of time – consider the possibility that the internet connection might be down at precisely the time you need to submit your application.
- Check how you can be sure that your submission has been received – this might be an onscreen message, or an email. If you are unsure that it has gone through, check, via email or phone.
- If you do submit at the last minute, don't forget to take into account time differences, or you could miss the deadline.
- Print a copy for your records.
- Don't forget to send the relevant print documents as well, as required.

Mail applications

- Remember that international mail can take a long time to arrive, and leave sufficient time.
- Check addresses, accurately, and include all relevant postal codes.
- Mark the envelope clearly with your name and address.
- You might consider sending it by registered mail, so you can track its progress.
- If you have to send it by courier or other special service, you may need the name of a specific person who can sign for the package at the other end – this will often be at a different address from the postal address you have been given, so make sure you check beforehand.

Dealing with stress

Applying for programmes of study abroad can be quite a lengthy process, especially if you are applying for a number of programmes. If you are applying for post-graduate programmes, you might choose to wait until after you graduate, so that the time you spend on applications does not jeopardize your capacity to do well in your final undergraduate courses.

Tips for reducing stress in the application process

- Be organized.
- Keep a detailed calendar of what is due when. Doing this visually can be a good way of being able to keep this under control at a glance.
- Give yourself, and your referees, plenty of time.

- Don't be afraid to ask for help, and constantly expand the number of people on your 'team'.
- Keep your family and friends in the loop – make sure they know what is going on, and what your goals are, so that they can help you when things go wrong, and celebrate with you when things go right.
- Don't let your life get subsumed in the application process. Keep a balance. Don't put your normal life on hold in expectation of your study abroad.

When things go wrong

The likelihood is high that you will have to face unexpected challenges during the application process. Try to create a mental filter for these things, and ask yourself 'Do I need to panic or can this problem be solved?' When you have put so much work in and have a lot invested in the outcome, it can be easy to let things get out of proportion. It is not unusual that a document fails to arrive on time, despite your best efforts to be organized. Most of the time, the department (or programme or faculty) will let you know that there is a document missing and ask you to rectify the situation.

When things do go wrong, don't be afraid to ask for help. There are numerous people who might be able to assist you. Your departmental secretary, whether in your home university or the one you are applying to, can help you with all sorts of problems if you communicate clearly what has gone wrong. If you find yourself having to ask referees for a reference at the last minute because of some unforeseen situation, smile at them, explain the situation and be grateful when they offer to stay up until midnight writing on your behalf. Things happen and even the best organization in the world cannot always prevent these things happening. Bear in mind, though, that you are much more likely to get the help you need if you have treated your team with respect along the way and kept them in the loop.

TIP Keep back-ups and photocopies of ALL your documents.

Almost everyone we know who has done a few applications to universities has had last-minute challenges. Most students seem to have stories of a terrifying phone call from a (sympathetic) committee head just hours before the selection meeting, or of a twelfth-hour email indicating an incomplete application. In almost all cases, the students utilized the help of their team – including partners taking a morning off work to drop off an application, mothers pitching in by calling a courier, departmental secretaries going in to bat for them, departmental heads making exceptions, or roommates offering to retype lost files – and suffered no long-term consequences. It's horrible at the time, but try to keep it in perspective and see it as just a glitch in the process. Whatever happens, don't assume that it's all over, don't give up, and don't try to solve it all by yourself. (And if someone around you has the same problem, be the one to offer help, even if it is inconvenient.)

> **Heads up**
>
> Once you have submitted your applications, make some preliminary enquiries into the procedures for obtaining a student visa, and organize any documentation you will need, to do this, while you are waiting to hear whether your application is successful.

The outcome

At some point, probably several months after you submit your application and usually later than you were expecting, you will receive an email or a letter telling you whether you application was successful.

If you were unsuccessful

You have probably already started to plan your trip and visualized it in your mind, and so finding out that you haven't been successful can be quite painful. Tell your team the outcome. Students sometimes fear telling their advisors or friends that their application has been unsuccessful because they feel ashamed or embarrassed. But far more people around you will have received rejections throughout their life than you will ever know about, so they are likely to be sympathetic. Give yourself time to grieve over the outcome.

When you are ready and have taken the time to re-focus your energy, there are some steps you can take to continue to pursue your goal.

TIP   Most importantly, don't give up – keep going after what you want.

- Ask your advisor(s) for advice about what the weaknesses in your application might have been.
- Find ways to strategize about how to strengthen the areas you have identified. For example, if your grades could be better, an

extra year could give you a chance to raise them, as well as giving your referees more time to get to know you and your talents.

- Often, students are unsuccessful simply because the programme they applied to was not a good fit for their interests, background and needs. Keep researching to find programmes that match up with your abilities.
- Cast your net more widely – apply to a wider diversity of different programmes, to increase your chance of acceptance.
- If the programmes you applied for initially were highly competitive, consider programmes that might not be as competitive, or which have different criteria.
- Take the time to work on your weaknesses and prepare an application that is as strong as possible.

You may have to reconceptualize your plans the second time around, but many students are ultimately successful in their plans to study abroad if they are persistent and don't let a negative outcome deter them from their goals.

If you have been successful

Congratulations!

Letters of offer

Clarify anything you don't understand in your letter of offer.

The tone of the acceptance letter will vary depending on the university culture. Your letter might tell you that you are outstanding and be very laudatory about your potential. However, if your letter is much more distant and merely informs you that you have been accepted, don't assume that this means that the university is any less interested in you. Different universities have different styles.

I received offers for my master's from both Canada and the UK. The Canadian universities sent me very laudatory letters of congratulation, telling me what a terrific student I was. My acceptance from the UK was almost deadpan and began 'I am writing to inform you that your application has been successful.' Luckily, they liked me just as much as the Canadian universities – the letters just reflected a cultural difference.

Author insight: Caroline

It is quite likely that you will receive several offers and will need to make decisions. Take your time making those decisions. Don't try to make a decision until you have heard from all the universities you have applied to.

There will often be a deadline for making a decision. It is perfectly reasonable to ask for more time to make your choices, especially if you are waiting to hear from other universities. The answer might be no, though, in which case you will have to decide how to proceed without losing your offer.

- Don't be afraid to ask questions and follow up with the contacts you have made.
- If your offer is conditional on your completing certain courses, clarify what those expectations are, so you are clear on what you are being asked to do.
- Never accept more than one offer. This is bad form and can damage your reputation. Wait until you have made a final decision before accepting an offer.

Being placed on a waiting list is common. It does not necessarily mean that the university does not value what you have to offer. Many departments have quotas according to students' areas of specialization. On the other hand, if you have numerous offers, it may be worth your while to choose a department which has offered you a place straight away; sometimes this indicates that they will support you more down the road in terms of further scholarships and opportunities and so on. If you are put on a waiting list, make sure you clarify when you can expect a final decision. Sometimes, departments have been known to call on students on the waiting list only a few weeks before classes start, which for an international student is almost always an impossible situation.

As soon as you have decided not to accept an offer, let the university know (politely); other students may be waiting for that spot.

If you are going to a particular university only because you want to work with a specific faculty member, make this clear and confirm with the faculty member that they will be able to supervise you. It is not unusual for academics to move from one institution to another, or to take extended leave. You don't want to find yourself at a university that your mentor has recently left, or to be very enthusiastic about writing your thesis with a faculty member who is about to take three years of parental leave.

And finally:

- Never make ultimatums.

- Treat everyone with whom you have contact with respect, even if you are turning down an offer from them.
- Check the fine print – especially whether what you are being offered lasts for the duration of the programme or only for part of the time.
- Enjoy the excitement of the offer, but don't ignore potential problems that could come up later.

With your offer, you will probably be sent some more glossy brochures about your new university. Enjoy reading them and allow yourself to get excited. Send off your official acceptance and take some time to enjoy the anticipation of your new opportunity. Tell your friends and family, and celebrate a successful application. When you are ready to think about practicalities again you can start 'Preparing for Departure'.

In the meantime, congratulations. You made this happen.

6 Preparing for Departure

You've been accepted into a programme and now you have the chance to turn your dreams into a reality. This chapter will guide you through all the things you need to do prior to departure that will make sure your experience studying abroad is a positive one. You will have to consider a variety of different aspects of your preparation. Read this chapter in conjunction with the relevant sections of 'Staying Healthy', as there are medical preparations you will need to consider as you prepare to leave.

> **Heads up**
>
> Remember that preparing for departure involves both practical and emotional aspects, so make sure you maintain a balance, and don't become so focused on the practical preparations that you neglect the emotional preparation, or vice versa.

Academic considerations

When your destination university sends you the letter of offer, you will probably also receive a package of other orientation information. If you have not already done so, make sure you fill in all the appropriate forms and send them back to the university. Pay any deposits or fees that need to be paid before you arrive. You might also drop an email to the relevant person at the university, letting them know that the paperwork is in the mail. Make sure

> **Heads up**
>
> If you have to submit an application for campus housing and haven't already done so, you should do this as soon as you receive notification of your acceptance.

you meet all deadlines, taking into consideration the length of time for international mail to arrive.

Immigration concerns

Organizing your immigration documents can be a lengthy process, so make preliminary enquiries while you prepare your application and wait for the outcome. As soon as you have the official letter of offer, you should begin the process.

Passport

If you don't already have a passport, you will need to get one now. This will involve completing some paperwork, providing documentation to demonstrate your eligibility for the passport you are applying for (in your country of citizenship), paying a fee and providing passport photographs. If your passport will expire before the end of your study abroad programme, it is worth renewing it before you go, to save you the hassle of having to do it while abroad. In most cases, this will be a requirement in order to be issued a visa.

Most countries have strict regulations about passport photographs, including size, colour, background, whether you are allowed to wear glasses or smile and so on. Check the requirements for your country before you spend the money on getting them, and make sure you include as many as you are asked for.

TIP   Get some extra passport photos while you have the opportunity. They will come in handy later for such things as an international student card, or a transit pass.

Visas

Even if you do not need a visa to visit your new country as a tourist, in most cases you will need a visa as a student. To get one is a similar process to applying for a passport – you will have to complete paperwork asking you about your plans and your history, offer supporting documentation, pay a fee (which can be quite expensive) and, in some cases, provide more photographs (which may or may not have the same specifications as the passport photographs, so make sure you check). It can take several months for a visa to be processed, and you will sometimes have to submit your passport along with the documentation (if you are planning to travel internationally in the meantime, you will need to check what your options are, since you will be without your passport). Increasingly, visas are being issued electronically; if this is true in your case, make sure you have some kind of confirmation of the visa being issued, just in case the computer system lets you down when you arrive in your new country.

In some cases, the process of getting a student visa is simple, but sometimes there will be a number of decisions you have to make. Things to consider include:

Does your student visa allow multiple entries into the country? Sometimes you will have to pay extra for this. Consider, for example, that you might have the opportunity to travel during your study abroad, or that you might need to return home unexpectedly in case of a family crisis and then re-enter the country.

Does your student visa allow you to work? Many student visas have considerable restrictions on where you can work (for example, on campus only, in fields related/unrelated to your area of study), and how many hours you can work. If you are planning to work to finance your study, you need to be aware of what restrictions there are, before you go.

How long is the visa valid for? Is it extendable? There may be occasions when you might need to extend your stay. In longer programmes, your study might take longer than you anticipated, and even in shorter programmes, unexpected events might come up. For example, there have been occasions when teachers have gone on strike for a period of time, and the school term has thus been extended. In longer programmes, especially at post-graduate level, you might only be granted a visa for part of the time of your study and will be expected to extend it (and pay another fee).

Find out how long the visa is valid for after you have stopped being a student. If you plan to travel after the end of term, you may need an additional visa to allow you to do so.

If you plan to travel while abroad, find out what the visa requirements are for each country you plan to visit and plan accordingly.

Heads up

Check your immigration status in your own country as well.

I left Canada as a permanent resident, and not as a citizen. I found out three weeks before I left the UK that I had to apply for a re-entry visa into Canada or I might be denied entry into my home country! It hadn't even occurred to me that it would be a problem. Believe me, the last thing you want to have to worry about while you are abroad is how to get home again.

Author insight: Caroline

Other travel documents

In order to apply for passports and visas, you will probably need some or all of the following documents:

Birth certificate
Marriage/divorce certificates as relevant
Immunization document
Residency documents
Citizenship documents
Proof of parental status, if you have a different surname from your child, as well as your children's birth certificates.

You should also carry certified COPIES (not originals) of these documents. You might need them for such things as opening a bank account, registering in your new university, or applying for government documents such as health care or a driving licence.

Heads up

If you do not have originals of these documents, you will probably need to apply to receive them in order to get your immigration documents. Bear in mind that this can take a long time, and can be costly.

Travel arrangements

When you are booking flights or other travel, bear in mind that booking well in advance can help you to take advantage of discounts.

Tips for booking flights

- Make sure you mention that you are flying for the purposes of study; there may be student discounts available. Many places have specialized student travel agencies, and these can be a good place to start.
- Shop around for price and convenience. The internet can help you to do this, but bear in mind that the best prices are not always those available online, especially for students, so make sure you check.
- Consider your stress levels. Numerous stopovers might make the journey a little cheaper in some cases, but might greatly increase your stress levels. Also, try to fly directly into the closest airport in your new country, so that you do not have to connect with many buses or trains, if possible.
- When you are choosing your departure date, try to give yourself some time in your new country before classes and other commitments begin; you will need it to get settled.
- Buy a return ticket, if possible. For longer programmes, this won't be possible, but customs officials in many countries might be suspicious of one-way tickets for shorter programmes – they want to know that you plan to leave again.
- Choose a ticket that allows you to change your return date easily and inexpensively.
- When considering the return date, remember that the last day of classes is not the same as the last day of term – most universities have examination blocks after classes end, for which you will probably need to be present.
- If you are travelling as part of an organized programme, make sure you know what date you are expected to arrive, and plan your travel accordingly.

TIP   If you have to book connections, give yourself plenty of time to get from one mode of transport to another. Connections that you could make quickly and easily in a place you are familiar with will take much longer in a new place, and delays are common.

Travel and medical insurance

Before you leave, you should consider your needs for insurance. You will need medical insurance (see the chapter on 'Staying Healthy'), but you may also need travel insurance, to cover you for delayed flights, missed connections, lost luggage and so on. Although insurance can be expensive, it can be much more expensive not to be properly covered. Again, shop around, to make sure you have the cover you need.

> **Heads up**
>
> Your visa may be dependent on proving that you have insurance – another reason to research this well in advance of your leaving date.

International student identity card

The International Student Identity Card (ISIC) is an internationally recognized proof of your status as a student. It will give you access to student discounts, and will often be recognized even when your university student card is not. When you purchase it, you will usually receive a booklet outlining the discounts it offers. As well as offering discounts, the ISIC offers, in many countries, a 24-hour emergency assistance phone number, which can help you to find emergency medical or legal assistance. It is worth getting the card before you leave – not only can it help you to get discounted flights and other pre-departure benefits, but you may not be eligible to get it in your new country. ISIC cards are typically valid for one year, and there is usually a small fee for purchase. Check your university or student travel agent for information on how to get one, or search online for outlets in your area. Other companies also offer similar cards – find out if they will be recognized in your destination country before you buy them.

> **TIP** If you are planning to travel while abroad, talk to a travel agent about membership of an international hostelling organization. Memberships will save you money when you stay in youth hostels. In addition, ask about travel passes (bus passes, rail passes); these can also save you a lot of money and inconvenience as they are specifically designed for budget travellers. Both hostel memberships and travel passes are often only available to purchase in your home country, so organize them before you leave.

Housing

One of the decisions you will need to make about studying abroad will be the kind of housing you stay in. This might include long-term accommodations –

TIP Most universities will have resources dedicated to student housing. Take advantage of them, and ask for help when you need it. Many university websites will have a list of frequently asked questions about student housing.

where you will stay for the duration of your programme – and possibly short-term accommodations – where you will stay when you first arrive if your long-term accommodation is not available. If you are joining an organized exchange programme, your accommodation might be organized for you, but you will probably still have some choices to make.

Options for long-term accommodation

Living on campus

This might include dormitory-style living, or having your own room, or sharing with a small group of others. You might have meals provided for you, or have access to a kitchen which you share with others.

Advantages	Disadvantages
Close to campus.	Potential lack of privacy and freedom.
Opportunity to participate in activities.	Can be expensive.
Social opportunities; chance to make friends.	You may have to share with others.
It can be a cheap option.	It can offer distractions to studying.
It is easy to organize.	Not often suitable for students with partners and families.
Meals may be included.	Often requires early application and/or competition.
Cleaning, maintenance etc. may be done for you, or shared among several students.	May not be available during holiday periods, or may cost extra at these times.
Furniture and household items are usually provided.	Little choice or freedom.
	Other students might be significantly younger or older than you, depending on the culture of the residence.

If you have to find a place to stay on your own go in advance to the country. If possible, before the local students start searching for lodging. It can be very difficult to find a room/flat if you are not in the country. It was more expensive to rent a flat than I had expected – probably because I was quite late in searching for one, when the cheaper ones were already taken. Some students shared a flat which is a good idea if it's possible to find a larger one.

Aisa, studying in Aix-en-Provence in France

Living off campus, in your own flat, apartment or house
This may be by yourself, or with one or more other people.

Advantages	Disadvantages
Privacy.	You have to find and organize it yourself.
You have your own space and freedom.	You do your own cleaning and maintenance.
Choice over flatmates.	You do your own cooking.
Access to your own kitchen, chance to cook.	Potentially expensive.
Potentially more suitable for families.	You will have to commute to campus.
Greater access to the world beyond the campus.	You may have to sign a fixed-term lease
Available year-round.	Socializing may take more effort.
Some choice about furniture and household items.	

Homestay

Homestay involves living with a local family.

Advantages	Disadvantages
Chance to learn about your new culture.	You may not get on with the family (sometimes, homestay students are seen as nothing more than a source of income).
Chance to practise the language.	Potential lack of freedom to make decisions.
Living with a family that treats you like a family member.	Potential lack of privacy.
Inclusion in family activities.	Possible commute to campus.
Chance to learn about the day-to-day aspects of your new culture.	Less social interaction with other students.
May be a financially viable option.	You will have to conform to family rules.

Heads up

If you plan to stay in a homestay situation with a local family, you will probably go through an organization of some kind to match you with your new family. Find out what screening procedures are used to check compatibility. It is worth choosing a reputable organization to help you with this process. Talk to your university's housing officer/office if you have any concerns.

TIP You will have your own priorities when deciding where to live. Come up with your own list of pros and cons to help you decide.

Your housing priorities

- Do you want to live alone or with other people?
- Do you want to live with other students or non-students?
- If you choose to live with other students, consider whether you want to live with other international students, local students, or students from your own country. (Living with students from your own country might be fun and help you to feel safer, but can also be quite limiting as it can isolate you from your new culture.)
- Do you want your meals included, or do you want to provide meals for yourself? If meals are provided, find out what flexibility is available if you want to eat out, or if you want to come home late in the evening – some meal plans can be quite rigid about attendance and timing.
- Do you have any particular food concerns? How might these be addressed?

Heads up

If you are staying in a college, or in a homestay position, you may have little control over the meals you are given. Although this can be a wonderful opportunity to experience new cuisine, it might be difficult to negotiate if you have particular food concerns, for example if you are vegetarian, or have food allergies or religious restrictions. Find out in advance whether you can be accommodated, and consider how you might negotiate this, by cooking some of your own food for example. In a homestay situation, consider how you might negotiate your dietary needs with your homestay family without causing offence.

- Do you want to have furniture provided, or do you want to buy your own? The answer to this might well depend on how long your programme is going to be, and how much money you have.
- Do you want to be able to speak your home language where you live, or are you comfortable being immersed in your new language (if applicable)?
- Are your stress levels higher or lower if you have a lot of people around? What are your needs regarding 'personal space'?
- What kind of housing will be most financially viable, in light of the

other things you want to do while abroad (socialize, travel and so on)?

● How long do you want to live there? Consider what your plans are. If you want to travel during university holidays, a room which you pay for over the whole year might not be the best choice. If you plan to stay during the holidays, find out if this costs extra and whether all the services will be available. If you stay off-campus you might have to sign a minimum-length lease – will this fit in with your plans?

● Do you want to be able to have friends visit you? Can this be accommodated?

● Do you want to live in a single-sex environment or are you comfortable living with both men and women?

● Do you have any special needs due to health/disability issues?

TIP Find out what the most common housing options are for students at your destination university. If almost all students live on campus, you may feel left out if you don't. Some campuses have very few students living on campus, in which case you may feel isolated. Take advice from people you know who are familiar with the culture of the place you are going to.

Questions to ask about potential accommodation

Once you have worked out your general needs, you will need to consider specific options that are available to you at your destination university. As you explore your housing options, find out the following:

● How close to campus is it? (Consider, too, that the size of the campus might be a deciding factor in evaluating the answer to this question – some campuses are huge.)

● How secure is it? Is it in a 'safe' neighbourhood? What efforts are made to keep it safe?

● What does rent include? (Check whether it includes electricity or gas, water, heating, hot water, phone, internet, cable television and so on.) If it does not include everything, see if you can find out – realistically – how much extra you are likely to have to pay.

● If meals are included, find out what meals. Many meal plans exclude certain meals, or certain days of the week. Or you may find that the main meal is included but that you are expected to pay for extras such as drinks or desserts. Be clear about what exactly is included, and whether that fits your needs.

● Is it on a direct bus/train/subway route? Can you get around easily?

- Can accommodations be made for health or disability concerns (e.g. allergy-sensitive meals; wheel-chair access, etc.)?
- What furniture is included, if any? Is there a work space, with a desk?
- What appliances are included (fridge, stove, toaster etc.)?
- What is available in the kitchen, if anything (cutlery, crockery, pans)?
- Will you have access to telephone, internet connection, cable television etc.?
- Do you need to provide your own linen and bedding?

TIP If you have to provide your own linen and bedding, we recommend that you buy it when you arrive, rather than trying to take it with you. Not only is bedding bulky to pack, but bedding sizes vary from country to country, so your bedding might not fit your new bed. Consider taking a blanket or another small piece of bedding if you would like the familiarity, and then buy the rest when you arrive.

- What laundry facilities are available? (Are there facilities on site? Will you need to take your clothes to a laundrette? How much will it cost to do laundry?)
- Is it a smoking or non-smoking environment?
- How old are the buildings (especially if you suffer from allergies to such things as dust and mould)?
- What services are nearby (restaurants, supermarkets, shops, exercise facilities and so on)? Are there budget-conscious options nearby?
- Is there parking (if you intend to drive)? How much will it cost? Will your car be safe?
- Who is responsible for damage repair and what is the procedure for repairs? (For example, will you have to pay if the plumbing goes wrong through no fault of your own? How long might you have to wait if the fridge stops working?)
- What are the rules and guidelines for tenants?
- What are the major concerns for current tenants, (noise, pest control, security and so on)?

Heads up

Bear in mind that there is often a correlation between safety and cost – for example, cheaper areas are often in less safe districts. Bear in mind, too, that personal contents insurance might cost more if your areas is deemed to be in a less safe area, so it can be worth choosing a "better" area from the outset.

Short-term accommodation

You may have to stay somewhere temporarily while your permanent accommodation becomes available, especially if you arrive in your new country well ahead of the start of the new school year or term. Cost may be an important factor in your decision-making, but don't forget that there are other things to consider. There will be a lot you need to do in your first few days, so choose somewhere reasonably close to campus or easily accessible by transport. Find out if it has kitchen facilities – it can be very expensive to eat out for every meal, even just for a few days.

If you have applied for some kind of housing, but haven't heard anything back, don't assume that it is all taken care of. Get confirmation of your accommodation before you leave, if you can. If you have to wait until arrival before you can organize your permanent accommodation, make sure you have your temporary accommodation booked and have a plan of what you need to do after you arrive.

When I first arrived in Toronto, my partner and I stayed in an immigrant's hostel in one of Toronto's distant suburbs; our permanent accommodation wasn't going to be available for several weeks. We had found the hostel on the internet and it was cheap. We soon found out why – it was a long way from anywhere and was in very bad condition. There was so much dust in the mattress we woke up in the middle of the night wheezing and coughing. It took well over an hour to get into campus, on three different kinds of transport. We lasted three days before we had to find a new place to stay. If I was doing it again, I'd be more realistic about our needs, and maybe less concerned with saving a few dollars.

Author insight: Anna

TIP Don't forget to check what to do when you arrive at your new housing: for example, how you pick up keys and what days and times you can access the building.

Driving

If you intend to drive in your new country, either your own car or a rented one, find out what the licensing requirements are. You might be allowed to drive on your home licence for a specific period of time before applying locally for a licence, or you may have to apply for an international driver's licence. Do this well in advance of your departure date, and take the opportunity to find out about the road laws of your new country. Make sure you check the applicable ages for certain kinds of licences as these differ enormously from place to place.

Researching your new home

One of the most fun things prior to departure is researching your new home. You have probably already started to do this as you decided where you wanted to go and put together your application. Try to learn about the culture, the economics, the politics, the history, the geography, religions, social structures, and education systems. Some tips:

- Read all the information your university sends you. This will almost always be very upbeat and positive and will tell you how wonderful your new university is.
- Tell people you are going. You'll be surprised at how many people you bump into who have been to your new country and can give you advice. You don't have to act on it all, but there may be some consistent features that come up.
- Read travel guides for your new country. These will give you all sorts of tips and tidbits about your new country, and may inspire you with options of places you can travel to in between studying.
- You might be able to listen to a local radio station via the internet. This can be a great way of familiarizing yourself with popular culture and the local news, as well as getting used to the language, accents and cultural idiosyncrasies.

- Talk to students or teachers at your university who have studied in your new country. They can be a valuable source of 'insider's information'.
- Read books and magazines about your new country. Some of the detail might not be important to you, but you will probably learn a lot anyway.
- 'Chat' online to someone from your new country.
- Ask for information from travel agents or tourism bureaus, in both your country and the country you are going to.
- Read newspapers to get a sense of where your country fits into international news and politics.
- If there are language differences, practise the new language as much as you can before you leave.
- Read novels or watch films set in your new country.
- Research the climate and weather.

I managed to contact a girl from my home university who was in the exchange programme the previous year and it turned out that she was the most valuable source of information about life abroad, study, parties and everything else one has to know before leaving home and starting a new life in a foreign country.

Tallina, on exchange

Find students currently enrolled in the programme you are thinking of pursuing, and get in contact with them. Faculty want to recruit you as an international student, as you bring in substantial funding. Students, on the other hand, will give you the real dirt.

Tim, completing a one-year master's degree in the UK

How much do you know about your new country?

- What are the country's major religions? What are the major religious practices? What levels of education are common in the country? What age do children start school? How old are they when they go to university? What different kinds of schools are there?

- What does a normal daily schedule look like? What hours do people work?
- What foods are most commonly eaten? What rituals surround eating?
- What are the society's major taboos?
- What are the important holidays/rituals? What are their histories? How are they observed?
- How are men and women treated differently?
- Is your new country currently at war with any other country? Why?
- What is the national anthem of your new country?
- What sports are most popular?
- Who are regarded as the country's heros (sports people, politicians, artists, scientists and so on)?
- How do people greet each other?
- How are children treated in your new country?
- What is the history of the relationship between your country and your new country?
- Are there many immigrants in your new country? Have many people emigrated from the country?
- What is the economic status of your new country and how does this affect its people?

As you find the answers to these questions, you will also find other useful bits of information.

Living abroad is complicated, at times difficult and often surprising. It is harder than one might think to leave home for an extended period of time even between countries as apparently similar as Canada and the US. If you will be somewhere for the length of a degree, it is vital to have some sense of where you are going before leaving your familiar surroundings. Talk to people, both at home and abroad, and do as much research as possible.

Chelsea, a Canadian, in the US to do her PhD

Your own country

When you are studying abroad, you will probably find that people ask you about your own country. You might want to do some research so that you can sound knowledgeable about your own geographical region. Especially, try to keep up to date with current affairs, so that you can discuss them with others. Educate yourself about the history of interactions between your home country and your new country as well as the opinions and stereotypes that people might have about your own culture.

Legal and practical preparations

> **TIP** Before you depart, consider giving a family member or close friend the legal authority to represent you so that they can act on your behalf while you are away. Choose someone you trust and make sure that you understand fully what the implications are of doing this.

- Prepare or update your will before you leave.
- Consider what you will do about your tax return while you are away, if applicable. Can you ask someone to lodge it for you?
- Consider contacting the embassy or consulate for your home country in your new country and letting them know that you will be living in the country for a period of time.
- Notify your banks of where you intend to travel. Banks have been known to cancel credit cards that are suddenly being used in a different country, because they assume fraud or theft.
- Make copies of all your tickets, passports and documentation and leave them somewhere safe, perhaps with a friend or family member.
- Don't forget to cancel all your services (such as newspaper delivery, internet provider, telephone, electricity and so on) and pay any outstanding bills.
- Have someone take care of any outstanding mail; you might need to provide a forwarding address to the post office.

Academic preparations

- Complete all official university registration.
- Get your credit approved through your home university.
- Choose your courses, and check for scheduling conflicts.
- Practise your language skills, to make sure that you can communicate using basic, everyday phrases and requests. Listen to

language tapes to help you to practise understanding, and to help you to get used to the accents you might hear.

- Read the chapter on 'Living Abroad', and learn what you can about the academic context you are going into.

You might ask for reading lists for courses ahead of time, and start to do the reading, especially if your programme is likely to be intense or challenging. If you are nervous about the academic side of things, this can also help you to build your confidence. If you are a post-graduate student, make contact with your new department.

Heads up

Increasingly, registering for courses is done online. Sometimes, places in the course are allocated on a first-come, first-served basis. In these cases, you might have to go online to register at a specific time. Be vigilant about this, or other students might get the places you want. Don't forget to take into account the time differences. This might mean having to register for courses at 4am, rather than waiting until the next day. Have the appropriate phone number available, in case there is a connection problem and you have to make a phone call.

Put the effort into figuring out which classes you want to take, how they will fit into your overall degree programme/academic goals, and find out if they are available when you need them. Sounds simple, but can turn out to be a bit of a jungle.

Jemima, who spent a year on an exchange studying anthropology, Spanish and psychology

If your new country uses a different language, make sure that you purchase a good dictionary which includes both your own language and your new one, if available (you might not be able to get one in your new country). You might have to order this if it is not available in your local shops.

TIP Plan to buy your academic stationery in your new country, rather than before you leave. Paper and binder sizes might be completely different in your new country, and these items are often heavy and bulky.

If you haven't already, make sure to learn some of the language before you go. It will make the transition to living in a new country much nicer and will give you a head start on connecting with residents of the country. Read about the culture and way of life of the people who live in the country you will be studying in. It will really help you become adapted and may even help you understand what not to do!

Claire, a Korean-American studying in France,
among other countries

 Packing

As your departure date approaches, you will need to start thinking about what to pack. This can be a lot of fun, so think about what you will need to pack ahead of time in case there are things you need to buy.

Choosing your luggage

Use a bag that is comfortable for you. For some people this will be a suitcase, for others a backpack might be the way to go. Think about what will be easier in a variety of situations, from catching buses to going travelling while abroad. Some tips for choosing a bag:

- Make sure it is good quality. You don't want it to rip while you are away. Especially, check that the zips are strong and unlikely to break. You need the bag to last and a warranty is no use if you are abroad.
- Is the bag flexible? Can you wheel it as well as carry it? Can you put it on your back or throw it over your shoulder? In different situations, you may need your bag to be able to do different things. Variation may also help your body not to get too tired when you carry your luggage.
- If you are buying a backpack, try it on first yo make sure it fits properly.
- Does it have multiple compartments and pockets? – These can help you to stay organized.
- Don't buy the cheapest bag unless it is also good quality, but you might not have to buy the most expensive either. Work out what your needs are.

How much you pack will mostly be determined by how much you will be allowed to take on the flight. Most airlines have a limit of two bags per person, and these must conform to weight standards as well. However, sometimes it is possible to request an extra weight allowance for your outbound trip if you are traveling for the purposes of study, so check with your airline.

Give yourself plenty of time to pack; trying to remember everything the night before is quite stressful.

Considerations for what to take

- You might not have easy access to ironing boards and washing machines, especially in the first few days. Take clothes that don't require huge amounts of maintenance. Dark clothes are less likely to show stains.
- Take clothes that have several functions and that can be 'dressed up' or 'dressed down' depending on the occasion. Choose items that you can mix and match.
- Choose clothes that are appropriate to the climate and season you are going to. You may need to buy some clothes once you arrive as well.
- Choose clothing items that you can layer for different temperatures. For example, rather than taking one thick jacket, take two or three items that you can wear at the same time.

TIP Having a selection of small, inexpensive presents from your home country might be useful. You can give them to people you meet as a gesture of good will.

Pack comfortable walking shoes.

Heads up

It is rude in some cultures to wear shoes indoors, but going barefoot might also be inappropriate. If this is true for where you are going, consider packing a pair of slippers, or be prepared to buy some when you arrive.

Remember that you will want to bring things home with you, so leave enough room to do so. Try to avoid packing things just because you *may* need them. If you know you need them, pack them. Everything else can be improvised, borrowed or bought later.

Don't pack any more than you yourself can comfortably carry. If you pack too much, you will increase your stress levels and put a lot of strain on your body. Will you be able to carry your luggage up stairs if you need to? Can you take all of your luggage with you into a public toilet? Most students over-pack and regret it later. Having too much luggage also puts you at risk of theft, because you may not be able to watch it adequately when you are focused on something else.

- Have one outfit which is more formal, including shoes.
- Pack a waterproof jacket.
- Pack a small travel alarm clock – your body clock will be very confused by the time changes and jet lag.
- Pack a towel.

Consider what you need academically. Don't forget to pack your dictionary, the course information, subject guide, or credit-transfer paperwork you will need, and any other documents or materials from the university you will need.

Be practical, but don't forget the emotional aspects of packing as well. For example, small items from home such as photos, or a familiar blanket, might help you to feel more settled in your new home. Avoid taking expensive or valuable items, though, as they might get stolen.

Notebook computers

If you have a notebook computer, find out what computer facilities are available at your new university, to help you to decide whether to take a notebook with you. Even if there are desk-top facilities for student use, you may have to wait in long queues to use them, or have access only at certain times of day. You might find it more convenient to take a notebook computer, especially if your housing offers wireless internet. Consider whether you will be able to get technical help in your new university if something goes wrong with your computer. Or you may decide that the added security risk and inconvenience of taking your notebook is not worth it, and you are better off leaving it at home. If you do choose to take a notebook with you, there are a few things you should consider:

- Have it listed separately on your travel insurance for its full worth.
- Make sure you have a good quality multi-voltage electrical converter that is designed especially for your lap top (a cheap converter might not be sufficient).

- Pack a conversion electrical plug so that you can recharge the lap top battery (you might be able to buy this at the airport, but it will probably be expensive and you might not find the one you need; it's better to plan for this in advance).
- Carry your notebook in a backpack that is not clearly identifiable as a computer case. That way, your hands will be free to do other things, and you are less likely to be the target of theft.
- When you travel, do not advertise that you have a computer with you; this may compromise your safety. You may choose not to use it in public for this reason.
- Carry your notebook in your carry-on luggage to avoid damage.

TIP Scan all your important documents and email them to yourself. Then you will be able to access them whenever you have internet access. You should do this in addition to leaving copies of your documents with family/friends at home.

Appliances

With the exception of your notebook and a camera, it is probably unwise to carry electrical appliances with you. If you do, bear in mind that your destination country might well operate on a different voltage system. If you plug your appliance into the wrong voltage, you can damage the appliance. It might also be a fire hazard. You can get around this by using converters and adapters. These are two different things. A converter will convert the voltage flowing into your appliance. Converters come in two kinds: lightweight and heavy duty – make sure you use the right kind for the appliance you want to use. An adapter simply changes the power plug to fit the shape of the prongs in the new power outlet. An adapter will NOT convert the voltage. Bear in mind that your warranty will not be effective abroad in most cases, and if your appliance breaks, you might not be able to find someone who can fix it, because brands vary from country to country.

Some packing tips

Heads up

Security measures in airports are constantly under review. Find out what you are allowed to take in your carry-on luggage and in your checked luggage.

Checked in luggage

- Pack shoes in bags to avoid dirtying your clothes.
- Pack heavier items first.
- Pack items you may need immediately on the top, to avoid you having to unpack your whole bag.
- Buy travel toiletries, rather than wasting space with full-sized bottles. Pack them in sealed plastic bags; the pressure change can cause them to leak or even explode.
- Make sure that you attach tags to your luggage with your name, address and contact details, in case your luggage goes missing. Repeat this information on the inside of your luggage. Try to buy tags that fold in half, so that casual passers-by cannot read your contact details.
- Using luggage straps can help to prevent wear on the zips of your luggage.
- Consider putting locks on your luggage.
- If you must take scissors, knives or other sharp objects, pack them in your checked-in luggage; you won't be allowed to take them in your hand luggage.
- Pack breakable items in between clothes for extra protection. Small items can go in a shoe to save space and for extra protection.

If you want to take guidebooks with you, consider how much space they take up. You might consider tearing out the pages you think you won't need. Bear in mind that the cover of the book will indicate that you are a tourist – many travellers take the pages they will need and put them in another binding for extra security.

If you want to take unusual items with you, check with the airline whether they can accommodate you. You may have to pay an extra fee.

Carry-on luggage

Make sure that you have with you:

- Passport.
- Visa (often this will be in your passport).
- Letter of offer and registration – you may need to show this to the customs official in your destination country.
- Travel tickets.
- ISIC card.

Heads up

If you have a student visa which does not allow you to work in your new country, and do not have a separate work visa, do not carry a copy of your curriculum vitae with you; this is likely to be interpreted as you intending to break the rules (consider emailing it to yourself, so you can access it later, if necessary).

- Money and credit cards.
- Insurance documents.

Heads up

It's a great idea to have a security pouch that you can tuck under your clothing (around your neck or waist, for example) to keep all your important documents and money in.

- Personal toiletries needed on the flight, if you are allowed them.
- The address of your accommodation, whether temporary or permanent. You will probably need to declare this when you arrive, and of course will need to know where you are going!
- A guide book for the city or country you are travelling to (these will often have maps in them, although you may also need to buy one when you arrive).

TIP Make sure you have a phone number of an appropriate campus contact (the international student centre, for example) with you, so that you can contact them if you have any difficulties when you arrive. You should carry your travel insurance documentation with you, including the emergency contact numbers, and be familiar with what you are covered for.

- Lap top computer, if applicable.
- Enough prescription medication to get you through the first few days in your new country. See 'Staying Healthy' for more information.
- Prescriptions and doctor's notes for all medications (including translations where applicable).
- A change of clothes.

TIP Consider what you will do if your checked-in luggage gets lost. Make sure you have everything you need to get through a few days in your new home.

- Whatever you need for the flight (for example, a book, magazine, toothbrush and so on).

Heads up

> Don't carry anything sharp or that can be construed as a weapon in your carry-on luggage. Even if you have a good reason for having it, it will probably be confiscated as a security risk. If you need needles on the flight for health reasons, make sure you have a doctor's note to explain why.

Emotional preparation

While you are getting excited about your upcoming trip abroad, it can be easy to focus so much on practical details that you forget to take some time to consider the emotional aspects of what you are doing.

You

Take some time to reflect on the opportunities that are coming up for you. You might like to start a study abroad journal early, and reflect on your dreams, goals, aspirations, hopes, worries and fears of the upcoming trip. This may be a good resource for you to refer back to later when you are homesick or experiencing culture shock. Take the time to breathe and to enjoy the anticipation and excitement, and to stay in touch with your own feelings; don't let yourself get lost in the flurry.

Take the time to set your goals. What do you want to achieve from your study abroad? What are the things that you must do to feel that your trip is worthwhile? What will you be disappointed about if you don't do it?

Take a deep breath, step forward and enjoy! Think about what you want to achieve and what kind of travel you want to have before you leave, because then you can choose your friends from people who have similar goals to yours.

Brigitte, a second-year biology student

Prioritize what it is that you wish to achieve before you leave home; you will inevitably find that you do not have time to do everything, although you will wish to do so.

Thomas, studying for a year in the Czech Republic

Also, take some time to consider what you see as the role of the international student. Inevitably, you will come across aspects of your new culture which you don't agree with. If you can see your role as one of learning and openness to difference, you might find that you have an easier time than if you see your role as being to educate and change your new environment. In fact, going in to your new environment with the goal of changing it is likely to set you up for alienation and isolation, and probably won't do much to counteract any negative stereotypes your new culture holds about your home culture. Think through what kind of international student you would like to be, and how you see your role while you are studying abroad. Consider how you will deal with potential conflict between your personal values and beliefs and those in your new country, in a way that will maintain your own integrity while also respecting those around you. Doing this before you leave is a good idea, before you get caught up in the excitement of your first few weeks.

Friends and family

Your friends and family are probably happy for you and want to help, but they may also be sad that you are leaving, especially if it is for a long programme. Be sensitive to what those around you are feeling. Tell them as soon as you know that your departure is definite, so it doesn't come as a shock (remember that gossip travels quickly). Find the time to spend with family and friends before you leave. Allow them to help you in whatever ways they can, whether it is emotional or practical.

Also, try to spend some time with friends and family where you are NOT focused on the date of your departure, and try to stay tuned in to what is happening in their lives as well. Reassure them that you care and will stay in touch.

If you are travelling with a partner and/or children, remember that they may have mixed feelings about going abroad. Take time to talk about the feelings that arise, and make sure that they have time and occasion to say goodbye to people and find closure. Children especially might be very sad and might be reluctant to leave; be supportive of their feelings and don't

Heads up

> Don't promise your friends and family that you will be just the same when you return. This is probably not true. You will still be YOU, but you will probably have changed and grown. In our experience, people tend to know this anyway, so be truthful about it, and reassure the people who care about you that you will still care about them even if you do grow while you are away.

assume that this means that they won't enjoy the experience and settle into their new home.

• • •

You may find, on the day you actually have to turn up to the airport to begin your new life, that you don't want to go. This is completely normal. It's OK to be sad as you say goodbye to the people you love and to the familiarities of your home life, and it's OK to be scared. It is normal to question why you are going and even to entertain the idea of changing your mind. Feeling several emotions all at once is not unusual, but most students we have talked to are very glad in the end that they went. All the preparation you have done will give you the best possible chance of having a terrific time studying abroad.

Further resources

- Project Visa
- www.projectvisa.com/
  This site lists embassies and visa requirements for countries worldwide. Use this site when you are exploring your options, but make sure you check official government immigration sites to ensure information is up to date.
- www.embassyworld.com
  Offers a database to locate your country's embassies in countries worldwide. Provides links to the embassy's official sites.
- Beverly D. Roman, *Home Away from Home: Turning Your International Relocation into a Lifetime Enhancement* (BR Anchor, 2006).
  A useful guide to relocating abroad. Includes strategies for negotiating the needs of children, partners and families.

7 Living Abroad

There will come a day when your pre-departure planning comes to an end. Whether you have done everything you intended to or whether you haven't, your departure day will arrive. You will turn up at the airport, probably feeling nervous and excited and, after anywhere from a few hours to a few days of travelling, will arrive in your new country. You'll have the chance to put all your plans and goals into practice, discard some of your plans in favour of new ones, and learn how to live in your new surroundings.

Heads up

You will probably be eager to get to your new university and start to settle in. Bear in mind, though, that it is likely that you will arrive in your new country with a lot of adrenalin in your body from the excitement, as well as jet-lagged and tired from tying up loose ends over the past few days. And even if you are a seasoned traveller, arriving in a new country as a student and not a tourist can be quite different: this is, after all, where you will live your life for the next few months/years and you have probably done a lot of planning for this moment. You will also have said goodbye temporarily to friends and family. So be aware that you will probably be in a heightened state of emotion, and that this may manifest itself in feeling disoriented, overwhelmed or just exhausted when you first arrive. Be gentle with yourself, and give yourself what you need to get ready for the opportunities that are coming your way.

Before you leave it is stressful, when you arrive it is stressful . . . one week later you are having the time of your life and won't look back.

Kylie, who has studied abroad several times

Settling in

Arrival and customs

When you first arrive in your new country, you will have to be cleared by Customs and Immigration. If you have travelled before, you will be used to this, but remember that every country is different and has different procedures and laws.

As an international student, clearing Customs will probably be more complex than if you were entering as a tourist. You will have to show all of your documents – including passport, student visa, possibly your immunization documents and evidence of your acceptance into an institution as a student. In many places, you will also be asked to complete an Immigration and Customs declaration form. You may have to undergo an interview, where you will be questioned and have your documents reviewed. There may be fees payable at this time, which sometimes involves waiting in yet another queue. Depending on the country and the time of day, this process might be simple, or quite involved and lengthy.

Tips for negotiating customs

It is very important that you do not make any false statements in your documentation. Be polite to customs and immigration officials, but don't be over-talkative or long-winded.

If the documentation is in a language that you are not yet comfortable with, see if it is available in your own language, or find someone who can help you so that you can be sure that you understand what you are declaring.

Never make jokes about having bombs or weapons in your luggage; customs officials are obliged to take all comments seriously.

Once you have been cleared by Customs, you will be allowed to officially enter the country, at which point local laws come into effect. You will then have to pick up your luggage, and it will probably be inspected and X-rayed. You may be asked to unpack your bags – if you are asked to do so, be polite and patient.

Unexpected events

The chances are very high that, if you have prepared well, there will be no difficulty in clearing Customs and Immigration. However, if something goes wrong, it is important that you have researched beforehand what your rights are. You might be asked, for example, to have a private interview, or to be searched in detail. This may even include a strip search. It is important that you don't panic, and you will have to use your own intuition and discretion to work out what is going on. The rights that you have in this situation vary from country to country, but you should feel free to ask politely what the problem is, and you might be able to make a phone call if the problem does not get immediately resolved, or ask the person dealing with you to call your embassy for assistance.

In and around the airport

Whether you are being picked up, or finding your own way to the university or your accommodation, the first thing you should do after clearing Customs is to organize some cash, if you are not already carrying local currency. Bear in mind the following:

- Airport exchange rates are notorious for being high. Change only enough money to get you through the first day or two of your trip and organize the rest later.
- Be conscious of security – there may be pickpockets around. Don't leave your luggage unattended.
- If you have to catch public transport, try to buy something small in the airport, so that you can change your large notes; many buses and trains require exact or close-to-exact change and may not be able to handle a larger note.
- If you need to use the phone, consider buying a phone card, or make sure you have the correct change.

As you leave the airport and travel to your destination, bear in mind that your body might be exhausted or jet-lagged, as well as running on adrenalin from the nerves and excitement. All of these factors can affect your decision-making abilities so be aware that your judgement may be affected, and take extra care.

If you have to cross roads, remember that drivers might be on the opposite side of the road from what you are used to, and that you might find the traffic around you unpredictable. Be especially vigilant until you get used to it.

The first few days

Occasionally, you may be thrown right into your programme on arrival, especially if you are part of an organized exchange. In most cases, though, you will have a few days before your official commitments begin. During this time, there are a number of things you might do to help yourself feel more comfortable and confident in your new surroundings.

Safety

Register with the police, if applicable. This may be mandatory for all foreign visitors, required only of visitors from certain countries, or not necessary at all. To register, you will usually have to go to the police station and show your passport and documents of student status, and might have to fill out a declaration form about your background and intentions in your new country. In some cases, you will be able to register by phone or through a hotel or other accommodation. (If you are travelling with a partner and/or children, you will all need to be present to register.)

Register with your embassy/consulate, if applicable. Most students never do this, but if you are in a place where there is political or civil unrest, letting your embassy know that you are in the country can provide an extra level of safety and protection. Phone them first to find out how to proceed.

Call home to tell your family/friends that you have arrived safely.

Orientation

Attend any orientation workshops offered by your programme or university. It is worth attending them even if you think you already know the content – you might learn something, and it is a good way to meet people in a similar situation and staff and faculty who may be able to help you. You might also take advantage of a guided tour of your local area and/or campus to help you to orientate yourself geographically.

Practicalities

Organize your health card, if applicable. This may include both temporary health care and applying for longer-term cover, if you have not been able to do this from home.

Open a bank account. This might be especially important if you are staying for a while. Make sure you have all your documentation with you. Be prepared for the process to take longer than you anticipate.

There can be a lot of bureaucracy to battle when living outside your home country. Opening a bank account, renting a flat, obtaining a national insurance number were all more difficult for me. It was very frustrating and took a lot of patience.

Annabelle, a Canadian student studying in the UK

If you have to buy new clothing when you arrive, you may need to to do this in your first few days as well. Ask around to find out where to shop for the best prices and quality.

Transport

Get to know your local transport system. How will you get to the campus? What routes go to the local shops or other facilities? How early and late does public transport run – on weekdays? on weekends? Find out about the most efficient and cost-effective way of using public transport. Can you buy a transit pass? Are there student discounts available? Should you buy tickets ahead of time or when you get on? How do transfers work, if applicable. (You might need one of your passport photos for your transit pass.)

University

Follow the instructions you have received from your university as to how to register your arrival. Organize your

> student card
> library card
> computer access
> sports facilities card
> other relevant documents.

Pay any fees you need to pay. Get receipts.

If you have not yet chosen your university courses/subjects, do this as soon as you can. Find out how to register in the subjects you want and do this. Find out if you have to sign up for tutorials, or laboratories, and do this – remember that these may be separate from lectures. Make sure there are no clashes in your timetable.

When you have received confirmation of your enrolment, buy the relevant textbooks, stationery and equipment.

Get to know the libraries around you. Which catalogue system do they use? What are their opening hours? Will you use one library in particular, or will you need access to several different ones. Are there computer facilities you can use for word processing, internet? What are the restrictions? If applicable, find out whether there are libraries in the community which have resources in your home language, if you need them (these may be part of the university, or may belong to a community organization).

Socializing

Take the time, in your first few days, to introduce yourself to those around you, including your roommates, neighbours, programme organizer, departmental staff and so on. You may find yourself doing a lot of 'extroverting' in your first few days – if this is exhausting for you, make sure you also give yourself time to yourself to rejuvenate.

Housing

You may have to do an inspection of your new housing, and report its current condition. It's important that you do this accurately and promptly – if there is damage when you leave, it will be assumed that you caused it unless you reported it in the initial inspection, and you will have to pay for it.

When you arrive in your 'permanent' accommodation, or if you are staying in temporary accommodation for more than a day or two, unpack and try to personalize your space. Putting up some photographs or favourite pictures on the wall, and perhaps having your favourite blanket on your bed, can help you to feel more settled.

> **TIP** If you are staying in temporary accommodation, don't forget that you will have to update your address when you know what your permanent address will be. You will need to tell the university, your service providers (phone, internet and so on), the police and embassy (if applicable), banks and, of course, your family.

Depending on your housing situation, you may have to organize a telephone account, an email account, rent payments and so on. Try to avoid signing up for services without shopping around; other students especially will be able to offer suggestions about convenient and affordable service providers. You may have to wait for some services to take effect.

You may have to buy furniture. The university may be able to give you advice about how to get the kind of furniture you need. Don't forget about second-hand furniture from other students.

> **Heads up**
>
> Many students report that dealing with bureaucracy in their new country is the most challenging aspect of their experiences abroad. Sometimes, you will just have to patient and keep trying until you are successful; sometimes you may have to enlist the help of the appropriate person at your new university to help you. These problems can be exacerbated by language problems, so enlisting the help of a local can sometimes be the only solution. Try to be patient.

Rubbish and recycling

Find out what is expected of you in terms of disposing of rubbish and/or recycling. Many countries have fines for littering and strict guidelines for disposing of waste. You may have to pay to have your rubbish removed. There may be recycling plants or systems you can take advantage of, which you will need to know how to use.

Laundry

Find out where you can do laundry. How do you pay? You might be able to get a pre-bought card, which can save you money, or you might need coins of a particular denomination. Planning this in advance can save you hours of wandering around shops asking for change every time you do your laundry. Check whether there are dryers available.

TIP Many students report that backpacks make an excellent temporary laundry basket.

Culture shock

At some point after arriving, possibly almost immediately, you are likely to experience culture shock. This is the term given to the feelings associated with learning to adjust to new culture, lifestyle, climate, food, and expectations. If you are working in a different language, it might be even more challenging, but culture shock can be just as significant without the language challenges.

Important things to remember about culture shock:

It can affect even very experienced travellers.
It is a normal and necessary part of an experience abroad.
It is not a sign of weakness.
It will probably subside with time.
It is sometimes sudden and unexpected, but more frequently sets in slowly, perhaps without you even realizing it is happening.

There are various stages of culture shock. You may experience all or some of these stages, possibly in different sequences.

It is common to feel excitement, possibly even euphoria when you first arrive in a country. This may last several weeks. At some point, though, it is likely that the novelty of your new surroundings will wear off and you may find yourself feeling sad or frustrated with the differences in your new country. Sometimes, this can manifest itself in depression or mood swings. It is important to remember that you will adjust, although perhaps only partially, and that this is a normal part of the process.

The first month will be great, the second and the third can be hard because it is no longer exciting. You may get lonely or even bored. If you can get through these feelings, you will have a great experience.

Chantal, a Swiss student on exchange

One of the defining characteristics of culture shock is that the small, everyday things you take for granted become a big deal. This can leave you feeling exhausted and stressed, without really knowing why. For example, going into a supermarket and being faced by different colours and different brands can leave you overwhelmed, but it is easy to dismiss your feelings as being silly ('I just went shopping! What's the big deal?') If drivers drive on the other side of the road in your new country, you will find yourself having to override your instinct whenever you drive or even cross the road, which can leave you physically and mentally exhausted. It is important not to underestimate how difficult these small things are in a different place, and how much stress they can put on you and your relationships.

You may be suffering from culture shock if you:

Feel extreme homesickness.
Feel depressed.
Have difficulty concentrating.
Find small things overwhelming and seemingly impossible.
Find that your self-esteem has gone down and you have lost your confidence.
Are tired and/or having difficulty sleeping.
Find that you have lost your sense of humour.
Feel frustrated or hostile towards your hosts or host university or country.
Find yourself avoiding new situations, including socializing.
Develop unusual health concerns or physical problems.
Are having fights or disturbances in your relationships.

The cultural differences sometimes show up when you least expect it. The things that might seem the most natural to you could be weird or even rude to people from other cultures.

Jakob, in Hungary

Heads up

The 'curve' associated with culture shock is well documented because it is such a common experience. If you see it out, it will get better, although you may not believe that until you have gone through the curve.

Negotiating culture shock

Time will help, but there are also a number of things you can do to mitigate the effects of culture shock.

- Gather as much information about your new country as you can. You will be faced with surprises, but you can also prepare yourself for what will come. Being prepared will help to make those situations less stressful, and may give you some guidance as to how to behave in a particular situation. Especially, be aware of the dos and don'ts of a culture. Ask questions in your first few weeks to find out what is acceptable and what is not.
- Be aware of your new country's attitudes towards people from your home country.
- Make new friends in your new country. Ask them about appropriate behaviour.
- Don't be afraid to talk about how you are feeling. The International Student Centre may provide opportunities to share your emotions with other international students. Try to keep these conversations positive – keep the focus on how you are feeling and how you can cope, rather than on all the shortcomings of your new country.

 You can look forward to great experiences – but prepare yourself to be lonely too. Once in a while you feel down and cry a little, but that's part of the experience. When you think back, you only remember the good stuff.

Christopher, who has studied abroad three times

- Contact your family and friends back home.
- Try to understand the reasons behind the things you see around you. This will help to counteract the sense of their strangeness and unfamiliarity, and may make them less confusing or threatening.

Heads up

We know family members back at home who have been so concerned that their loved one is suffering from culture shock and/or homesickness they have offered to pay for them to fly home again! This is rarely a useful solution, even if it is tempting at times. If you can make it through, things will improve and you will learn about yourself in the process. If you give up, your self-esteem and confidence might be affected and you might not want to take the risk next time. (With longer programmes, by all means go home for a holiday, but it is a good idea to wait until your initial period of adjustment is over.)

- Be positive about your new country, and try to avoid constantly comparing your new country with your own.
- Keep a journal to record your feelings.
- Exercise and get plenty of sleep (more about this in 'Staying Healthy').

TIP   As soon as you can, try to establish a positive routine for yourself. Make sure you include in your routine things that make you feel happy, energetic and strong. Try to stick to your routine even on days when you are feeling sad or overwhelmed. Having a routine will help you to feel grounded, as well as helping you to be more productive once you have study commitments to get through.

- Take breaks – read a book in your own language, watch a favourite movie, or talk to others who speak your language or who come from your own country. Be aware though, of not letting this become a crutch which prevents you from having to adjust to your new culture.
- Keep your long-term goals in mind. If you remember that this process is part of who you want to be and who you want to become, you will find the short-term challenges easier to cope with.

TIP   If you are in a longer programme, especially at the post-graduate level, you may find the effects of culture shock lingering long after you are over the initial adjustment phase. If you find that you are physically or mentally suffering from culture shock over a significant period of time, you may need to seek help from a doctor or a counsellor.

*Remember that just because somebody does something in a
different way does not make it wrong and it doesn't make it
right . . . it is just the way it is. Go into another country with an
open mind and learn something from your experience.*

Nira, a US student in Sweden

Social conduct

Culture shock affects every bodily sense. You will be experiencing new
smells, new sights, new sounds, new tastes and new tactile experiences. But
one of the most challenging aspects of culture shock is that you have to
adjust to new rules of social conduct.

There is no definitive list of dos and don'ts for adjusting to a new set of
guidelines for social conduct. Like all communication, what is deemed

Heads up

One of the most frustrating things students report about
being abroad is being faced with stereotypes and inaccurate
representations of their home country. For example, we have
been struck by the number of Canadians who genuinely
seem to think that kangaroos hop down the main streets of
Sydney (we tell them that the kangaroos are treated the
same way as all the bears walking down the streets of
Toronto . . .). You will rapidly work out your own ways of
dealing with these kinds of stereotyped questions. It can be
fun to work out where the stereotypes are coming from (for
example, a famous movie or book). Be patient and maintain
your sense of humour. On more serious issues (politics,
cultural assumptions about beliefs or social structures), you
may feel the need to 'defend' your country. Be clear that you
are speaking only for yourself and that you do not represent
an entire nation. Try to avoid giving more information than
the situation demands, or you might be perceived as socially
awkward. It can help to remember that the person you are
talking to is probably not trying to be offensive or rude. If you
need to give vent to your feelings, do so in your journal. Be
aware of your own tendency to stereotype and be willing to
have your beliefs about your new country challenged.

appropriate is contextual and shifts according to who you are talking to and what you are saying. However, the following are some things to be aware of.

Greetings

Learn the appropriate ways of addressing people for the place you are in. There may be different greetings for different levels of authority, job type, gender, and so on. If you are overly casual, you may offend. Make sure you understand the differences between addressing the people you know and those who are unfamiliar to you.

Language

Try to use local phrases even if you do not speak the language properly. You may be invited to speak your own language, but your effort to use your new language will usually be appreciated. Remember that some languages differentiate between informal and formal address. Expect to make mistakes, and don't be afraid to take risks. Try to avoid using slang expressions or cliches, as these can often be misunderstood.

Physical contact

You may find that expectations around appropriate physical contact are different from what you are used to, and you may feel uncomfortable. Remember that this discomfort goes both ways – the person you are talking to may also be uncomfortable. You may also have to adjust to different levels of physical distance when having a conversation, and you may find that people will change how they are positioned when they are talking to you. For example, in some cultures, it may be inappropriate to stand when someone else is sitting, or to be at a higher level that the person you are conversing with. Take cues from the people around you.

Negotiating prices

Be attuned to whether it is socially acceptable to negotiate over the price when you are making a purchase. In some places, this is a necessary part of the process; in others it might be insulting to the seller. It is often all right to politely suggest that the price is a little more than you were hoping to pay, and then take your cue from the seller as to whether this can be changed.

Subtext

When you are trying to cope in a second language, or even if you are working in your native language, you may not be attuned to the subtleties of language such as subtext and euphemism. It may seem that someone is saying one thing on the surface but actually means something entirely different. Don't assume that the people around you are doing this to make you feel left out – their meanings are probably just taken for granted.

Dating

The unspoken rules of dating and sexual conduct differ enormously between countries. Be aware that your behaviour might be misinterpreted as a result of different cultural 'signals'. The expectations surrounding how a date might proceed, and who pays for what, might be different. Rules surrounding appropriate physical and sexual contact might also be confusing. Be clear about what you want and be assertive if you feel that your boundaries are not being respected.

Taking photographs and other recording

Avoid photographing people without permission. Some people – such as street performers – may demand some form of payment if you want to take a photograph. Respect this. Be aware that some buildings or artefacts may have religious or cultural significance and it may be offensive to take photographs. Copyright protections might also limit what you are allowed to record; this is often true in museums, art galleries and theatres. Err on the side of caution and people will usually tell you if you have made a mistake. Always obey signs that specifically ask you not to take photographs – and don't try to cheat by taking photographs with your phone or other unobtrusive technologies.

Time and clocks

You may have to adjust to different expectations around time and punctuality. In some places, you are expected to meet someone or turn up at a party at exactly the time mentioned, or even early, while in other places, this is a rough guide only and most people will be much later. Public transport systems may also be affected by these assumptions.

Drugs and alcohol

Laws about who is allowed to drink and when differ enormously in different parts of the world. You also need to be aware that, beyond the legal restrictions, different cultures have different attitudes towards what is appropriate behaviour and usage.

Conversation

Casual conversation is often full of cultural and local references, which can make you feel very left out. You will have to choose whether you ask about them as they come up, or go along with it and figure it out later. You will

Heads up

Many students report feeling that they lose some of their identity when they are studying abroad, at least initially. You may find that you are not as confident as normal, or that things you are usually good at are an effort. Most notably, students often report that their sense of humour gets lost for a while – this can be because of language challenges or simply because your sense of humour is culturally specific. It might also be because you are stressed and absorbing a lot of newness. It will come back.

often be able to find some friends you trust who will happily fill you in. Making friends can be a crucial part of overcoming culture shock, too, so it is worth taking the time to understand what they are talking about.

Dress codes and fashion

You will quickly get a sense of what people around you are wearing, and whether your own dress codes are appropriate. You may need to ask for some guidance on what to wear on particular occasions, especially if you are unsure just what is meant by phrases such as 'formal' or 'informal', which are often very specific to certain social groups or contexts. Many dress codes will be culturally specific, so research how your dress code might be perceived.

Politics

If you are unsure of your environment, expressing your political beliefs may serve to alienate you despite your best intentions. What you feel comfortable talking about will depend on your context, including how long you are in your new country. If you do offer political opinions, make it clear that you are offering only your own perspective and that you do not speak on behalf of your entire country or community. Bear in mind that, in some places, you can be arrested for expressing certain political beliefs. Be clear about what those issues might be before you arrive. You might find a discernible difference, too, between what you feel comfortable discussing in the context of the classroom and what goes on in social settings.

Gender issues

The ways in which particular genders are treated and expected to behave may vary enormously from your home country. Sometimes you will find gender roles very well defined and in other places expectations around gender will be more subtle. You may be accorded more, or less, freedom than you are used to. Ask appropriate people at your university for guidance about what is expected of you. Differences you might encounter include: who has authority and how this authority is exerted; expectations around social behaviour; assumptions about interests and hobbies; acceptable conduct around personal space and body-boundary issues; what kinds of friendships and relationships are socially acceptable; expectations around levels of education and potential career paths; assumptions about parenting roles and so on. Bear in mind that gender rules may or may not be applied to 'foreigners' in the same ways as to locals. In some cases, your new country will afford you a freedom you are not used to – take some time to figure out what these freedoms are, rather than assuming them.

> **Heads up**
>
> Culture shock can be significantly exacerbated if you face some of the additional challenges we discuss later, including having a disability, identifying as lesbian, gay, bisexual or trans, or facing discrimination based on your race, skin colour, ethnicity or religion. Read our discussion of these in 'Additional Challenges'.

As a girl from a traditional family, sometimes I couldn't 'relax' enough. Some of my friends and housemates from other cultures told me that I was too conservative. I wanted to stay true to my upbringing and to what my parents had taught me, but I wanted to be able to make friends and have fun too. It was hard to work it all out. These kinds of cultural challenges were quite difficult.

Fatima, a Malaysian student, living in student
accommodation in Ireland

Foreign laws

When you are in another country, the laws of that country apply to you. Make sure you are aware of them. Even if you break the law unintentionally, you are still responsible for your actions.

Housing

When you travel abroad, you are likely to experience culture shock in relation to your housing and accommodation. You may be staying in a form of accommodation that you are unfamiliar with, but even if you are staying in a very similar style of housing to what you are used to, it will probably be very different. If you are sharing with other students, you are likely to find that language and culture differences affect a variety of different concerns, from study habits, to meal arrangements to personal hygiene, to furniture choices to meal times.

Conflict resolution

You will probably also encounter differences in the way people resolve conflict, especially when you are sharing housing. Patience and strong communication are probably the best tools you can use to counteract these problems.

> **TIP** There are many housing difficulties which you will need to learn to negotiate and which are just part of your experience studying abroad. However, if you find that your housing situation puts you in a dangerous or unsafe position, don't be afraid to pursue other options. Advisors at your university will usually be available to help you with this. Emergency housing is sometimes available.

● Building community

One of the things that will probably be important to your capacity to adjust to your new home will be the ability to build community. This involves not only making friends, but also having social contact and getting to know the people in your area, even if they are not necessarily friends. Community is not just something that happens. When you are abroad, you will probably have to make the conscious effort to get to know people and build community. The following offers you some ideas about how you might do this.

You meet lots of people but become close to only a few of them. Having good friends is essential, but rushing to become close to people is not the solution.

Amy, a post-graduate student in France

Building community is not just about making friends. It's also about feeling as if you belong, and know the local area. Take the time to introduce yourself to local shop assistants, for example, or the staff in a local coffee shop. You may never say much more to them than a few words of polite conversation, but being recognized can help to make you feel like you belong.

Take every opportunity to find out about events on campus. At the beginning of the school year or term, there may be some kind of fair which will give you information about all the student groups on campus. See what's around, join a few things you are interested in, and sign up for some email lists.

Heads up

Many student groups these days will have listservs, email lists or online forums, which you can sign up to. Getting onto them can be an important way of finding out about upcoming events, and getting involved in discussions, so make sure you sign up.

Check out student notice boards in the library, in common eating areas, in your department, in your college or residence, as well as bulletin boards in the local shopping centre, community centre, church and so on to find out what is going on.

Choose some events that seem interesting. Make the effort to go and chat to people. Go to departmental parties or events, even if you don't know anyone.

Heads up

Get involved with social activities as soon as you can – many students report that friendships are formed quickly and that it is easy to be left behind if you wait too long to get to know people.

Try to attend some regular events. Often, you might not get to know someone until you have both been going to the same event several times. There is something about seeing someone over and over which tends to open up the possibility of friendship.

Be open to a diverse group of friends and people to have fun with. Try not to restrict yourself to people from your home country or people who speak your language.

> *Don't just hang out with other exchange students, although it might be tempting. Take the the the opportunity to get to know the locals. You'll want people to visit when you go back for a holiday!*

Zivon, from St Petersburg, studying in Buenos Aires

Make the effort to talk to a classmate in a break during lectures or before a tutorial. Invite people to share meals with you.

Get to know people in the wider community. Find out about community events that interest you and attend them regularly. It can be great to meet people who are not students – it gives you a break from thinking about your studies, as well as helping you to meet more locals.

Heads up

Don't be afraid to let people know that you are new to town. People often enjoy sharing their home town with visitors, and might offer to show you things you would never find on your own.

Take advantage of trips and excursions organized by your international student centre, or residency – these are often great ways to explore your local area and meet people, and are often reasonably affordable.

Volunteer for an organization you care about in your new community –

Heads up

If you are an introvert, it can be very exhausting having to be sociable a lot of the time. You may find that you need to 'extrovert' more than you are used to. Make sure you give yourself time to yourself to rejuvenate, but try not to let yourself get isolated. You could tell yourself that you will go to a party, for example, for one hour and then see how you feel. You might stay longer, and you might not, but you are at least making contact with those around you.

this can be a terrific way to stay active, get to know people and learn about your new environment, as well as helping to keep your self-esteem high.

It takes time to build community and even longer to make friends. You may not make a huge number of very close friends, but it shouldn't take too long before you start to feel a bit more relaxed in your new environment. Make sure you keep up the attempt to socialize beyond the first few weeks and make it a priority for your whole study abroad.

Academic adjustment

University cultures differ not only from country to country but also between universities. In order to adjust to a different university culture and make the most of your time abroad, there are a number of things that you need to be aware of. Knowing the right questions to ask can be most of the battle. Some of the questions will be specific to your particular discipline or field of study.

Student participation

Is your study based on lectures, tutorials, practicals, lab work? Each of these has different expectations regarding student participation. Lectures, for example, often ask students to listen and take notes, whereas a tutorial might demand active participation and discussion. Find out when it is appropriate to ask questions, and to discuss.

Are you expected to be active or passive as a student? Are you expected to quietly take notes, or can you ask questions? Are you responsible for your own learning or are you led through the process more directly?

What kinds of participation are expected? Students who are used to being silent and taking notes are often shocked by some universities' cultures of rigorous debate and questioning. If you are used to discussion, it can be hard to adapt to a more reserved educational atmosphere.

Should you raise your hand before you speak? Some teachers encourage open debate; others regulate discussion in various ways. The students will often determine what goes on in the classroom in this regard.

> **TIP** Even if your destination university seems very similar to your own, it is worth checking basic guidelines for conduct.

Teacher/student relations

How are you expected to treat your teachers? Find out what you should call them. In some places, teachers are called Professor or Doctor, while in other places it is more appropriate to use first names. There may be a difference between how you are expected to interact with senior faculty and with more junior members.

Is it appropriate to email or phone your teachers? Do they hold office hours? Do you need an appointment? When are you allowed to talk to them? (Tip: Make sure you use appropriate email communication. This usually involves fairly formal language, and a clear, precise style.)

What are appropriate modes of conduct towards teachers? For example, in some countries, it is impolite not to offer teachers expensive gifts or tokens of appreciation. In other countries, this might be highly inappropriate (or just unnecessary).

> **TIP** If you want to continue some of your traditions in a context where they might not be understood, explain why you are doing it and what it means to you. For example, we know a number of students from Hong Kong and China who like to give their professors little gifts, and find that explaining this cultural tradition to their western professors helps them to avoid any misunderstandings.

Is it OK to argue with your teachers? In some universities, it is a sign of respect to agree with your teacher's every statement; in other universities, it is expected that you will engage and argue with your teachers, and your teachers may make provocative and controversial statements to get you thinking.

In Australia, I called all of my university teachers by their first name, but in North America, I had to find out on an individual-by-individual basis what to call my teachers. Some were fine with being called by their first names; others were offended. It was also a huge shock to me that even post-graduate students raised their hands in class before speaking and waited to be called on, rather than regulating their own discussion.

Author insight: Anna

Assessment

How are you being assessed? Is success based on memorizing large amounts of information and reproducing this in an exam or are you expected to synthesize, analyse and offer your own opinions? What is the grading scheme you are being assessed with? How does it work?

When I first arrived in Paris, I had to figure out everything by myself; to speak to each teacher to find out how many pages I had to write and what was expected – there were no standards for that. It was a great challenge to have to write two big essays in French at a high level; I had never handed in a paper in French before. But I worked really hard, studied at the Pompidou library and had a Russian friend who studied linguistics correct my papers. (I took her out for a night of free Danish beer afterwards.)

Ingrid, studying in Paris

What are the different genres you are being asked to work in? An essay is different from a report. An oral presentation has different rules from written work. Are you expected to make use of technology (for example, graphics, powerpoint presentations, computer software)?

The main challenge I had was to learn how to write 15-page research papers on literature in a language that wasn't my native language, and to actively take part in classes: the teaching methods were very different from back home. It turned out to be extremely gratifying and valuable in the end.

Jaqueline, studying in Canada

Ideas and research

What is your university's attitude towards using other people's ideas without referencing your sources? In some universities, it is regarded as commonplace to use other people's ideas in your papers, but in many universities, this would be regarded as plagiarism (and therefore a form of cheating). Penalties for plagiarism can be very high – so make sure you know exactly what that means in your university.

What level of research is expected? This will often be made clear by your teachers but there might be assumptions made of which you are not aware. You might find yourself spending hours researching your topic in the library only to find that you were supposed to discuss your own ideas, or you might write a personal essay when you are expected to integrate extensive secondary sources.

Deadlines

What is the attitude towards deadlines in your programme? In some places, deadlines are a rough guide only, while in others you will be penalized for handing work in late. If you have to hand in work late due to a personal emergency, or health issues, find out whether you can get an extension or special consideration, and what you need by way of documentation. Don't make assumptions either way.

Getting help

Where can you go to ask questions? Familiarize yourself with the 'chain of command'. Who is the first person to go to for help? Who should you go to if there is still a problem?

What campus resources can help you academically? Are there tutors available for you to talk to? Writing centres? Faculty advisors who can help? Peer counselling? Workshops on developing academic skills? Is there help available for students who are working in a second language?

> **TIP** Don't be afraid to ask, if you are unsure. Your colleagues and teachers will usually be happy to lead you in the right direction.

Many of these expectations are likely to vary from class to class or discipline to discipline, as well as culturally. You will get a very rapid sense of the culture you are working in. Sometimes you will make mistakes; that's fine. Just remember that there *are* differences, and that these can take a while to get used to.

In my own university, I had teachers and people I could ask when I was making decisions about what classes to take, or how to do the work. Before I left for New Zealand, I planned everything beforehand, but then things changed and I had to make new decisions. I missed being able to get help from the usual places. It was probably good for me, but I still found it hard.

Judith, a South African student studying environmental science in New Zealand

Heads up

You may find your academic work more challenging while you are abroad, and your grades may suffer as a result, along with your self-esteem. This is partly because you will be under more stress than usual as you deal with cultural adjustment and so you might not produce your best work. You might also be struggling with language differences, as well as a different set of expectations. It can take time to adjust to the new system.

If you find that these challenges start to affect your self-esteem, make sure you get involved in activities outside the classroom that can help you to feel good about yourself. Stay in touch with family and friends who can remind you of your strengths and what they love about you. You might also consider getting in touch again with your referees – they believed in you and supported you so they may be good people to remind you of your potential. Don't be embarrassed to talk to your supporters if you are struggling – they may have helpful advice, and many will have gone through similar situations and will be able to relate to your experiences. You might also consider talking to a learning counsellor at your university if possible, who may be able to offer you both practical and emotional help with dealing with your academic challenges. Bear in mind, too, that the students around you have had a lot longer than you to get used to the expectations and possibly the language. Be patient and give yourself time to adjust, and find ways of valuing yourself that aren't linked just to your academic work. There are so many things you can learn from studying abroad – enjoy them and allow yourself to grow and change as you go. And you may find that studying abroad gives you the chance to excel in new ways and with new opportunities.

The language was a challenge to me. In the beginning I was really worried and I was so afraid to speak during seminars and classes. It was also quite a challenge to write academic English. But it was a great challenge, and I enjoyed seeing how I improved, month by month.

Sara, a Scandinavian student studying in the UK

● Practicalities

Driving a car

Some countries will allow you to drive using your home driving licence for a designated period of time. Beyond this time, you will probably need to get an international licence. If you are in a longer programme and can prove residency, it might be possible to apply for a local licence. This may involve re-sitting the driving test.

A few things you need to know:

- The country you are in may drive on the other side of the road from what you are used to. This can be quite disorientating.
- The local road rules and etiquette might be very different. Take time to familiarize yourself with the official rules of the road AND talk to a local about particular habits which you need to know about.
- Make sure you know what age you must be to drive, rent a car and so on – regulations differ from country to country.
- If you do intend to drive a car, make sure you have the relevant insurance. Insurance you hold at home might not be sufficient.
- If you are travelling with children, make sure that you have adequate seat belt and safety provisions that conform to local and international standards.
- Remember that culture shock and jet lag can leave you tired and disorientated, which may affect your safety on the road.

Riding a bike

If you plan to ride a bike, or if you find that everyone around you owns a bike, ask round to find out where you can buy an affordable one. Find out:

- Are there bike paths you can use?
- What are the laws about helmets, bike lights, reflective gear?
- Where can you go to get help with your bike if you have a problem?
- What precautions can you take to prevent your bike being stolen? (It's worth investing in good locks if bike theft is a common problem, as it is on many campuses.)

Finding the things you need

Linguistic difficulties aside, it can be very challenging to find the things you need in a new country. There are often different kinds of shops, so you won't always know exactly where to look for what you need. In addition, there will be things available that you can't get at home, and other things that you might take for granted but that just aren't available in your new country.

The best way we have found of coping with this is to ask questions and to give yourself lots of time. Remember, too, that shopping might be a completely exhausting undertaking for a while until you get used to it, so try not to attempt too much at once and give yourself a break when you need to. Become familiar with the opening and closing times of the shops and restaurants around you, as these may be different from what you are used to.

The best thing, and the most challenging thing, is that everyday life is suddenly exotic – even grocery shopping.

Sam, an undergraduate living off-campus in the UK

Money revisited

Hopefully, you have arrived in your new country with a detailed plan of how much money you have available to you and what your expenses will be. It is important to revisit this budget and see whether it works in practice. One way of doing this is to keep a detailed record of everything you spend over your first few weeks. Make sure you include every detail – even just very small things such as a few pages of photocopying or the cost of running your clothes through a washing machine. Don't forget to include the cost of phone calls home. After a few weeks, compare what you have spent with your budget and make whatever changes you need to make. Revisit your budget periodically throughout your study abroad.

> **TIP** When you first arrive in a new country, you might be tempted to buy all sorts of new things and spend your money. Remember that you are here for a while and you have to make your money last. If there are things you really want to buy to take home with you, there will be time to do that later on. For now, be careful with your money until you work out what you can afford.

Tips for saving money

As well as a budget for the whole of your trip, create weekly and/or monthly budgets. Stick to them!

Be aware of currency exchange rates. If you are continually changing money from your home currency to your new currency, but aren't taking into account the fees you are paying, in your budget, you may have less money than you think you do.

Take advantage of student discount and special rates, for meals, entrance fees, attractions and so on. Sometimes, for example, museums may offer free or reduced-price-entry on particular days or at certain times, and the international student card might give you access to a variety of discounts.

Try to reduce costs by preparing your own food. It is often cheaper to take your own lunch, for example, than to eat in a café or restaurant. Eating places on campus may be cheaper than others, and your university may have special food plans which you can take advantage of. You might also split costs with a roommate or friend. Eating as a group can be an excellent way of saving money, dividing cooking responsibilities and making friends.

Take advantage of free community entertainment. Universities will often run free or cheap events for students.

Try to avoid convenience stores or specialized stores; often the same goods are available at cheaper prices in markets or supermarkets. Ask around to find out where other people shop.

Don't carry large amounts of cash around with you, and have a back-up source of money in case your credit cards, bank cards and so on are stolen or lost. Use credit cards sparingly – it can be very easy to load up a credit card without realizing how much money you are spending.

Many countries will offer return of sales taxes on particular goods when you leave the country. Find out whether this is possible in your new country. You will need to retain the receipts in order to claim the tax back.

If/when you travel, stay in youth hostels and student accommodation rather than the more expensive bed and breakfasts and hotels.

Hang out with other people who have similar financial situations as your own, to avoid being in situations where you are expected to spend a lot more money than you can afford.

Join university and local clubs and organizations which can help you to socialize and meet new people without over-spending.

TIP Many phone companies will ask for an expensive security deposit if you want to be able to make international phone calls. There are many ways around this, including using service providers who allow you to pay-as-you-go, or phone cards which require a security number and offer reduced rates. If you have access to a computer with internet access, email or computer-generated phone calls can also be much cheaper than regular phone calls. Ask around and see what options are available to you.

Find cheap ways of contacting your family and friends back at home – international phone cards, email, or online call programmes can be much cheaper than regular phone bills. Mobile/cell phones are rarely budget options.

Heads up

In some countries, such as Singapore, Israel and the UK, among others, you have to pay for a licence to own or to use a TV. In other places, especially North America or cities with high-density housing, you might have to pay for cable television in order to get any reception. Both of these things make watching television a much more expensive form of entertainment than it might be elsewhere.

Balancing study with work and travel

Heads up

We know many students who had many great intentions of travelling while they were studying abroad, but found that they did not have the time, money or energy to do so. Perhaps they didn't budget thoroughly enough, or had unexpected financial challenges along the way. Often, their attempts to earn more money in order to allow them to travel or to deal with unexpected costs left them with no time to get away. In addition, the stresses of dealing with culture shock while trying to study in another country often leave students with no emotional or mental resources or energy left to negotiate yet more travelling or more cultural shock. Planning ahead might help you to mitigate this, but your plans might need to change; try to be kind to yourself if you have less energy, time or money than you had hoped.

Balancing study with work and travel can offer multiple benefits:

- Having a job is not only helpful for your budget, but can also help you to learn a language faster, to get to know more local people, and to learn more about the place you are in, and help to over-come feelings of isolation and loneliness.

- You might make some friends.
- Having a job can also help you to feel more grounded, and less vulnerable to problems you might face in your study or in your housing situation.
- Travelling can help you to understand the place you are in at a much deeper level, you might make friends along the way, which can keep your stress levels down and your excitement levels up, and travelling can even help you to negotiate financial problems, as well as giving you some relaxation time.
- Both having a job and travelling can also boost your self-esteem and your confidence, which may help you to cope better with your university work.

I found my study abroad really expensive. The UK cost much more than I anticipated. I worked out that if I spent my winter break – when I had no classes – in the Czech Republic, I could travel and also save some money, since Eastern Europe is cheaper. I flew with a budget airline and stayed in youth hostels. I also found someone else from my university who wanted to travel. I didn't really know him very well before we left, but we ended up becoming friends.

Mike, a student from New Zealand studying in the UK

Coping with holidays

One of the challenges facing international students is often what to do with university holidays. During holidays, local students may leave campus and return home to be with family. As an international student, you might be left on campus with nothing to do but imagine the fun your friends are having with their family, and getting terribly homesick for your own life at home. These can be times of terrible depression and disillusionment for international students.

Try to plan in advance what you might do. For example, find out what locals do to celebrate. Are there public festivities you can go to (perhaps with some friends)? Are there rituals and traditions that are public events that you can be part of?

If many of your friends will be going to spend time with their families, are there other international students you could get together with? Even if you don't know them well, you might still have fun, and maybe make some new friends. Between you, you could cook a meal. If it is a holiday that is celebrated widely around the world, you could each cook something from your own culture that marks the occasion, and share it.

> **Heads up**
>
> If it is a holiday you celebrate at home, don't expect it to be the same as it is at home. You will probably only exacerbate your homesickness if it does not match up to your memories. Take the opportunity to create something new.

- Are there any resources on campus for international students during holidays?
- Could you volunteer your time to a local organization during the holiday (spend time with children in a hospital, or elderly people in a retirement home, or help out in a homeless shelter)?
- Could you take advantage of the holiday to go travelling (taking into account that the holiday might be celebrated across the whole country, and therefore limit your travel options)?

TIP   Try to avoid the temptation to use holidays as a chance to 'catch up' with work; you may be setting yourself up for isolation and loneliness. Plan a way to have some fun, even if you can't be with your family.

Changes at home

It can be particularly challenging to be abroad when important events or changes are happening at home. You may feel alone and may find that your experience of culture shock is made worse when you are emotionally vulnerable. Try to find support, from a friend or a professional counsellor who can help you through the situation. Find ways to have frequent contact with those back home, and make sure they know that you are thinking about them.

You might face pressure from family or friends to return home before your programme ends, which you may or may not be able or willing to do. Try to think through the implications of your choices; you may need to get help doing this if you are very emotional. Try to weigh up the pros and cons of returning permanently, returning for a short period or staying. Whether you stay or leave, seek help from an appropriate staff member on campus, who can help you to make arrangements, for example helping you to contact your teachers for extensions on your academic work. You may be able to access emergency funding from your university if needed. If a member of your family dies while you are abroad, you may be able to request a bereavement fare for the flight home – this can be cheaper than the normal fare (although often a student fare is still cheaper). Your travel insurance might pay for a return trip home in this scenario.

Setting goals

Most students report that their time abroad went much more quickly than they anticipated. Try to keep a clear vision of your goals. If there are particular things you want to do or places you want to see, do them as you go, and plan how to fit them in. Remember that you might not get another chance soon to do some of the things that are unique to your area. Don't leave everything for a few weeks before you fly home again. You might need to come up with a detailed plan for each weekend, or holiday, so that you don't keep putting things off and never actually getting to them. When you arrive, it will feel like you have a long time to fulfil your goals, but the time will pass quickly once you are involved in studying, building community and your new life.

Maintaining flexibility

In the first few chapters of this book, you probably noticed that we emphasized careful planning and meticulous organization. At some point or other, though, almost inevitably, your good intentions will fly out of the window because you will face unexpected challenges. Whether this is because the housing you accepted triggers off an allergy and makes you sick, or your passport is stolen, or a crucial course is suddenly made unavailable the year you need to do it, at some point (or several) you will need to adjust your plans and muddle your way through whatever challenges are thrown at you. This is part of the experience. You can and will cope, although you may have days where you wonder how it will be possible. It is one of the joys of studying abroad – you simply cannot plan for every eventuality and you will have to take a deep breath and improvise. You will bring together whatever resources you have to work through whatever challenges are thrown your way. And it will make a great story when you get home again.

I had to become completely self-sufficient since I was basically on my own, and learned a lot from this. At one point, my passport was stolen a day before I was leaving on a trip. I had to figure out exactly who to talk to and what to do by myself, and had only part of a day to do it. I managed to get a replacement passport in time for my flight. I learned a lot from that experience.

Sally, a US student in Europe

Be aware that you can never be prepared for everything, and you will eventually be thrown on your own resources at some point – whether those resources are financial, emotional or psychological.

Jessica, an English student who went to Canada to do her PhD, and decided to stay

Your time abroad will go quickly, so make sure you take advantage of every opportunity that comes your way, and learn everything you can. To make sure you can do this, you will need to look after your health and to stay safe, the topic of our next chapter.

Further resources

- Craig Storti, *Figuring Foreigners Out: A Practical Guide* (Intercultural Press, 1999).
  A guide for business people on working across cultures, but useful for anyone dealing with cross-cultural communication. Storti's other books might also be useful.
- *Culture Shock!* Country Guides (Graphic Arts Books).
  www.gacpc.com/culture_shock/cs.htm
  An excellent series of books offering advice on negotiating the local customs and etiquette of countries worldwide.
- The 'Living Abroad' series (Avalon Travel Publishing).
  http://www.travelmatters.com/livingabroadin.html
  A series of books offering comprehensive advice on living abroad in countries worldwide.

- The 'Live and Work' series (Globe Pequot).
  www.globepequot.com
  A series of books offering comprehensive advice on living and working in countries worldwide.
- H. Ned Seelye and Alan Seelye-James, *Culture Clash: Managing in a Multicultural World* (McGraw-Hill, 1995).
  Offers discussion of negotiating cultural difference. Aimed at business people, but nonetheless useful for those studying abroad.

8 Staying Healthy

Staying healthy is an important component of your experience studying abroad. Maintaining your physical, mental and emotional health will allow you to have more fun, take advantage of opportunities, take risks that will give you a chance to grow, be more focused on your academic work, have the energy to travel and explore your new environment, and be strong enough to develop and change as you need to. Staying healthy, though, is not something that just happens but takes conscious effort, and when you are in an unfamiliar environment, it can take even more effort than normal. Your mind and body will be going through a lot of adjustment, so you might need to develop a plan for how you will look after yourself, and revisit the plan throughout your study abroad to check that you are giving yourself what you need to stay physically, mentally and emotionally healthy.

● Before you go

Immunizations

Talk to your doctor or a travel doctor about immunizations and vaccines you might need before you leave. In some cases, these will be immunizations you choose to have in order to decrease your risk of getting sick; in other cases, they will be a requirement of entry into the country (that is, you won't be granted a study visa until you can prove that you have had them). The immunizations recommended and available to you will depend on both your home country and where you are going.

Make sure you talk to a doctor well in advance of your travel date. Some immunizations need to be administered several months before travelling, and some of them will have to be given in different stages over a period of time.

Keep a record of what immunizations you have and when. The 'International Certificate of Vaccinations' is available in many countries and is recognized internationally. You will need to get it stamped and dated by the doctor who provides the vaccine. In some cases, this will be the only proof of immunization that will be accepted by official agencies such as customs officials. You may need to know what immunizations you had as a child.

Bear in mind that vaccines can be expensive, and can cause side effects. If you choose to be immunized, make sure you use the same doctor for all your immunizations, so that the doctor can make sure that they are compatible with one another, and always tell your doctor about any medical conditions you may have, including pregnancy.

> **Heads up**
>
> We strongly recommend that you do not travel without health insurance. An otherwise relatively insignificant sickness or injury could cost you a lot of money in medical and other costs if you do not have appropriate insurance.

Health insurance

Many countries have reciprocal health arrangements with other countries, so it is worth finding out what you are entitled to. In some countries, you will be entitled to some health care as part of your student visa or residency. You may still need travel insurance. You should make sure that you are covered from the day you leave home to the day you arrive back. Your university may also give you partial or full cover, paid for by student fees. This may or may not be mandatory. In other places, you will have to pay for some kind of health cover. Find out what these schemes cover. Even if you have some kind of cover through your university, you may still choose to take out additional insurance through a private organization. Private insurance can be quite expensive, so if you are studying abroad for any length of time, make sure you research other options.

Make sure you understand how your insurance works. Some companies will have an emergency number you can call from anywhere in the world

> **Heads up**
>
> Even if you are a citizen of your new country, do not assume that you will be entitled to the same health care as locals – many health schemes differentiate between residency and citizenship, and you can be resident for some purposes, such as tax, without having all of the rights of a resident.

and will help you to organize payment for your health care. Often, you will get the health care and then receive a bill later. Sometimes, when the amounts are small, you will have to pay the money upfront, and then submit the receipts to your insurance company for reimbursement. So, always keep receipts and whatever other documentation the insurance company needs. Bear in mind that reimbursement can take quite a long time. If you face a medical problem, call your insurance company – or ask someone to call for you – as soon as you can and inform them of what is going on.

Be clear before you sign up for insurance what exactly is covered. For example, many health insurance policies specifically say that they do not cover 'dangerous' activities as part of the plan. These often include such things as bunjee jumping, white-water rafting, parachuting, deep sea diving and so on. You may have to pay extra to get these activities covered. Bear in mind that you might very well want to do these kinds of activities as you travel. Chances are high that all will go well, but we strongly recommend that you have some kind of insurance to cover you if it doesn't.

If you are a post-graduate student, and will be working as a teaching or research assistant, you may have additional health insurance. Find out what this covers and when it applies, so that you don't pay for cover you already receive. Check, though, that international students are eligible, and how many hours you need to be doing to be covered. Find out if your cover applies during holidays or if you are traveling.

Dental work

Have any necessary dental work done before you leave your home country. Leave plenty of time before your departure – some treatments take several months to complete, and some dental procedures can prevent you from flying.

Check that your travel insurance covers dental work. Many policies will cover 'emergency work' only; clarify what this includes and decide whether you feel satisfied with the coverage.

Medical bills and a visit to the dentist may set you back a fort-night's budget on groceries so brush your teeth 3 times a day and floss too!

Derek, who has studied on three continents

Glasses and contact lenses

If you wear glasses, make sure you pack an extra pair – you probably don't want the hassle of having to have an eye check and buy a new pair of glasses while abroad. If you wear contact lenses, have a pair of glasses as back up. Bear in mind that contact lenses may not be available in your new country, or may be more expensive than you are used to.

Pre-existing health problems

Pre-existing health problems are unlikely to magically disappear simply because you go abroad, so be prepared for them. Think through the issues that might come up, and how you will deal with them.

Carrying a summary of your medical reports might be useful – this can help a doctor in your new country understand what the problem is and how it can be treated effectively. If you are travelling alone, you might consider letting someone you trust in your new country know about your medical condition. If you are part of an organized exchange programme, you will probably have to complete a medical health form, but if you are studying independently, you might talk to a study-abroad advisor, or a flatmate. You might consider wearing a bracelet or necklace that indicates a particular medical issue, in case of an emergency.

If you have a disability that requires technological accommodations, research beforehand whether you will be able to get what you need to run your equipment. Consider where you might buy new hearing aid batteries, for example, or where you might go for technical assistance if your electric wheelchair needs repair work. Your new university might have an accessibility centre that can give you advice on how to negotiate these challenges; don't wait until you are in dire need before you work out what you can do. See the section on accessibility in 'Additional Challenges' for further information.

Medications

If you are going for a short time, consider taking enough prescription medications to cover your whole stay. This will avoid the problem of having to replace them in your new country.

If you are going for a longer period, it will probably be impractical to take a full supply. In this case, make sure that you have enough medication to get you through the first few weeks/months abroad. Ask your doctor to provide you with a clear indication of what the drug is and its ingredients (including amounts). Drugs will often be known by different names in your new country, and the dosages might be very different. Make sure you know the generic name of any medication you take, as well as the pharmaceutical name.

Always carry a supply of any life-saving medication on your person, in case your luggage gets stolen or lost.

Make sure you carry a note from your doctor indicating what you are carrying and why – customs officials may otherwise be very suspicious of your medications. Carry them in their official containers, with all labels intact. Do the same with any equipment you might need, such as needles, ventilators and so on. You might consider getting the doctor's letter translated if you are going to a place where a different language is spoken – this might help to avoid long delays at the airport, and will also help you in the case of an emergency.

Heads up

> Sometimes, in order to get to your new country, you will have to fly through one or more other countries. If you have to clear Customs in other countries (and not just stay in transit), make sure you research the drug laws and policies in ALL of the countries you must fly through, to avoid any problems with your medications being confiscated.

In some places, the medication you need will simply not be available in your new country. You might consider having it shipped to you from your home country. This can be risky, though, because you need to know that Customs will let your package into the country, and you need to be able to rely on the postage system to deliver it on time. Also, this can get very expensive. If it is a drug which you cannot do without, make sure you research beforehand how you will cope.

Once you have started to get settled in your new country, visit a doctor and discuss your needs – he or she will probably be able to help you find an equivalent medication. Bear in mind that your body may take some time to get used to a new drug and in some cases, you will have to experiment with different ones to find one that matches the efficacy of your old one. Make sure you keep your doctor up to date with your symptoms and any side effects you might be experiencing.

As you are travelling to your new country, or if you travel once you have arrived, don't forget to take account of the time-zone changes – this will affect when you should take your medications. If it is important to take them at regular intervals, keep a watch set to a single time zone and keep a record of when you have been taking your medications, to make sure the time zones do not interfere with your dosages.

Research what you are allowed to take into a country. Bear in mind that a common medication available over-the-counter in one country might be illegal in others.

NEVER carry illegal drugs into your new country. Check beforehand what is regarded as illegal. Having even a small amount might be a convictable offence.

Recreational drugs in your new country

In some parts of the world, some kinds of recreational drugs are widely available and perfectly legal. Make sure you know what the laws are in the place you are going to. Don't assume that a drug is legal just because it is widely available or widely used. Even if a drug is legal, bear in mind that concentrations and purities differ from place to place, and your body might have difficulty adjusting. Don't forget that many drugs can affect your capacity to make good decisions.

In an emergency

Before you need help, think about what you will do in an emergency. You will need to plan for this both before you leave, and in the first few days after arrival.

Medical emergencies

Consider how you might negotiate a medical emergency by thinking through the following issues.

- In a medical emergency, does your insurance cover ambulances or other kinds of emergency transport?
- Where is the nearest hospital? Will it accept your health-care coverage (some hospitals won't treat international students, for example)? In what circumstances is this the best emergency option?
- Does the community have medical centres? (These can be useful if you need a doctor, but don't want to have to wait at a hospital.) What are its opening hours? How far away is it?
- What is the emergency number for police/fire/ambulance?
- If language is a problem, is there a facility that is more likely to speak your language?

Heads up

Emergency numbers differ from country to country. Make sure you know them. They are usually listed in the front of phone books or in public phone booths.

Other emergencies

In other kinds of emergencies – for example, terrorism, natural disasters and disease outbreaks – have a way of making contact with your home government. Find out where the embassy or consulate is for your home country. Some countries will share an embassy with another country, an arrangement whereby in emergencies, citizens of one country can be protected by another country's embassy; find out if this is the case for you. It is often possible to register with your country's embassy so that you can be contacted in case of an emergency. You should take advantage of campus resources for help with most problems, but if you have some kind of emergency, the embassy will be able to put you in touch with people who can help you, including doctors who speak your language, if available. The embassy is unlikely to cover costs or expenses.

Plan these aspects of your safety before you leave, and revise your plans as you get to know your new environment.

Staying healthy abroad

There are a number of things you can do to maintain your health during your time abroad.

Doctors

It is remarkably common for otherwise healthy students to get sick while they are studying abroad. This is often due to a combination of unusual food, reactions to water, stress, problems sleeping. Many students find that this passes by itself, while others have to seek medical attention. It can be absolutely awful to be sick in a strange environment, without your usual support, but most students get through it somehow, and it makes an interesting story later.

In non-emergency situations, the best way to find a doctor is probably to ask your university for help. In many cases, the university will have a medical centre. Make sure you take any relevant medical documentation with you to your appointment. You might have to ask around for a doctor who speaks your language; alternatively you might find a translator who is willing to help you explain the problem. Make sure that your doctor's appointment will be covered by your health insurance plan or you may have to pay for it yourself.

Seeing a doctor in a new country can be very difficult. There may be very different expectations around patient care, the use of technology, and the conditions under which you are examined, as well as the kind of training the doctor has. You will have to make a judgement about what you feel comfortable with, and whether you feel safe. Many hospitals will see non-emergency cases, although the waiting periods can be very long.

In some places, you will be required to register with a particular doctor for the time you are in the country. The choice of doctor will often be based on your geographical location. In this case, you will need to go to that doctor first; if you feel very unhappy with the treatment you receive, it might be possible to change.

Heads up

Students often report facing long waiting lists for doctors, counsellors, psychiatrists and other health providers on campus. If you need help more quickly, ask the receptionist 'to fit you in' or consider using resources off-campus which have shorter waiting lists, if this is viable for you financially.

Food

It is very likely that you will be eating food that your body is not used to in your new country. Even if it seems familiar, there will be differences that will take your body time to get used to. Differences in food can also contribute to culture shock, so be patient with yourself.

Some food tips

Raw foods may be contaminated. Bear in mind that, even if the locals can eat something happily, you might not be able to as your body will be used to different things. Raw foods may include uncooked vegetables, salads, meat, chicken, fish, seafood, and unpasteurized dairy products (including milk). Some of these things you may have to avoid the whole time you are away, while others your body might get used to.

Don't expect to be able to get the same kinds of foods that you get at home. In some cases, there will be little discernible difference, but in others, much of your food might be very unfamiliar. Sometimes, you will be able to find specialist supermarkets that sell particular kinds of foreign foods. These may be able to satisfy a craving you might have for familiar foods, but might be expensive.

Try to keep an open mind about new foods. Allow your new friends to introduce you to new things.

Try to avoid foods that have been hot but are now cold. This could indicate that they have been sitting for a while, and might be bacteria-ridden. This is especially true of street foods and market foods. Even countries that

Heads up

If you have food allergies, make sure you research the food regulations of your new country. For example, are food producers required to list all the ingredients, or only the main ones? How can you find out what chemicals have been used to make the food? Make sure you learn the words for the foods you are allergic to in the new language, so that you can ask about them.

have strict health codes for restaurants and coffee shops, might not extend the same codes to street vendors, whether it is hot dogs in Toronto, fried rice in Hong Kong or kebabs in Lebanon.

If something seems to have upset your body, avoid it for a while.

TIP Don't get so scared of potential problems that you play it too safe. You will have the chance to experience a variety of foods that are not only safe but are also delicious. Be sensible, but be willing to step outside your comfort zone.

Water

If the people around you are not drinking the tap water, you are asking for trouble if you do – the water may not be safe to drink.

Even if the water is safe to drink for locals, your body might still react negatively to it, because you may not have the same resistance to certain kinds of bacteria. If you have doubts, boil your water before drinking it, or drink tea or coffee made from boiled water. Beer and wine are often safe options. You might also drink bottled water. (Make sure the cap is sealed properly, so you know the bottle has not been refilled from a local tap.) Carbonated drinks can also be a safer option.

Avoid sharing plates, utensils and so on that are not washed thoroughly in hot water and detergent. Be wary of unclean glasses or bottles in restaurants.

Avoid ice. We know many people who diligently asked for a carbonated drink, in order to be safe, and then got sick from it.

If you decide that the water is unsafe to drink, remember that this includes washing your food with it, or cleaning your teeth with it. You may also choose not to swim in it. In some places, you can buy iodine tablets to clean your water. Make sure you read the directions and follow them carefully.

Other health tips

If you are in an area prone to mosquitoes and other insects, wear insect repellent, sleep underneath a mosquito net, and wear long sleeves and trousers tucked into your boots to avoid exposing your skin.

Wear good shoes, which will protect your feet from bacterial infections in very wet areas and from other health problems. Good shoes will also prevent you from getting sore feet, sore legs and back problems if you are walking a lot. Wear footware in shared showers to prevent athlete's foot.

Try to avoid handling animals in your new country. Even healthy domestic animals could cause health problems for you if your body is not used to their particular kind of bacteria.

Exercise

Obviously, while you are abroad, you will still need to exercise, just as you do at home. Don't make the assumption, though, that whatever you do at home will be available to you in your new country. Many sports are culturally specific. You might love to play soccer or cricket, only to find that the only people who play in your new country are international students. You might get your exercise by bike riding, only to find that it is much less of an option in a city that is not designed for cyclists, or which has a lot of steep hills. Even something as simple as walking might be hard in a city at a much higher or lower altitude, or which is more polluted, or which is more unsafe for pedestrians than the environments you are used to.

Since exercise is often useful for stress-reduction as well as for physical health, it can be quite disorientating if you can't rely on the physical activities that are usually part of your regular routine.

If you are in a large city, you might be able to find resources more in line with what you are used to. Bear in mind, though, that these options may be expensive and you might have to travel to other neighbourhoods to participate. Also, be aware of isolating yourself from the local culture. Doing what you do at home might be a good way to meet other people from your own country but might not be the best way to meet the locals.

Studying abroad can be a great chance to learn new skills and try new sports. If you have grown up in a hot climate, for example, you might have the chance to join all the local three-year-olds in learning to ice skate. If you have grown up skiing, it might be your chance to discover that surfing is not as easy as it looks.

Make sure you are clear about what is included in any team membership or gym membership you choose to buy. Is equipment included? What about transport to out-of-town games? Can you use the pool at the gym, or just the machines? Will you need to purchase expensive shoes, or uniforms?

Many universities have gyms, athletics facilities, pools and sports teams or a combination of all of these. Take advantage of them when you can. However, bear in mind that, while some universities include access to these facilities as part of your student fees, others charge extra for use of sporting facilities. Make sure you take this into account in your budget.

Sleep

In the excitement of being in a new country, especially with new housing arrangements and study commitments, it can be difficult to get enough sleep. This might affect your mental health, your ability to cope with your new environment, your ability to have fun, and your health.

Try to make sure your new bed is not dusty or mouldy; this might especially be a problem if you are living in student accommodation. It might be worth buying a plastic undersheet to cover your mattress.

It is not unusual to find that your sleep is disturbed and restless for the first few weeks. This may in part be because of jet lag, but may also be because you are in a new bed, with strange smells and sounds around you.

You might find that you need more sleep while you are away – it gives your body and mind a chance to recuperate while you adjust to the changes around you. You will adapt eventually.

Climate

Chances are high that the country you are going to will have a different climate from what you are used to. In hot countries, you might be at risk of heat stroke, dehydration, sunburn or skin cancer. Make sure you check the UV indexes, as ultraviolet can be high even when it doesn't feel very hot. In cold countries, frost bite, hypothermia, snow burn, and ice-related injuries might be issues you will have to contend with. Check for wind-chill, since this is a more accurate measure of conditions than temperature alone. Listen to local knowledge for tips about how to deal with the climate, and bear in mind that the locals will be more used to it than you and so you may have to take extra precautions.

If you are moving to a place that is colder than you are used to, or where it rains more often, or the days are shorter, or there is less light, you might find that your mental well-being is affected, and you might not even realize why. There is not always a lot you can do – although good lighting, special lights which emulate the sun, and indoor sporting activities might help – but sometimes recognizing that these factors are contributing to your feelings can be helpful in itself.

Potential health concerns

Chances are very high you will make it through your study abroad with only minor health concerns. However, the following are some health challenges of particular concern when you study abroad.

Diarrhoea

It is fairly common for travellers to get diarrhoea, as a result of unfamiliar water and food. There is a good chance that it will go away by itself. These are a few things you should do if you find yourself afflicted:

- Maintain adequate fluid intake to prevent dehydration. If you suspect the water has caused it, try to stick to hot drinks, bottled water, pre-packaged fruit juices or carbonated drinks.
- If you think the cause is something you have eaten, try to avoid the food you suspect until you are feeling better, and then experiment with small quantities.
- If your diarrhoea lasts for more than a few day, or if there is blood and/or mucus in your stools, or if you have a fever, or have shakes, consult a doctor.
- Make sure you wash your hands carefully, to avoid spreading infection.

Tetanus

This is commonly known as 'lock-jaw' and is an infection caused by a contaminated wound or injury. It can be fatal if untreated. If you have an open wound, make sure you clean it thoroughly. Try to avoid contact with animal faeces (which may be present in contaminated water). Immunizations are available and need to be re-administered every ten years. If you get an injury in a region where tetanus is a high-risk, clean the wound and see a doctor to get an anti-tetanus boost. Make sure your tetanus boost is up-to-date before you set off.

Hepatitis A

This is most prevalent in areas of North Africa, the Middle East and the Caribbean, but you may encounter it anywhere. It is transmitted orally through contaminated food or water. In addition, seafood, especially shell fish, might be sources in contaminated areas. Symptoms include fever, loss of appetite, nausea, abdominal pain and yellowing of the eyes (jaundice).

Malaria

Malaria is transmitted by some mosquitoes, and is most prevalent in parts of

Heads up

If you will be spending time in a hospital, science lab, child-care centre, prison, a homeless shelter or other similar places, you will need to seek specialist health advice before you leave to make sure that you neither pick up a disease, nor transmit one.

the Caribbean, Latin America, Africa, the Middle East and Asia. Anti-malaria medication is available and, in some places, required. Make sure you read the instructions carefully – you will probably have to take the medication before you leave, during your stay and for a few weeks after you return to your home country. Make sure you sleep under a mosquito net to avoid being bitten, and you can use insect repellants on your skin as well.

Tuberculosis

TB is a pulmonary infection transmitted through the air, from someone who is infected. It is not transmittable through dishes or food, but can be transmitted through unpasteurized dairy products.

Be aware if you are going to a high-risk area, and seek medical assistance. Antibiotics are available. Immunizations are available for infants and children, but seek medical advice before proceeding.

Heads up

Some viral, bacterial and parasitic infections might not produce any symptoms for several months after your study abroad. If you find that you get sick later, make sure your doctor knows that you have been abroad, and where you have been – this will help the diagnosis process.

Sexual health

Sexually transmitted diseases/infections (STDs)

These are known by various names – both generic and specific. They are infections which are transmitted through sexual contact, which may include kissing. When engaging in sexual activity, use appropriate protection (condoms, mouth dams, gloves and so on) to avoid having contact with sexual fluids. It is unwise to take your sexual partner's evaluation of their health at face value – they may be lying, or may have an infection they are not aware of. If you do contract an STD, contact a doctor or sexual health clinic. A pharmacist may also be able to assist. There may be a centre at the university that can advise you about sexual health treatment and disease prevention.

> **Heads up**
>
> The use of safer sex methods (e.g. using condoms, mouth guards, birth control) can be culturally specific. You may find yourself pressurised to engage in unsafe activities and may need to assert yourself to make sure you are safe

HIV/AIDS

HIV/AIDS is transmitted through body fluids, through having unsafe sex, sharing needles, or through blood transfusions. Anyone can be at risk of HIV/AIDS, no matter what gender you are, who you have sex with, what your sexual orientation is, or how old you are.

In some countries, you are unlikely to contract HIV/AIDS through a blood transfusion, because donated blood is thoroughly checked beforehand. In other countries, donated blood might not have been so thoroughly checked, and so you may be at increased risk.

You may be at risk if someone uses a contaminated needle to give you accupuncture, inject you with vitamins or other nutrients, give you body piercings or tattoos or carry out medical procedures, through blood donation or in any other situation which involves you being pricked with a needle. Never allow someone to use a needle that has been used on someone else, and that is not medically sterile.

HIV/AIDS has been proved NOT to be transmittable through skin contact, shared water or food, contact with inanimate objects, air conditioning, or mosquitoes.

If you have any contact with another person's bodily fluids through sexual contact, regardless of the gender of the person you are having sex with, use protection.

> **Heads up**
>
> Women – the birth control pill does not protect against sexually transmitted diseases so you will need to use another form of protection to avoid the transmission of STDs.

Heads up

Some countries will screen incoming travellers on the grounds of HIV/AIDS status, and can deny access to those who are HIV positive. Sometimes, countries will also deny access on the grounds of perceived risk-factors. You may have no legal recourse to counter this, so make sure you do the research before you leave. If you are HIV positive, bear in mind that health care varies enormously from country to country and make sure you are prepared for whatever care you need. Clarify whether this care will be included in your insurance and health plan.

Pregnancy

Needless to say, a woman can get pregnant wherever she is in the world and however inconvenient it may be. Make sure you use reliable contraception if you want to to avoid pregnancy.

Safety

You might be very good at keeping yourself safe in your home environment, but being abroad can raise new issues concerning personal safety.
Some tips:

- Be vigilant. Until you get used to your new surroundings, don't take anything for granted. Be aware of whether you 'feel' safe. Listen to local advice about where you are safe and trust your own instincts as well.
- Keep your money secure in a money belt. Try to avoid showing people where you keep your money. If you are in a place where you have a lot more money than those around you, be very cautious about letting people know how much you have.
- Divide up your money instead of keeping it all in one place, so that you have back up if some of it is stolen.
- Beware of pickpockets and bag-snatchers. This is especially a problem in crowded areas such as trains or markets. Be aware that you might get distracted as you try to read a map, or work out directions. Be especially vigilant of children, as they might be used as a distraction.
- Try to avoid sticking out as a foreigner. This might include adapting your clothing to fit local standards.

Heads up

If your passport is stolen, you will need to report it to the police and to your embassy or consulate. Make sure you get an official police report, if possible. You will need to apply for a new passport as soon as possible – sometimes emergency temporary passports are available. If you have credit cards stolen, report them as soon as possible to the banks involved – many companies have international emergency numbers you can call. It is important that you do not treat this casually since unreported stolen credit cards can be used fraudulently. Try not to carry all your important documents and cards around with you all the time – this increases the chance of losing everything. Leave copies of all your documents with someone at home.

- Be confident. Even if you are feeling scared, try to make it look as if you know where you are and what you are doing.
- Use a lock on your bags.
- Avoid isolated areas. This might include train carriages with few people in them, or areas of the city which seem deserted.
- When travelling, take the time to read the safety material. Often, diagrams will be used, which will help you to get around potential language barriers.

Heads up

Stay in regular contact with your family and friends back home. If you travel during your study abroad, leave the details of your itinerary with someone – a flatmate, a friend, a host family and so on.

- Learn basic phrases in your new language which will get you help. For example, police, hospital, fire, help.
- Do not hitchhike.
- Explore and socialize with a friend, especially in bars or nightclubs. Make a commitment to watch out for each other.
- If you are meeting new friends, do so in a public place.
- Do not agree to carry packages for strangers.

- Be aware of the local laws and know how they apply to you.
- Even if you are not driving, accustom yourself to road rules and etiquette to avoid road accidents. Especially, check which side of the road cars drive on, as this might be different from what you are used to.
- Learn about taxis in your new country. Some countries have marked taxis which are strictly regulated. Other countries have unmarked taxis, and you will have to decide whether you are safe or not.
- Learn about the risks that are particular to the area you are going to. Are you likely to encounter animals that might be dangerous (anything from elephants to spiders)? Are you in danger of drowning or getting caught in a riptide or strong current? Avalanches? Cyclones? Natural disasters? Find out how you might deal with these scenarios. ,
- Find out which parts of town are regarded as safe and unsafe. Bear in mind that this may be affected by such factors as your physical appearance, skin colour, racial characteristics and so on.
- If you are a member of a particular group that is likely to make you more vulnerable to safety concerns in the country you are going to, read the 'Additional Challenges' chapter.

Drugs and alcohol

Alcohol and drugs are some of the biggest risk-factors for students studying abroad. Away from your usual communities, and your normal supports, you might take risks with alcohol and drugs that you would never take at home. This is one area where risk-taking can be hugely detrimental to your health and safety.

Heads up

Wherever you go, be cautious about accepting food or drink from strangers. Never leave a drink at a bar unattended. People have been known to slip drugs into drinks that will leave you unconscious or unable to make good choices. This can lead to dangerous situations, including rape or theft. These drugs are sometimes called 'rape drugs'. If you suspect that you have been given a drug of some kind, contact the police, and talk to someone you trust who may be able to help.

If you are under the influence of drugs or alcohol, you are more likely to find yourself in dangerous situations, and your judgement might be impaired. This can affect everything from road safety, to 'stranger danger', to your sexual health. Maintain moderation, and try to be around people you trust who will help you out if you need it.

Mental and emotional health

Although it is a very important aspect of health abroad, maintaining your mental and emotional health can be quite challenging, especially if you do not acknowledge it as something that takes time and energy.

Tips for mental and emotional health

Make sure that you keep family and friends up-to-date with who you are and how you are changing. Phone calls, letters and emails are not perfect, but can communicate a lot.

Commit to regular activities where you will see people regularly. This might be a hobby, or sport, or volunteer work – it doesn't matter what it is. Seeing people regularly will help you to make friends, and spending time with people can stave off depression.

Do things that are fun. Take some time off. This will help your mental state as well as making you more productive when you are working.

Make some friends beyond your programme at the university. Community groups or hobby groups can help to create variety in your life and will give you a chance to surround yourself with people who may not be doing exactly what you are doing. This may help the kind of insular vision that can grow from sustained programmes.

If you feel anxious or depressed, talk to people about how you are feeling. Don't try to deal with it alone. Make contact with your international student centre; other international students will probably understand some of your feelings, and the centre might have resources to help you.

Get out and be active even if you don't feel like it. Turn off the television and find some company.

Decorate your new home with pictures of your family and friends. Keep small things around you that remind you of home and remind you that you are loved. If you feel disillusioned, remind yourself of your goals and reasons for studying abroad. Don't be afraid to revise your goals and plans as you grow and change.

Celebrate your own holidays and special occasions, and find ways of cele-brating the special occasions of your new country. Don't expect the celebrations to be just the way they are at home – this is a chance to create something new.

Create routines and give yourself something to look forward to. For example, regular meals with friends, Friday night movies, Saturday morning sport with friends.

Find a place that makes you feel peaceful. Examples might include a local church, a park, a river, or a coffee shop. Give yourself some time alone in this place regularly.

Be mindful of the importance of time management. This will help you to keep on top of your academic work while still having time to have fun and make friends, and will help to reduce stress.

Keep a journal of your experiences. It will help you to record your study abroad, and remind you of things you want to share with your family and friends. It can also be a great way of venting and getting your feelings out, and tracking how you have changed. If you find yourself suffering from depression, keeping a journal can help you to see the way your feelings shift and remind you that you are not unhappy ALL the time, and it can help you to plot what makes you feel better. If you have regular email access, keeping an online journal/blog can also be a good way of keeping in touch with people back at home. A journal might include just writing, or might contain photos, pictures, ticket stubs, postcards and other memorabilia.

I wrote a web blog during my stay, which helped a lot to stay in touch with friends and family. And it also helped me to sort my impressions and photos. And now I can always read about what I did on each day.

Allan, a computational linguistics student from Germany

Keep your eyes open, and your mind open. When you go abroad, imagine yourself as a big sponge. Absorb everything you see, hear and experience. Remember to take a journal with you. When you're all saturated, at the end of each day, wring yourself out by writing everything down in your journal, drawing pictures, getting your travelling companions to write in it too. Share your deepest thoughts with your diary, and your experiences with those travelling with you. At the end of your trip, you'll have a record of a wonderful journey that you will remember for the rest of your life.

Amir, who has lived and studied in a variety of countries

Heads up

Relationships continue to grow and change wherever you are. If you are travelling with a partner or family, make sure you continue to protect those relationships. It is possible that you may have to go through a break-up while you are abroad. Don't try to negotiate this without the support of good friends and maybe a counselor. When you are ready, tell your family back at home, so that they can support you as well.

Longer programmes

A student on a relatively short programme may suffer from mental and emotional issues no more severe than culture shock and homesickness. If your programme is longer, especially if it lasts several years or more, it is possible that you may suffer from such concerns as depression, even if you have not suffered from mental health problems previously – many students we know in longer programmes report having difficulty coping.

Post-graduate programmes seem to be especially challenging in terms of mental health at the best of times, and these difficulties can be compounded for international students. As a post-graduate student, you tend to spend a lot of time working alone on your research, and working long hours. You may have to deal with relationship or family issues without the help of your usual support networks, and you may find it hard to develop the kinds of friendships that can sustain you when you are having a hard time (casual friends to have fun with are generally easier to find than friends with whom you feel comfortable sharing difficult emotions). If you find yourself dealing with mental health issues, you may start to question why you chose to study abroad and you may feel anxiety about your programme and your future career. Your self-esteem may also suffer as a result. Over the length of a long programme, things may also change at home, leaving you feeling powerless and 'out of the loop'. You might find that your emotions feel out of control and that you are experiencing emotional highs and emotional lows. All of these feelings are not only normal, but seem to be quite common for international students in long programmes overseas.

Recognizing burn-out

The combination of culture shock, being away from your support networks, a challenging academic programme and the stress of planning your study abroad might leave you vulnerable to 'burning out'. The following experiences might be an indication that you are burnt out:

You feel depressed and tired.
You find it hard to motivate yourself.
You find yourself getting isolated.
You are not enjoying your studies.
You feel like university is taking over your life, and you have no free time for fun or relaxation.
You feel overwhelmed.
Your creativity seems to have gone on a long holiday – without you.

Strategies for protecting your mental and emotional health

If you are in a long programme, plan to go home regularly if you possibly can. This might only be as frequently as every two years, but even this can help you to reconnect with people who care about you, and remind you why you made the choices you made.

Invite friends and family to come and visit you in your new country. Show them your home, take them on a tour of the campus, show them how you spend your days, take them to your favourite places. This will help them picture where you are, and can help you to appreciate your new country and to feel more 'grounded'.

Take breaks and holidays. Travel in your new country. You have worked hard to get here so it can be difficult to take a break, but you need to if you are going to make this sustainable.

Be patient. It takes time to turn acquaintances you have fun with into friends who will be there when things are not so much fun. Try not to put pressure on these friendships; allow them to grow naturally, and accept that really good friends can be rare. Stay in contact with friends in your home country, but acknowledge that these friendships, too, will not be 'frozen' but will change as you both grow.

If depression is getting in the way of your relationships, university work, personal life or happiness, seek help from a counsellor or psychiatrist. Your university may have resources to help you with this.

• • •

Most students studying abroad seem to go through a range of emotions while they are abroad, and many report that their emotions are more volatile and inclined to change rapidly. But most also say that they are glad they studied abroad, even if they did have to face the challenge of depression or other emotional issues. Remember that even negative feelings can teach you about yourself, and that most emotions will shift again eventually.

Further resources

- Deborah Mills, *Travelling Well: The Essential Handbook for Healthy Travel* (published by the author).
  www.travellingwell.com.au
  An excellent book on healthy traveling. Available online, as well as in print.
- The 'Healthy Travel' series (Lonely Planet).
  www.lonelyplanet.com
  This is a comprehensive series on health and safety for specific countries and regions.
- The Foreign and Commonwealth Office.
  www.fco.gov.uk
  Targeted at UK nationals, but its travel advice by country has wider applicability. Contains general tips for travel safety and health and also stresses the importance of obtaining adequate health insurance before you travel.
- Travel Alone and Love It.
  www.travelaloneandloveit.com/
  A resource to help solo travellers make the most of their travel. Includes safety advice.
- Sara's Wish Foundation
  www.saraswish.org
  This site offers safe travel tips, as well as some scholarships for women.
- Association for Safe International Road Travel.
  www.asirt.org/
  Dedicated to reducing road traffic accidents including travellers, with a section for students studying abroad. Offers specific road reports as well as general safety advice.
- US Centers for Disease Control and Prevention
  www.cdc.gov/travel/
  Offers country-specific health advice, as well as advice about vaccinations and other health concerns.
- World Health Organization.
  www.who.int
  Useful for finding out about current epidemics and world health issues, including travel advice and medical information.

9 A Changing Relationship to Home

When you get near the end of your programme abroad, and it is time to think about going home, you will probably find that there are a lot of practical details to negotiate, as well as emotional and psychological challenges you might face. On the one hand, you will probably want to see your family and friends and to resume your 'normal' life. On the other, you might just be starting to feel at home in your new country and be reluctant to have to pack up, say goodbye to your new life, and leave. You may also be concerned about how you will re-adjust to life in your home country, and how to incorporate what you have learnt into your life on a more permanent basis. There are a number of things you can do to make the transition back home go smoothly.

Practicalities

Return flights

When you book your flight home, give yourself enough time to pack up and say goodbye to friends after your classes, final papers and exams are over. This will not only help ease your stress levels but will also allow you to create 'closure' with your new life.

Bear in mind that flights get very full at certain times of the year, so make sure you book the return flight well in advance.

Remember that you will need time at home as well, to settle back in before your study or work commitments begin again.

> **Heads up**
>
> Changing pre-booked flights can be quite expensive, so try to plan ahead as much as possible and try to avoid making last-minute changes.

Travel

Many students take the opportunity to travel after their programme ends. Keep in mind the following things.

- If you want to travel before returning home, make sure you check the provisions of your visa before you make these plans.
- Make sure you give someone you trust a copy of your itinerary, and arrange to 'check-in' regularly while you travel.
- Work out what you can do with your luggage. Will you take everything with you when you travel (this could be heavy and cumbersome, and if you have a lot of stuff, could pose a security risk)? Do you have the option of leaving some of your luggage and picking it up before you fly?
- If you are taking a flight home from another city, plan carefully and remember that delays, strikes, accidents or other mishaps might make it difficult for you to find yourself in the right city at the right time, particularly at busy times of the year. Book trains or buses in advance to avoid finding that they are overbooked.

Belongings

Consider what you will do with the belongings you do not want to take home with you. For example, you have probably accumulated some household items. Consider donating these to a charity or to other students. Many universities will have some kind of system for passing on used goods to others.

If you plan to sell your belongings, find out the best way to advertise these, and leave yourself plenty of time to find a buyer.

When I went home to Canada after living in the UK, I had accumulated a lot of books. I had planned to ship them home, but it would have cost so much money. I worked out that, on an international flight, I had a total baggage allowance of 64 kg (32 kg per bag). So I travelled home with a single change of clothes . . . and 63 kg of books! The rest of my clothes and personal belongings arrived later, having been shipped for very little cost. The only time I regretted my decision was when I had to pull my suitcases off the luggage carousal! My shoulders ached for days.

Author insight: Caroline

> **Heads up**
>
> Make sure you hold on to any official university paperwork, as well as taxation information, pay slips and so on that you may need later.

If you have bought a lot of things that you want to take home with you, keep in mind the weight limits imposed by the airline. You might consider shipping things home but bear in mind that this can get expensive.

Be aware of what you are and are not allowed to take either (a) out of the country or (b) back into your home country; it is very frustrating to carry something internationally only to find that you have to place it in a bin before you are allowed to clear Customs. This might include food, wood products and plant matter, for example.

Academic loose ends

Academic material

It can be easy, at the end of term, to be reckless about your academic textbooks, handouts, papers, exams and so on. There are a number of reasons why you should consider keeping them:

- If you are claiming credits from abroad for your home programme, these course materials might be important in clarifying what credits you should receive. It is common that your work will be assessed by someone in your home university before a credit is granted.
- You might find it interesting to look back on them in the future.
- They might prove to be useful in your future studies.
- They are artifacts of a different culture and you might want to refer to them if you write about or present on your experiences abroad.

Don't forget to:

- Order a transcript, if relevant, from your university.
- Provide a forwarding address for the university.
- Pay any overdue library fees or academic fees (if you don't, you might not be sent your transcript or other important documentation).
- Organize to have your certificate forwarded to you, if you have undertaken a full programme and are unable to be there at the graduation ceremony.

- Pick up any essays or exams left outstanding, or provide a stamped addressed envelope and politely ask your teachers to forward them once they have been assessed.

Heads up

> Remember that you might want to return to your new country at some point, so it is important to leave with a good credit rating and all your bills paid (including phone, electricity, internet and so on). You also stand to lose your new friends/room mates if you leave them with unpaid bills!

Preparing to be back home

You may need to make plans for your life at home while you are still abroad. This might include such things as

Organizing a place to live (whether you are renting or living in residence).
Organizing utilities.
Registering for the following term, if you are still studying.
Choosing subjects and enrolling in them.
Working out how to access your money back at home (if you have been using a local bank).
Putting in applications for jobs or scholarships.

If you wait until you get back before thinking about these things, you might miss some important deadlines and then spend time playing 'catch-up'.

Saying goodbye

By the time you leave, your new country will probably feel like a second home. You might not even realize how much you're going to miss it until you think about leaving again. It is worth taking the time to say goodbye to your life abroad.

In the last few weeks

- Take lots of photographs if you haven't already done so.
- Buy souvenirs, gifts, pictures and so on, both for yourself and for your family and friends.

- Take the time to thank the people who have helped you, for example your homestay family, your advisor, or the international student centre staff.
- Revisit your favourite places in your new home.
- Spend time with your new friends; let them make a fuss of you if they want to.
- Make plans with friends and family at home for after you get back.

The thing that surprised me the most was how hard it was to go back home. Having spent fifteen months abroad, I was very pleased to see friends and family again. But during my entire stay abroad I knew that they would always be there. That doesn't work the other way around. When you leave the country where you've been on exchange, you leave behind a bunch of friends, from all corners of the earth. And you have no way of knowing whether you will ever see them again. The one thing you do know is that it is unlikely to have the same group of people reunited (even though we try . . .). It is great going home, but it is terrible to leave.

Detlef, after fifteen months studying in New Zealand

I really enjoyed everything except going home.

Daniel, who studied in China for six months

Personal reflection

Many students report that their experiences abroad were life-changing, and find that they feel that they have changed in profound ways while they have been away. Starting to work out how you have changed before you leave might help you to re-integrate into your home life. So before you leave and arrive back among your family and friends and your 'old' life, take the time to reflect on your experiences abroad. Some questions you might consider:

What have you learnt from your experiences?
What is the biggest change you feel in youself?
What is the biggest change other people might see in you?
How have your opinions changed?

How has your view of your home country changed?

How have your politics changed?

What skills have you learned or developed?

What hobbies and interests have you developed?

What have you learned academically?

How has your view of yourself changed?

How has your perception of your past and your family background changed?

How have your plans for the future changed?

What have your new friends taught you?

What were the biggest challenges of your experience?

What have you managed to do that you never thought you would?

Try to record your responses in some way. You might forget your answers when you return, and it could be useful to be able to trace how your answers change as you get back home and re-adjust to your home life.

I loved meeting new people. I learned more about my country from being abroad than from staying at home. It was difficult at first to get used to an entirely new system, but as I adjusted I started seeing that it was possible to do things in different ways that are equally valid.

Gillian, a Canadian student in New Zealand

It was a difficult but important experience, both personally and professionally. Much had to do with expectations – the things I expected never happened; the things I came to value were totally unexpected and unanticipated; I had expected the PhD to be hard work, but it was much harder than I expected; I learned so much, but not what I had expected to learn. I learned much about the world, about culture shock, about different institutions, about different values, about different histories, about different self-conceptions. I also learned much about myself, about my weaknesses and strengths, about my limitations, about the conditions I need to thrive, about the things I value and the kind of community I want to live in.

Thomasina, a PhD student in the UK

Arriving home

Arriving home is not necessarily the end of your experience of study abroad. In fact, many students have told us that they learnt more from going back home again than they did while they were away, and that their growth and change was ongoing. There are a few reasons for this, including reverse culture shock, changes at home and for your family and friends, and, of course, the fact that you have changed.

Reverse culture shock

We discussed the emotional and practical aspects of culture shock in 'Staying Healthy', and most students expect to have some kind of culture shock when they go to a new country, but they are often unprepared for the shock of returning home again. This is often called 'reverse culture shock', and is very similar to the initial culture shock you might have experienced. You may feel disoriented and as if you don't really belong. Things that were once familiar might seem strange to you, and you might have the experience of seeing things with 'new eyes', which could make you feel critical of things in your home country you have always taken for granted. In addition, you might have difficulty settling in to your old routines and connecting with your family and old friends.

In some ways, reverse culture shock can be even more challenging than the initial culture shock you experienced. There are a variety of reasons for this:

- Your study abroad was for a limited period of time, and so you could anticipate the end of it when things got rough. When you go back home, there is no sense of this being temporary.
- You are returning home to things that are familiar, and so the feelings of displacement can be quite confusing and disorienting because you may not be able to identify what is feeling strange.
- People expect study abroad students to feel culture shock and you may have been able to access support on campus to help you to deal with it. When you return home, however, your experience is officially 'finished'; you might not get institutional support and your family and friends might be confused – even hurt – that you are experiencing reverse culture shock.

Both you and those around you have changed, but these changes may not be immediately apparent, so you might all try to proceed as you did before you went away.

Indications that you are suffering from reverse culture shock include:

> You find yourself critical of how things are done in your home country.
> You feel claustrophobic or lonely.
> You miss your new friends.
> You wish you were back in your study abroad country.
> You feel misunderstood.
> You have the urge to explain how things are so much better in your study abroad country.
> You are irritable.
> You feel disoriented or confused.
> You find it hard to communicate or connect with your old friends.
> You feel that your family no longer knows you, or that you no longer belong in your old community.
> You feel restless and unable to focus.
> You feel that the way you are behaving and what you are thinking are not in line with one another.
> You feel that others have expectations of you that no longer seem to 'fit' who you are.
> You get frustrated that people don't understand you.
> You feel fragmented or like something is missing.
> You don't know who you are or what you want.

For example, you might have become more independent, more assertive and more confident, only to find that the people around you still treat you just like they used to.

It can be easy, though, to believe that all the changes are in you, and that everything else has stayed the same. You will discover quickly that things have been changing at home while you were away, and it might be you who has to adjust to new situations and to the changes around you.

Some tips for dealing with family and friends while you re-adjust:

- Consider their point of view.
- Communicate with family and friends and let them know when they are making assumptions about you which are no longer true. Try to listen when they do the same to you.
- Listen to what the people around you have to say; they too have lived their lives while you have been away. Take the time to catch up with who they are and how they might have changed.
- Talk to your family and friends about your experiences abroad, so that they can understand how it has affected you.

When I was in high school, my sister spent a year studying in Russia. I missed her a lot and was really excited that she was finally coming home. But the first thing she said when she got off the plane was that she wished she had stayed there and that she was planning to go back to live! It would have been nice if she had been pleased to see me and glad to be home for a few hours at least.

Author insight: Caroline

- Talk about things *other* than your study abroad.
- Keep writing in your journal, so that you can stay in touch with how you are feeling.
- Be patient
- Make contact with other study abroad students who might be going through the same thing, and compare notes.
- Try not to be judgemental or critical.
- Find outlets for the new parts of your identity that your family and friends haven't quite caught up with.
- Reassure your family and friends that you are happy to be home and that you missed them.

Heads up

Your family and friends might feel that you have changed but not be able to identify how. They may be experiencing all sorts of emotions with regards to you, and not know how to deal with them. For example, they might be jealous that you have been abroad, or resentful that you left. They might wonder if you still care about them, or feel insecure that you have 'outgrown' them. They might simply have moved on with their own life and have to readjust to having you back. They might question whether you are still the person they love. You might wonder the same thing.

You are still YOU, but you have changed, and so have the people around you. In our experience, the most successful re-adjustment occurs when you acknowledge that you have changed and take the time to get to know your family and friends again, rather than trying to 'go back' to the way things were before. This might mean that you really don't connect with some of your old friends any more or that your relationships change.

 Being in a different country in itself is a remarkable experience, and it has been quite nice to experience different cultures. Also, since I am from South Africa, I have not experienced snow, so that was lovely. It is all in all an opportunity of a lifetime, so whatever you do enjoy it. But I am homesick a lot and the language barrier is keeping me from fitting into this society. But there's no place like home. Home is where the heart is, and although this is a lovely country and they gave me the opportunity to get a degree, my heart is in South Africa.

Hamisi, a South African student studying in Europe

Exacerbating factors

You may find that your reverse culture shock is exacerbated by particular situations or events that have happened while you were away. These might include variations on the following.

At home:

While you are away, a family member or friend might have died. You will know this logically, but it might still be a huge shock when you go home and have to face it in reality. Other family members will have gone through a different kind of grief from you. They may have visited the person in hospital or nursed them while they were sick. They will probably have gone to the funeral. When you come home, either to stay or just for a visit, you may find that you have to grieve in a different way from the way you grieved while abroad, and it may be challenging that you are at a different 'stage' from those around you.

Family relationships might shift. Couples might break up, or family members might have new partners. New members of the family might have been born. The dynamics of the family relationships might have changed as a result and you will need to work out where you fit with the new structures.

Friends might have moved away, changed jobs, made new friends, had babies and so on. You might have to work out what your place is in their new lives.

The political climate in your home country might change. Even if you keep up with the news of your home country, significant economic or political changes can make you feel extremely vulnerable and may even leave you unable to return home, in extreme situations. If you do go home, you may suffer from extreme reverse cultural shock because your country has changed so much.

Abroad

You might make decisions or discover aspects of your identity that your family finds challenging. Studying abroad often gives students the chance to grow and develop in ways that might not be possible at home. Anything from deciding that you want an entirely different career from the one your parents have always wanted for you to coming out as gay can be challenging for family and friends and cause them to wonder if they 'know you' at all. We know many students who have made major life changes while studying or travelling abroad and it can take quite a while for families and friends to catch up.

You might fall in love. Sometimes this will be beautiful, but fleeting, and you will return home with fond memories. But it is also quite common that students abroad, especially if they are in longer programmes that allow relationships to mature, might find someone who becomes their partner. There are a number of issues that can arise from this:

- Your new partner may give you a different perspective on whether you want to return home at all, and where you want to live. We will come back to the options and possibilities if that happens.
- Your family and friends may have to adjust to a new, very important person in your life whom they haven't met. If you bring this new person home with you for a visit, family dynamics can quickly become challenging. It is hard for families in these circumstances because they have to get to know you again, as well as your partner, and haven't had the same time to adjust to how you have changed that you and your partner have had.
- You may have to face issues from both of your families around cultural difference if your new partner is from a different culture from your own. You may face a lack of understanding or even racism in these circumstances.

In any of the above situations, you may need to seek help from counsellors or other professionals who can support you as you work through your feelings. It can be challenging to hold onto your own dreams and goals if you are facing emotional pressures from your family at home; try to talk through the issues with someone who can help you.

Academic re-adjustment

You may find that returning to study in your home country may also trigger reverse culture shock for you. You might feel frustrated with the way you are being taught, or with your classmates (who may not share your global view of the world). You may also have to find ways of translating your qualifications so that they are meaningful in your home context. Make sure you do everything you need to do in order to claim credit from your study abroad, including adhering to important deadlines.

The most important aspect of coping with reverse culture shock is to recognize it when you experience it, and trust that it will ease with time and energy, just as it did when you arrived in your new country.

● Staying abroad

If you are in a short programme, the chances are high that you will go abroad, have fun, learn a lot, and then go home.

But if you are in a longer programme, especially a post-graduate programme, you might find yourself in a situation where you want to stay in your new country and make a life for yourself. Maybe there are more work opportunities for you in your new country, maybe you have fallen in love, you can't return home for some reason, or you just love what your new country can offer you. If you want to consider staying in your new country, consider the following.

Legal and practical considerations

You will need to find out whether you can legally change your status in the country. Find out:

- Can you apply for 'permanent residency' or citizenship? You will have to check whether you are eligible – eligibility is often based on a combination of education, language, work experience, age, health/medical issues and other factors. Applying for residency is often a lengthy process and may involve a considerable amount of money.
- Does your funding or scholarship allow you to stay? Some scholarships specify that you must work for a period of time in your home country after returning.
- Is your programme or funding or scholarship contingent on being an international student? What are the implications of changing your status?

Financial considerations

Applying for residency (which is often necessary before you apply for citizenship) can be very expensive. You may have to pay an application fee (which may or may not be refundable if your application is unsuccessful), a residency fee (often separate from the application fee), as well as costs associated with photographs, medical checks, criminal-record checks and postage. You may also have to pay for legal advice. If you are applying with a family or partner, these costs will be multiplied.

Emotional considerations

In many cases, friends and family are aware that permanent immigration might be an option before you even leave. If you decide to change your status during your programme, though, be prepared for some resistance from your family. It can be quite a shock for the people who love you to find that a temporary study trip abroad becomes a permanent arrangement. Take the time to explain what it means to you to stay in your new country. If they express concerns, listen to what they say. Bear in mind that they might cite practical/safety concerns when really the issue for them is emotional. If they are open to the idea, it can help for close family and friends to come and visit you to see what your new life is like (and to see that you are happy). Sometimes, it just takes time for people to get used to the idea.

● Keeping your second home close

If you do return home, you will probably want to maintain contact with the country of your study abroad. You probably don't want to lose the language skills you have acquired, will have friends you want to stay in touch with, and may have the opportunity to utilize your knowledge of your second country for future jobs. Here are some tips for keeping your second home close.

Keep in contact with friends in your second country – emails, letters and phone calls can all help you to stay in touch and can help you to re-adjust to home life again. The frequency of this contact is likely to ease off gradually as you get back into your normal life, but you can still keep in touch. Remember that all relationships require nurturing, and be conscientious about keeping them going.

Invite your new friends to come and visit you at home. Most people won't take you up on the invitation, but some people might, especially if they have got the 'travel bug'.

Read newspapers or go online for news of your second country, to help you to stay connected to what is going on. Visit online chat groups of people interested in your second country, and share your experiences. Volunteer to share your experiences of studying abroad with students who are planning their own trips. You could speak at study abroad fairs, or write a piece for the campus newspaper. You could also become a peer advisor for international students.

Share aspects of your new culture with your family and friends. Cook national dishes or visit a restaurant where you can share the cuisine of your new culture. (You can show off your language skills as well.)

Find people with whom you can continue to practise your new language. Without practice you might lose it. You could take some advanced courses or, if you are fluent, study the literature of the country you have been to. If there are students from that country currently at your university, you could offer to be a conversation partner. Read novels or other books in your new language.

Make contact with the local community in your home country of the place you have been to, and see if there are events you might be involved in. These might be clubs, film nights and so on. Listen to music from your new culture. If it is familiar music, this will have the added advantage of triggering memories of your study abroad.

If you have learnt new skills abroad, find opportunities to use them and enjoy them. You might have to think outside the box a little to find opportunities. Incorporate your study abroad into your academic programme, if you can. You might do some elective courses in the history or politics of your region, for example.

● Marketing yourself

Your study abroad is a valuable asset when it comes to getting jobs, identifying volunteer opportunities, applying for post-graduate work, and getting scholarships.

Make sure you include your experience on your CV, and don't rely on committees to find it from a line on your transcript. However, study programmes abroad vary enormously, so it might not be immediately apparent how your study abroad relates to the position you are applying for. To remedy this situation, consider the following suggestions:.

Tailor your application to the position you are applying for. Work out what aspects of your study abroad are most relevant and highlight them. You might focus on language skills, academic aspects of your experience, or the personal skills you displayed and developed while abroad. Explain what you learnt while you were studying abroad and how it is relevant to the position you are applying to.

> *I suppose the fact that you have the courage to live and study in a foreign country for a period of time separates you from the rest.*
>
> Martin, on a master's degree exchange programme

When referring to your language skills, be clear about what level you have achieved. If you have not completed formal credentials in your second language, specify whether you have conversational language skills, are fluent in the language, have functioned in academic contexts in your second language, or have written papers and examinations in that language. If you have studied at a highly specialized level in your second language, make that clear. (Be truthful; you need to be able to follow through with your claims.)

Explain how your insights into your discipline or subject area have benefited from studying abroad. Consider how this could be useful for the position you are applying for. If you have worked with specialists in your field and your application will be read by specialists in your field, you might mention your teachers by name. If you have done well, mentioning your academic success in your programme abroad can be indicative of your expertise in your area, as well as your ability to adapt to a new learning environment. You have probably developed considerable skills in intercultural awareness and communication. Explain how you demonstrated these skills, and how they might benefit you in your new position.

Consider how you can you use your experiences abroad to highlight the personal traits and characteristics that you are proud of, and which make you suitable for the position. If you organized aspects of your study experience abroad, for example, you could highlight your organizational ability or your initiative. If you have had experiences that have been particularly challenging or frightening, you could highlight your courage or your capacity to solve problems.

Consider the hobbies and skills you developed while abroad. While these may not be directly relevant to a position, they might highlight your team work, or your leadership, or your capacity to learn quickly. Did you do any volunteer work abroad? You could use this to show your energy and your commitment to giving back to whatever communities you find yourself in.

Consider whether your knowledge of your second country is potentially useful to your position. Explain how it might be relevant. If it is not specifically relevant, consider how your developing awareness of the role of your own country in international contexts may be useful.

If you volunteer your time after you return to share your experiences with others, remember that this can be used to reflect your willingness to help other people, your public speaking or writing skills, and your initiative.

Planning the next trip

What will be your next trip abroad? Will you study again? (Post-graduate work? A post-doc?) Will you volunteer abroad? Will you work in another country? Will you be a tourist? Will you go back to visit your friends? Will you go on an organized tour? Once you have studied abroad, the world will become easier to conceptualize and you may be flooded with possibilities. Give yourself a chance to rest, and then start planning again! Have fun!

Further resources

- Carolyn D. Smith, *Strangers at Home: Essays on the Effects of Living Overseas and Coming 'Home' to a Strange Land* (Aletheia, 1996).
  A collection of essays about coming home after living abroad. Includes advice for parents helping their children to negotiate the coming home process.
- J. Stewart Black and Hall B. Gregersen, *So You're Coming Home* (Global Business Publications, 1999).
  Written for business people, but useful in its discussion of returning home after working abroad.
- Craig Storti, *The Art of Coming Home* (Intercultural Press, 2001). www.ebooks.com/ebooks/book_display.asp?IID=218389
  A comprehensive book on reverse culture shock, including sections for spouses, teenagers and children. Available online as an e-book.

10 Additional Challenges

When you are studying abroad, you might find that there are additional challenges which you face. This section will give you a chance to think through some of the issues you might come across around race and ethnicity, disability, sexual orientation, and class, or if you are a woman, a mature student or travelling with your family, and offer some suggestions about how to negotiate the potential challenges. We recommend that you read this chapter even if it does not seem immediately applicable to your situation, since you may find yourself facing associated challenges, or socializing with others who are facing such challenges.

Many of these sections will intersect. For example, the fact that you are a member of an ethnic minority does not exclude you from being a mature student. You might be a parent who has a disability. Whatever your situation, make sure you talk to people who are directly affected by similar issues. An able-bodied person might reassure you that there is plenty of wheelchair accessibility; a white person might tell you that racism is simply not an issue; a Christian might be blissfully unaware of Anti-Semitism, and a heterosexual might be convinced that you can openly talk about your same-sex partner without any negative consequences. All of this might in fact be true, but might also be misleading and prevent you from considering scenarios that might affect you.

If you do face issues as a result of any of these additional challenges, there may be university resources that can help you. You might have to ask around to find out what they are called on your new campus. Potential resources include:

- The campus equity/diversity office.
- University task forces for negotiating particular issues on campus (such as racism), and student groups that focus on particular issues (such as an accessibility group, or a faith-based group).
- The ombuds office (often useful for helping you to ascertain your rights).

- Peer advisors working in the area you are concerned about.
- The student crisis centre (often excellent for putting you in touch with appropriate resources).
- Counselling services.
- Advocacy committees/groups.
- The family care office (if the issue concerns your partner or children).
- The women's centre/office.
- A union representative (if it is a matter related to a work situation).
- The housing office.

If you feel that your concerns are dismissed, keep looking until you find someone who is willing to help you. You may also find resources in the wider community that may be able to help you.

Don't let the fact that you may face challenges around these issues stop you from studying abroad. It is better to be over-prepared and pleasantly surprised than under-prepared and shocked.

Race and ethnicity

When you go abroad, you might find that you are in a racial or ethnic minority when you are used to being in the majority. This can be an incredibly eye-opening experience. You may find, on the other hand, that you are used to being in a minority but are in the majority in your new country. Or you might find that you are a minority in both places, but that the implications of this are different.

Heads up

Race and ethnicity shift across borders. A minority in one place might be a majority in another. In addition, what race and ethnicity 'means' in one culture is often very different from what it means in another. Ethnic and racial communities are encoded within cultural and social norms, which vary from one place to another. While your race will not change when you go abroad, the way you are treated as a result of your race may very well change.

Learning about your new environment

Questions to consider include:

- Is the place you are going to racially and ethnically diverse? What are the dominant races? Ethnicities?
- What other ethnic backgrounds are represented by large communities and resources in the area?
- What is the history of the place in relation to racial and ethnic conflict? What is the history of colonization in the place? How recent was this colonization and what historical effects has this had? What challenges is the place still facing as a result of colonization?
- Is there a social hierarchy that governs the interaction of people of different races and ethnicities? (For example, many cultures have histories of certain races being enslaved or in positions of servitude to a dominant group.)
- Are there different geographical areas associated with different ethnicities? What are they?
- What racial groups are represented on campus and in the wider community?
- What recent events have contributed to racial or ethnic tensions? What form does this take?
- Are there laws in place to protect racial and ethnic minorities? Are there policies in place on campus to protect marginalized communities?
- What stereotypes are prevalent towards other races and ethnic groups in your new country? What stereotypes are you likely to face?
- What are the taboos surrounding dating and socializing across racial divisions (many places, for example, still have strong taboos against 'mixed-race' or bi-racial dating)?

Heads up

Racial groups that are defined similarly in your home country might be regarded as belonging to a number of different groups in another country. For example, shades of skin colour might be used to make distinctions between people in one place, while in others no distinction is made. Perceptions of race may also be affected by your class, your financial status, gender and other markers of social difference. You might be mistaken for a racial identity that is not your own, and may be subject to the stereotypes associated with it.

- What are the laws surrounding race in your new country? Are the laws applied equally to all races? Which races are discriminated against? How?
- How do the police treat members of various ethnicities?

Strategies for negotiating potential issues

Find allies and supportive community. Remember that allies are not necessarily only people who have the same background as you – other marginalized communities (whether along racial lines, or through other forms of marginalization) may also be an excellent sources of support.

Know your rights and be willing to advocate for them, as appropriate.

Know who you can get help from, either for emotional support, for advice, or to help you assert your rights. As well as campus initiatives that may help you (such as the equity office, anti-racism initiatives and student groups), you may find that academics who specialize in your geographical region or racial history might be a source of support.

If there are members of your ethnic group in the area, try to make contact with them – they may be able to help you understand the social and cultural norms of your new culture and offer you support as you adjust.

Find out what words are used to describe particular racial or ethnic groups in your new country. Knowing the words used will help you to access appropriate resources.

If there aren't any campus groups that can support you, and you are in the programme for a while, you might consider starting up an anti-racism alliance or social group.

Observe how race, ethnicity and skin colour affect the opportunities of those around you in your new country. As an outsider, you may be much more tuned in to racial dynamics than you might be in the familiar environment of your home country, and you can learn a great deal from this kind of analysis to understand how societies negotiate (or fail to negotiate) inequities along racial or ethnic lines.

Be aware of the potential for discrimination on racial grounds, in terms of both your own racial identity and that of those around you. It might be quite overt or more subtle, but recognizing it for what it is can be a useful strategy for negotiating it.

> **TIP** If race or ethnicity are areas of academic study that interest you, you could look for programmes which will enable you to study subjects such as race studies, cultural studies, minority studies, or equity and diversity studies.

Heads up

If you are studying abroad in your ancestral home, even if you emigrated when you were young, you may experience a strange sense of both belonging and not belonging. Through your family, you may have an awareness of the culture of the country and may be fluent in the language. You may share physical characteristics, including skin colour, with the local community, and may have a name that is common in the local community. You may sometimes be mistaken for a local. Yet you are likely to have a very different cultural identity, and your expectations and assumptions might reflect the country you now live in rather than the country your family came from. Students frequently report that this can be quite challenging, since they are mistaken for a local but don't have the cultural knowledge to really 'belong'.

Further resources

- Salto-Youth Cultural Diversity Resource Centre.
  www.salto-youth.net/diversity/
  European Commission site for youth, dedicated to promoting equity and diversity.
- Marilyn J. Jackson, *Breaking the Barriers to Overseas Study for Students of Color and Minorities*.
  www.iienetwork.org/page/71532/
  Online article about minority groups studying abroad.
- Black College Online.
  www.blackcollegian.com
  A website for African-American students, with a section on study abroad and international travel. Some useful information on negotiating race while studying abroad.
- Anti-RacismNet.
  www.antiracismnet.org/main.html
  An 'international online network of anti-racism organizations and practitioners'. Useful for its list of international social justice organizations, as well as its international events list.
- Access International Education.
  www.ucis.pitt.edu/aie/
  Dedicated to 'Underrepresented Groups in International Education' in the US.

- Elaine Lee, *Go Girl! The Black Woman's Book of Travel and Adventure* (Eighth Mountain Press, 1997).
  A collection of stories from black women travellers.

Disability/accessibility

Many students with disabilities suggest that they have an advantage over other students, because they have already had to learn to be independent, to overcome stress and to work out ways of ensuring that their needs are accommodated in a diversity of situations. Having said that, as you work out your priorities and do your initial research, you will probably need to take your disability into account and may need to make different decisions to ensure that your experience is a positive one. We have talked to students who tried to ignore their disability as they were planning to go abroad to study and later regretted that they hadn't been more upfront with themselves and those around them in order to get the support they needed.

Anticipating your needs

You may take much of what you have at home for granted. When you plan to go abroad, it is important to take a moment to think about exactly what you need in order to accommodate your disability, and not just assume that your needs will be met.

What kinds of accommodation do you need?

If they are related to a physical disability, remember that the accommodation will need to apply to a variety of situations. Consider your needs in relation to:

- The campus (including your department, the library, sports facilities, social venues and other resources you will need to access).
- Housing (temporary and permanent).
- Dietary concerns (in a variety of contexts).
- The local community (including shopping centres, public transport, community resources).
- The wider area (including getting to and from the country, and travelling in the region).

What kinds of medical attention do you require?

Consider:

- Regular/routine medical attention.
- Emergency medical attention.

What kinds of supplies will you need, to manage your condition?

Consider such things as:

- Medication.
- Batteries.
- Replacement parts (if your supplies run out or get broken).
- Adaptive technology (including access to maintenance/technical support, replacement parts and so on, as well as the technology itself).
- Back-up options in case of damage to or theft of your equipment.

Do you have particular needs in relation to scheduling?

Consider such things as:

- Physical limitations (for example, if you were on a large campus, you might need extra time between classes to get from place to place).
- Fatigue levels (an intensive programme might not work for you; you might need to schedule rest breaks and so on).
- Medical needs (for example, needing a weekly medical appointment or needing to eat meals at regular times).

If they are related to a learning or social disability, what are your accommodation needs?

Consider:

- Classes (including lectures, tutorials, workshops and so on).
- Take-home assessment (such as extra time, help from a tutor, computer software and so on).
- Examinations (such as extra time, regular breaks, special conditions or rooms for sitting exams, and so on).
- Social situations.
- Housing (including what kind of environment you need to allow you to get your work done without distraction, and who you live with).

What kind of programme will best accommodate your needs?

Consider:

- How long the programme is (for example, if you need extra time for written work, a short, intense programme might be very stressful).

- The social aspects of the programme (for example, whether you will be socializing with a small group of the same people, or expected to meet lots of new people).
- The academic components of the programme (for example, whether the assessment is based on written work or examination-based).

> **Heads up**
>
> Consider how stress might exacerbate your symptoms, and try to strategize for what to do in those circumstances when you are away from your usual support networks.

Learning about your environment

While you are considering your options, it is worth researching your new environment to work out whether your needs can be accommodated. You might need to consider both the practical aspects of your disability, and the attitudinal components (that is, how your disability is perceived by others). Once you have a better sense of how your disability can be accommodated, you will also be able to anticipate potential challenges you might face.

Questions to consider include:

- Will your needs be able to be accommodated? What process will you need to go through to make this happen?
- Will you be able to access appropriate medical help?
- Will you be able to access whatever supplies you need (consider too, how efficient this is likely to be, and whether it will be affordable)?
- Is there housing available which can accommodate you?
- Will you have access to support for your disability? (Find out whether the university has a disability/accessibility office and what support is available.)
- Does the university have a disability policy that protects your rights?
- Are there government programmes/laws in place to protect your rights? Are you likely to be discriminated against on the grounds of your disability?
- What is your disability called in your new country? What are the prevalent attitudes and/or stereotypes towards it? (Bear in mind that possible discrimination may come from other exchange

Heads up

Many countries now have government-issued disability plans which specify such things as building codes and the kinds of accommodations that must be available for people with physical disabilities. Bear in mind, though, that these codes often apply to NEW buildings, and may not be effective for buildings built before a certain date. In addition, these codes often relate specifically to wheelchair access, and may not extend at all to other physical disabilities, or to environmental and learning disabilities.

students, not necessarily from nationals of your destination country.)
- If you are using a provider, is the provider willing to make appropriate accommodations for you?

Strategies for negotiating potential issues around disability

Make use of all possible resources. For example, if you have a disability advisor or counsellor at your home university, he/she might be invaluable in helping you to negotiate your new environment. You might even have regular contact with him/her while you are abroad. As well as campus resources, you might find local or national advocacy groups working with your disability, either in your home country or in your new country. Consider making contact with them for support.

Be clear (with yourself and with others) about what your needs are. Many people will be able to help you better if they know exactly what they are trying to achieve. Don't leave people trying to guess what you are thinking or what you need. Bear in mind that providers, teachers, administrators and others may not have expertise or training in negotiating accessibility issues, and might need some guidance.

Carry documentation with you from your doctor or accessibility advisor so that you are not left to explain it alone, either to other doctors or to those helping to accommodate you.

Try to find some sort of support for your disability, even if you think you have your accommodations under control. Having a plan for when things do go wrong is important, and sometimes just knowing you have a safety net can help you to relax.

Check your travel/health insurance and try to find a plan that is flexible with 'pre-existing conditions'.

Try to avoid pretending that everything is alright when it really isn't. Your study experience abroad could be considerably better if you have your needs met than if you are struggling to do it all yourself.

Heads up

> If you use a guide dog or other kind of animal support, you will need to check quarantine regulations, as well as finding out how you can best care for your animal while abroad. Remember that animals are susceptible to health problems similar to those of humans when in unfamiliar environments.

If you need to ask for accommodations from your teachers, try to do this before classes begin. You are much more likely to have your needs met if you alert the relevant people well ahead of time.

If having a disability is likely to affect your finances (for example, if you cannot undertake a full course load, you may spend longer abroad than you would otherwise need to), you may be able to get a bursary, from your home university, your destination university or an external agency. Government funding is also sometimes available. Make sure you explain that you have a disability; often, there are different regulations for students with special needs.

Further resources

- Laura Hershey, *Survival Strategies for Going Abroad: A Guide for People with Disabilities* (Mobility International USA).
  An excellent resource for students with disabilities as they consider studying abroad. Some of the same information is available online at www.miusa.org
- Access-able.
  www.access-able.com
  A website catering for travellers with disabilities. Particularly useful are its links to organizations and companies that assist disabled travellers, including a list of travel agents.
- Disability Travel and Recreation Resources.
  www.makoa.org/travel.htm
  This site includes a list of worldwide organizations that cater for travellers with disabilities, and a collection of strategies for negotiating travel as a person with a disability.

- Rick Steve, *Rick Steve's Easy Access Europe 2004: A Guide for Travelers with Limited Mobility* (Avalon Travel Publishing, 2004).
  A travel guide to Amsterdam, Bruges, London, Paris, and the Rhine for travellers with physical disabilities.

Sexual orientation/LGBT

If you identify as lesbian, gay, bisexual or transgendered, you may find that you have access to local LGBT communities, which can be a great way to meet people and make friends. Having said that, as you are no doubt aware, the level of acceptance and respect for sexual diversity differs enormously from country to country. When you are planning to study abroad, it is important that you consider these differences, as they might impact on such basic things as your health and safety. In some countries, you will be able to legally marry, have or adopt children and walk down the street holding hands with your partner. In others, you can be arrested – in some cases executed – for being LGBT, or even if you are suspected to be, with little or no recourse.

Anticipating your needs

Consider the following questions:

- How open are you willing to be about your sexual orientation/gender? What are the personal and psychological ramifications for you if you find yourself having to 'closet' yourself? Will this affect your mental well-being, your self-esteem, your relationships?
- What coping skills have you developed for dealing with different kinds of homophobia or transphobia? How does this affect you emotionally?
- How important is it for you to have contact with other LGBT people while studying abroad? How will you make contact with other LGBT students, or members of the local LGBT community, if that is important to you?
- Do you have the option of not revealing your sexual orientation? (For example, are you identifiable as LGBT even if you try to hide it? If you are travelling with a partner, it might be much more difficult to remain closeted.)
- How important is it to you that your housing situation and/or social life is reflective of your identity?

Heads up

LGBT students who study abroad and have to live with roommates who are homophobic often choose to hide their sexual
orientation. But many report that this is very stressful and
have attributed it to feelings of isolation and depression
while abroad. Being abroad is stressful in itself; ask yourself
whether this additional stress is one you are willing to negotiate.

Learning about your new environment

There are a variety of different aspects of your new environment you should
learn about in relation to LGBT issues, which include both the legal and the
attitudinal.

Questions to consider include:

- Are LGBT/same-sex relationships legal?
- What are the repercussions of being LGBT? (In some cases, the law
  might officially sanction against same-sex relationships, but may
  never actually act on it.)
- What are the laws that may be relevant to sexuality/gender? (such
  as public decency/indecency laws, age of consent laws)?
  Remember that the same law might be applied differently to
  heterosexual couples and LGBT couples.
- What is the police's attitude towards the local LGBT community?
  (Remember that some laws are enforced and others are not.)
- If you are harassed or discriminated against on the grounds of your
  sexual/gender orientation, are there legal recourses for you? Are
  these theoretical only or actually acted on?
- Are there resources, either on campus or in the wider community,
  for LGBT issues?
- Does the university have an equity and diversity policy that
  protects students from harassment on the grounds of
  sexual/gender orientation?
- Is the local LGBT community accepting of diversity within its own
  community? For example, is the community likely to be transpho-
  bic? Accepting of racial diversity?
- Is the LGBT community accepting of 'foreigners'?

Heads up

> Some of the answers to these questions will be easily available in guide books or online. Some of them you will need to find by talking to people who have experience of the local LGBT community. If you find it impossible to make contact with anyone in the local community, or there seems not to be a local community, this does not mean, of course, that there are no LGBT people in the area you are going to, but may mean that the community is 'underground', perhaps because it might be dangerous to be openly LGBT.

If you are traveling with your partner, do you have any rights? (Remember that if you are married or recognized by your home government as being in a civil union, your status may not transfer to a new country, where you may find that you have no partner rights. This can affect everything from whether you can visit your partner in hospital, make medical decisions, or act on each other's behalf legally and financially.)

Heads up

> If you identify as LGBT, and are travelling with a partner or with your children, make sure that you have all agreed on how you will present your family. This is not only for your own safety and protection, but will also prevent hurt feelings or confusion. If you are travelling with young children, seriously consider whether they are old enough to be discreet if you are travelling to a place where honesty could be dangerous. Also consider the impact of 'closeting' your family with regard to your relationship with your partner.

Strategies for negotiating potential issues

If you have to stay 'closeted' in your daily life (in the classroom or in your residency, for example), making contact with the local LGBT community may help you to stay sane.

Find out about the terminology used in your new country for talking about LGBT issues. Are these derogatory? How can you identify a partner as opposed to a friend?

When I first went abroad, I was really happy to be away from home, since I thought I would have more freedom to be myself. I thought that I could cope with homophobia and that it wouldn't be a big deal for me. But I found myself living with a homophobic roommate. There was no way I could tell her I was gay, so I had to listen to her bigotry on a daily basis. I found myself getting really anxious around her, like I couldn't relax in my own home. I got increasingly isolated, and started to feel really bad about myself. I found it hard, and a lot more stressful and exhausting than I had anticipated.

Maria, a post-graduate student

Check the definitions of the terms in your travel insurance. There may be clauses which refer to 'family members' or 'children', but your insurance might not recognize your partner or children as family. Even if your relationships are recognized in your home country, you might lose all your rights in the new country, so you need to plan for this. Clarify the definitions before you leave.

Consider setting up support networks for yourself before you leave. For example, you might have regular email contact with an understanding friend. Remember that phone calls in a homestay or roommate situation might not be private, so you might not be able to discuss these difficulties by phone.

Heads up

Bear in mind also that some cultural symbols do not translate. For example, if you are traveling from a place where a rainbow flag indicates a 'safe space', check whether this is true in your new country. Similarly, behaviour which you interpret as identifying someone as LGBT might not have the same meaning in your new country.

Consider how you might negotiate potential difficulties with airport security, security checks, borders and so on in relation to such issues as being LGBT parents, or issues surrounding gender.

TIP One way to combine your LGBT identity with study abroad is to study subjects such as sexual diversity studies, queer studies or the history of sexual activism. You can also find homestay opportunities where you stay with an LGBT family. This might especially be attractive if you are majoring in a related field, or have career goals that would benefit from this specialist academic knowledge.

Heads up

You may be more susceptible to reverse culture shock if you have been to a country where you have had more freedom as an LGBT person. You may have spent your time abroad being open about your identity, only to find that your openness ostracizes you when you return home.

In addition, being abroad is often a chance for students to work out who they are. You may 'come out' to yourself (and others) while abroad and then face the challenge of having to come out again when you return home. This is far more common than you may think. Your family and friends, then, not only have to come to terms with all the ways you've changed and how much you have grown, but also must face that you have identified some very important aspects of your identity while abroad. This situation can be even more difficult if you have fallen in love while abroad and have a new partner to introduce to the family.

If you find yourself in this position, try to find people to talk to. Connect with your local LGBT community and find other students who have dealt with similar challenges. You might also get support from your new friends in your study abroad country. Your family and friends may find it hard to accept that this is a permanent identity – they may see it as a 'phase' which will fade as you re-acclimatize to your home. It may take time for those around you to catch up with your new awareness of who you are.

Further resources

- Out and About.
  www.outandabout.com
  Online travel guide for the LGBT community.

- International Lesbian and Gay Association.
  www.ilga.org/
    An international organization devoted to gay and lesbian rights.
    Useful for finding out about safety concerns in particular regions.
- International Gay and Lesbian Human Rights Commission.
  www.iglhrc.org/site/iglhrc
    Provides information on human rights conditions in countries
    worldwide.
- Utopia Guides to Asia.
  www.utopia-asia.com
    A comprehensive series of travel guides about Asian countries
    for LGBT travellers. Available for a variety of Asian countries.
- Gay Guide.
  www.gayguide.net
    Comprehensive worldwide travel site for LGBT travellers.
- Damron Travel Guides.
  www.damron.com
    Travel guides for LGBT travellers. Books in the series include a
    city guide and an accommodations guide for LGBT-friendly
    places worldwide.
- Gay Middle East.
  www.gaymiddleeast.com
    A site devoted to LGBT issues in the Middle East. Excellent
    source for researching the laws surrounding LGBT issues in the
    region. Searchable by country.
- Behind the Mask.
  www.mask.org.za
    A comprehensive website devoted to gay and lesbian affairs in
    Africa. Includes a searchable database for researching the legal
    status of homosexuality in each country, a calendar of events,
    and an online forum.

Class/financial background

It is possible that your class status and your family background may affect
your decision-making regarding study abroad, as well as your experience
while you are abroad. For example, if other people in your family have not
studied abroad or do not value university education, you might find resistance from your family and pressure on you to stay at home. This can be
exacerbated if you have family responsibilities, such as working in the family

business, looking after children or helping with elderly family members. You might have to negotiate complex family dynamics to explain why you want to study abroad and to find ways of making it a viable option.

In addition, your family's financial background may affect both the practicalities of studying abroad and your attitudes to money. You might not need to apply for scholarships because you are confident that your family has the financial means to finance your study abroad. Or you might find that you have to work a lot harder to save the money before you leave than other people you know, or make decisions which cost less. While abroad, you might need to earn money (which will affect the amount of time and energy you have to study, and the amount of social time you have).

Heads up

Class, like race, is one of those areas which becomes very complex in the context of studying abroad. Although you may be seen as, and perhaps identify with, a particular class at home, being in a new environment might shift the categories. For example, you might be used to being less well off than many people around you only to find that in your new country you are regarded as very wealthy. Alternatively, you may be used to having a lot of class privilege (financial means and the power that comes with it) only to find that this does not translate in your new country and you are afforded no special treatment. Both of these scenarios can be disconcerting, especially if you aren't prepared for it. To make things even more complex, class is also often affected by nationality, race, religion, skin colour, gender, marital status, levels of education, language, family background and so on, all of which are interpreted in highly culturally specific ways. You might find that you are viewed as belonging to a particular class simply by virtue of the clothes you wear or the way you speak.

Learning about your new environment

Each university tends to have its own unique culture around money and attitudes towards wealth. Some universities attract students from very wealthy backgrounds, for example, and there might be a culture of wealth that prevails in everything from the cost of tuition to attitudes of privilege in the classroom. Other universities may have a culture of students working while studying, have affordable food and housing to accommodate a wider diversity of financial backgrounds, and have a classroom culture that coincides with the class assumptions of its students.

Questions to consider include:

- Is financial power linked to social power in your new country? Are there other criteria that determine who has power and who does not? Are foreigners held to the same criteria?
- What criteria are generally used to determine if people are well-off or not? How does the average standard of living in your new country compare with what you are used to?
- At the university or programme you are considering, are the students generally wealthy? Are they often supported heavily by their parents or are they more financially independent?
- Is there a culture of debt at the university? Is there an assumption that students will go into debt in order to fund their programme? Do many students have part-time jobs?
- What other factors most influence people's social standing in your new country?
- How is your personal wealth and family background likely to be perceived in your new country?

I got a scholarship to study art for two months in Italy. I saved up before I went so that I could go on a train trip through Europe for two weeks at the end. I kept coming across all these rich students who had everything paid for by their parents and I got really annoyed because I had to be so careful with my money but they got to buy anything they wanted. That was bad enough, but they didn't even seem to get how lucky they were. I'm glad I did it the way I did, though.

Jake, an art student

Strategies for negotiating potential issues

It can be helpful to find friends with similar financial pressures or attitudes towards money. It can be very stressful to socialize with people who have much more money than you, or who have attitudes towards money that you can't relate to. (Finding similarities along these lines does not necessarily involve making friends only with other people from your own country – most cultures have divisions along the lines of wealth, even if they define this differently; you might find you have things in common with local students and other international students on these grounds).

Be clear with yourself about what you can afford and what you can't. Try to resist pressure to spend more than you can afford, or to go into unwanted debt. You will have to live with the consequences of it.

If you find yourself relatively wealthy compared with the people around you, try to be sensitive to this, and try to avoid making assumptions about others based on their financial background.

Observe how class affects those around you in your new country. As an outsider, you may be much more tuned in to class dynamics than you might be in the familiar environment of your home country, and you can a learn a great deal from this kind of analysis.

Be aware of the potential for discrimination on class grounds. It might be quite overt or more subtle, but recognizing it for what it is can be a useful strategy for negotiating it.

Heads up

The financial background of your family is also likely to influence your attitudes towards money. You might find that your experience of culture shock is intensified if you are surrounded by people with very different attitudes towards money, work and spending, as well as values, ethics and assumptions about social relationships.

Women

You may find that your study abroad offers you freedom as a woman that you do not have in your home country, and in some countries you will have advantages that men do not have. Or you may find yourself in a country which has a high level of gender socialization and strict divisions along gender lines.

You may not find any problems at all, but it is best to be prepared and to inform yourself of the kinds of challenges you may face in your chosen country. These challenges can range from sexist attitudes and assumptions through to physical safety issues and harassment, and are likely to be extenuated when you travel alone. The fact that you will be studying may be a further reason why you might not fit in with gender expectations, especially in countries where education is still largely a male domain. Or you may find that there are many women in your university, but that you face hostility outside of the university for being a strong, educated and independent woman.

Learning about your new environment

Questions to consider include:

- What are the expectations around the role of women?
- What are the cultural attitudes surrounding women?
- How are women expected to respond to other women? To men?
- Are there many women in positions of power, both within the university and beyond?
- Do many women pursue higher education?
- Are there any prevalent stereotypes in your destination country surrounding women from your country?
- Are attitudes towards women affected by race/skin colour/ethnicity? How?
- Is it safe to walk alone, during the day? At night? (In some places, it is assumed that women alone are prostitutes, and behaviour towards you might reflect that.)

Strategies for negotiating potential issues

Before you depart

As a woman, you may face gender-related challenges before you even leave. For example, if you have a male partner and/or have children, you may face pressure and criticism from friends and family for wanting to study abroad. People may question whether it is 'right for the children' or you may be accused of being selfish and of potentially damaging your male partner's career prospects. If you are going abroad without your family, this may also generate criticism. If you do not have a partner or family, people might tell you that travelling abroad alone is too dangerous and 'inappropriate' for women. It is sometimes surprising how many of these attitudes come up even in cultures which are said to be liberal in their attitudes towards women. Try to find other women who have studied abroad who are more aligned with your own values. Seek out role models who will encourage you to take risks and encourage you in your dreams and goals. Read other people's travel books and experiences to keep you excited and inspired.

You may also face some challenges at the application stage. You may, for example, have to undergo an interview or interviews to get a scholarship to study abroad. Women are sometimes subject to different challenges than their male counterparts in these kinds of competitions, depending on the cultural assumptions (and legal protections) of their home country or their destination country. If you are asked inappropriate questions (for example 'Why should we give you a scholarship, since you will waste it by getting married and having children?' or 'How does your husband feel about the idea of you studying abroad?' there is often no right answer – the committee might be interested to see if you can maintain your composure and professionalism and whether you can negotiate complex social interactions. Stay calm and answer politely, in as much or as little detail as you feel comfortable with.

Safety

Review the tips for personal safety in the 'Staying Healthy' chapter.

Think through how you will negotiate potential safety issues. For example, the conventional wisdom concerning dealing with unwanted sexual attention from men is to ignore it and leave the situation. However, many female students report that they simply cannot ignore it, or that ignoring it actually makes them more unsafe. If you face frequent unwanted attention, you might get to the point where you avoid going out, or wish you were invisible. This is incredibly stressful. If this is the case, you will need to work out some better coping strategies. How do the local women deal with it (if they are subject to it; sometimes it may just affect foreigners)? Can you emulate them? Talk to female teachers or university staff or advisors. What do they recommend you do? Talk to other female international students, either from your own country or from others, and compare notes about what works and what doesn't. Your objective is to keep yourself safe, but deciding 'what works' will also be determined by how you feel about your actions and whether it makes you feel better or worse.

Personal questions

You may find yourself treated as something of a novelty and subject to some very personal questions, either from men or from other women, if you don't conform to the expectations of women in your new country. (Remember that being a foreigner might automatically make you suspect.) People might ask you about your marital status, your relationships, and even your sex life. The following are some tips for dealing with this.

Try to find out why people are asking the questions they are. Are they curious about your culture? They might have been taught stereotypes about women from your country and be checking to see whether they are true. Are they trying to find a way of having a conversation? Are they finding out if you are 'available'? Are they trying to teach you how things happen in their culture? If the conversation is genuinely one of exchange and curiosity, you too can learn a lot by asking similar questions. Remember that different cultures have different boundaries around what is a personal question or not – your questioner is not necessarily hostile.

Make decisions about what you will and will not talk about and express this. If you want to, you can make it into a joke and laugh it off. Saying 'Oh, I'm not going to talk about that' and laughing may have the same effect as being more serious. If pushed, though, you may have to assert yourself more seriously.

Remember that you don't have to tell the truth. While it may be difficult to make friends if you are not willing to open up, if the questioning makes you feel uncomfortable, you do not have to reveal anything you don't want to. If you are in a dangerous situation of some sort, you might have to say things that will keep you safe, rather than being honest.

Friendships with other women

While you may receive a lot of advice about how to deal with men abroad, many female students report that one of the most challenging parts of study-ing in some countries is how difficult it can be to make friends with the women. International students might be trying to 'immerse' themselves in the culture, but find that the local women are hostile to them, perhaps because they have learnt stereotypes about women from other cultures. Sometimes, you may make 'friends' in your classes, but these won't translate into friendships outside of class. You may find that your attempts to befriend other women may be met with hostility or dirty looks.

Consider being involved in a conversation partnership, where you meet up with a local woman and help each other learn your respective languages. This will help to increase your proficiency (and theirs) while giving you social contact.

Even in cultures where women seemingly have no freedom, you will still find strong women who are empowering themselves, although this may be in ways that you are not used to. If you can, see if you can find how the local women empower themselves, where they do have control and what they take pride in. This can give you valuable insights into your new culture, give you a new respect for the women around you, and help you to negotiate your own challenges.

Gender differences on campus

Be attuned to how men and women are treated differently, and behave differently, in academic contexts. Revisit the questions we asked in 'Living

Heads up

While immersing yourself in your new culture is something to be encouraged, and you will frequently be warned about the potential loss of opportunities if you only spend time with other international students, especially those from your own country, this is not always the best tactic, especially for women. If you find that you are receiving unwelcome attention from men which is affecting your self-esteem, your freedom and your enjoyment, and you feel isolated from friendships with local women, you may find yourself lonely, isolated and depressed. In addition, your sense of reality might start to feel like it is under siege, for example, if your views of gender, and on the role of women, are continually being contradicted. In these cases, making friends with other international students can help you to hold onto your own reality and give you a way of understanding the culture you are living in, and of dealing with culture shock. Holding onto the goal of complete immersion in the culture might not be the best course of action for you.

Abroad' about the kinds of cultural expectations in your new classroom surrounding discussion, argument, the role of the teacher and the place of disagreement, and consider that the answers to these questions may very well vary according to gender. You may need to make decisions about which expectations you will conform to and which you will not, taking into account the climate and tone of the classroom, the expectations of your teacher and the way in which you are treated by your classmates, as well as your own learning style and needs. The differences may be overt, in which case the equity office or women's office on campus (if there is one) may be able to guide you, but the more subtle gender differences you encounter may be harder to negotiate.

TIP   Many campuses have sports facilities for women only, or special times set aside where only women will be using the facilities. Find out if this applies in your new university, if this is a concern for you.

Clothing

Many guidebooks will advise you to wear clothing that is appropriate to the culture you are in, so as to avoid standing out. This is valuable advice and you should make every effort to do so. Bear in mind, though, that you may not have the option of 'blending in' if you are in a culture where you are in a racial or ethnic minority. The kind of clothing you wear might affect how you are treated by men, especially in relation to sexual assumptions. Strategize about how you can negotiate this.

I'm from Saudi Arabia. I spent a year in the US. I thought that it would be a year where I could learn about a new culture and have some fun, make some friends. But it was not long after 9/11. I don't know if people thought I was a terrorist; I think that they thought that terrorists were men. But they made so many assumptions about what I thought and what I believed. I found it hard to make friends, sometimes, and it was tiring constantly being stereotyped. It wasn't really the time I had hoped it would be.

Adara, a female student from Saudi Arabia, in a specialized English-language programme in the US

Body language

Body language is culturally encoded. Be conscious of how your body language is being read, and how it differs from that of those around you. Bear in mind that body language is frequently read in sexual terms, so be careful about what you are communicating. Smiling, laughing and physical contact might be read as flirtatious even if that is not what you mean. In some cultures, body language is related to social status and indicates respect. Eye contact is another aspect of body language which will be read according to cultural social practices. Take the time to learn and observe what it means.

Dating

Ask someone from the local culture you can trust about dating 'rules' and etiquette before you date. Expectations, assumptions and etiquette differ enormously from culture to culture.

Sexual health

Review the guidelines and tips in the 'Staying Healthy' chapter, including protecting yourself against 'rape drugs', sexual diseases and unwanted pregnancy.

Heads up

Be cautious of the reliability of the birth control pill while abroad. There are a number of things that can affect the effectiveness of the pill, including having diarrhoea and taking antibiotics. When you are abroad, you may be at increased risk for either of these situations. We know more than one child who has come into the world as a result of the pill's effectiveness being affected by a 'travel bug'. Make sure you have back-up contraception with you.

If you do get pregnant, bear in mind that most airlines have restrictions about pregnant women travelling after a certain period of time, so make sure that you fly home well ahead of time so that you don't unwittingly get trapped in your new country.

Sometimes the stress of being in a new environment can cause you to stop menstruating temporarily. This can be confused with the first signs of pregnancy. Take a pregnancy test if you have any doubts. In some places, pregnancy tests are widely available, and you might have access to the 'morning-after' pill, if you want it. In other places, you will have to see a doctor.

Heads up

Bear in mind that in some places, some forms of family planning might not be available to you, or may only be available if you can prove that you are married. Larger cities are more likely to have doctors who will be able to help you. In some places, contraception is illegal – research this before you go and make plans accordingly.

● **Further resources**

● *IIE Study Abroad: A Guide for Women* (The Institute for International Education).
www.iie.org
A comprehensive guide for women studying abroad, including pre-departure, interviews, overcoming barriers and accessing information.

- Thalia Zepatos, *A Journey of One's Own: Uncommon Advice for the Independent Woman Traveler* (Eighth Mountain Press, 2003).
  A practical guide to travel for women.
- Elaine Lee, *Go Girl! The Black Woman's Book of Travel and Adventure* (Eighth Mountain Press, 1997).
  A collection of stories from black women travelers.
- Journey Woman.
  www.journeywoman.com
    An online travel resource for women. Includes personal stories and advice columns, as well as advice on traveling with children.
- Women Travel Tips.
  www.womentraveltips.com/
    A site devoted to travel for women, including safety tips and information on travelling with family and friends.

Religion

Studying abroad can be a wonderful opportunity to learn about religions other than your own, or to go to places where you can learn more about the history of your own religion. Since religion is often at the heart of a culture's history, values and social relationships, whether overtly or in more subtle ways, any exposure to a new culture is likely to open you to religious diversity and difference. You may find that you practise a different religion from the majority of people in your new country, or simply that it plays a much more important, or less important, role in daily life than you are used to.

Anticipating your needs

Depending on your religion and what it means to you, and the religion of your destination country, you may find that religious considerations will affect the decisions you make as you explore your options.

Questions to consider include:

- Are you willing to be in a culture which has very different religious values from your own?
- What are your expectations and needs surrounding your religious practice (including access to places of worship, access to religious leaders/teachers, access to the religious community, recognition of religious holidays)?

- Are you willing to be involved in the religious practices of other religions? (In some places, religion forms the backbone of people's social lives and leisure activities.)
- What kinds of changes are you willing to make in order to fit in with the local religion (for example, wearing certain clothes)? What are you not willing to change?

Learning about your new environment

There are some places where religious difference might just make you feel uncomfortable, but there are others where religious tension is such that you may be physically at risk for practising a particular religion or even for coming from an ethnic background or country where your religion is practised, especially in places where civil wars are being fought over religion. Considering religion in your decisions about studying abroad is not only about your own practice, but also understanding how your religion might be perceived by those around you.

Questions to consider include:

- Will you be able to practise your religion as you choose? What are the opportunities and limitations on this in your new country?
- Does the university have student groups or associations for members of your religion? Are there groups within the wider community?
- Will you be welcome to join in activities associated with the local religion? Will you be isolated if you choose not to?

Heads up

Try to find out what the social scene is like in your programme. Social scenes which revolve around long nights at the pub drinking can be very alienating for students of a variety of religious groups which prohibit alcohol. If you find yourself in this situation, try organizing an alternative social event – you may be surprised how many people might be willing to do something different from the norm.

- Is there considerable religious diversity in the area you are going to? (Remember that there may be regional differences within the country you are going to.)

- What is the history of relationships between different religions in your new country? How does your own religion feature in this history?
- Has there been any recent conflict between members of your religion and those of other religions? What form has this conflict taken (intellectual discussion, physical violence, constitutional/legal cases)? (Consider, for example, the backlash against the 11 September terrorist attacks in the US, which has led to an increase in Islamophobia in otherwise racially and ethnically diverse communities.)
- What are the stereotypes surrounding members of your religion in relation to the dominant religion(s) in your new country?
- Do members of different religions generally live in different parts of the city/town you are going to?
- If your religion is the same as the dominant religion of your new country, what differences might you expect? (Remember that religions may be practised very differently, and that the doctrines of a religion may be interpreted very differently from place to place.)
- Are there any aspects of your identity which may be in conflict with the religious values of the place you are going to (for example, your marital status, your LGBT identity, your choice of clothes, your family structure, your politics)? What are the consequences for you if you hide these aspects of your identity, or if you do not hide them?

 There are always parties going on here and everyone is welcome. However, to be honest with you, if you belong to any other religion than Christianity you will find it difficult to find a temple or mosque for worship. In the UK there are many temples and even more mosques so if a person wants to worship there they can, but here I think it's difficult to find such places.

Alexander, British Muslim in Sweden

Strategies for negotiating potential issues

Find support on campus or in the wider community from people who have similar religious views to your own, if you are feeling isolated.

Learn as much as you can about the local religion(s), in order to understand the reasons for some of the differences that emerge. Find ways of

> ### Heads up
>
> You may find that your priorities or your values are in conflict with the religious assumptions around you (for example, such things as marital status, the size of the average family, or the role of women often have religious roots) and you may face anything from curiosity and surprise to hostility in your new country if your situation differs from the local norm. Try to avoid being defensive, and take the opportunity to learn more about the values of your host country. You will probably quickly develop strategies for negotiating conversations about these issues. It might help to talk to others in a similar situation (such as other international students), to find out what strategies have worked for them.

acknowledging/celebrating your own religious holidays. If you feel comfortable, participate in the celebrations of local religious holidays as appropriate. Many religious festivals have a strong community and cultural component which can be enjoyed even by those who do not practise the religion.

If you find that your religious practice creates a scheduling conflict with your academic work (for example, if you are supposed to be in class during prayer times, or to sit an exam on a religious holiday), find out what your rights are (many universities specify in their charter of student rights that you are entitled to religious accommodations). Approach your teachers and explain the difficulty you have or, if you prefer, approach the equity office and ask for advice on how to proceed.

If you find that your religious background is getting in the way of your academic work (for example, students of English literature are often expected to know the stories of the Christian bible and therefore recognize allusions in other texts, which often puts non-Christian students at a disadvantage), raise the concern with your teachers. It may be a good chance to learn more about your host culture. You may consider approaching the equity office if you feel that you are being unfairly penalized for your religious background in academic assessment.

If you have particular dietary needs based on your religion, you will need to check whether this can be accommodated by your residential college; do this well in advance of your arrival. Explain your reasons and get the answer in writing. If you will be cooking for yourself, find out if you will be able to buy what you need in your local area (remembering that it might be costly).

Partners and families

Increasingly, students are studying abroad with their partner and/or children. Many of the benefits that you will get from studying abroad will apply to your family as well, and it can be a wonderful opportunity to spend time together learning about a new culture.

Anticipating your needs

Probably the most important aspect of studying abroad with a family is communication at each point of the process. Include a partner and children (if old enough) in the decision-making process, rather than presenting it as a *fait accompli*. Give them the chance to do their own research, to make suggestions and to get excited and enthusiastic. Find out about any particular concerns they may have.

Questions to consider include:

- If you are travelling to a country which operates in a language other than the one your children usually speak, do you want them to learn the local language or to be educated in their own language? If you have the option of enrolling them in a school where they speak their own language, what opportunities can you find to give them a chance to learn the new language?
- What can you do to prepare your children for the social, academic and linguistic challenges of the new country?
- Do your children have any particular needs?
- What does your family need in order to function well as a family?
- What kinds of child-care or schooling do you want for your child?

TIP Don't forget to make plans for what happens when you return from studying abroad, for child-care or schooling.

Learning about your new environment

There are a number of factors you will need to research as you plan to study abroad with a partner and/or children, ranging from the legal through to the practical. Questions to consider include:

- How do children fit into the social structure of your new community?

- What kinds of activities are children expected to be involved in (for example, going to school, working, looking after siblings or parents, and so on)?
- If you are travelling with a partner, what is your legal status? Does immigration require you to be married? Does it accept domestic partnerships? What kind of evidence is required?
- What is the legal status of your family? If you are travelling with step-children, foster children, or other 'non-traditional' family structures, check that you will be recognized as a family for such things as immigration laws and travel insurance. Bear in mind that having a different surname from your children might cause problems with Customs and Immigration in some places, and you will need to show proof of your parental status.
- What employment rights does your partner have? While you will have a student visa, your partner will need the right to work (if he/she wants to). Check whether there are any limitations on this – are there restrictions on what field he/she may work in? Are there time limits? What do you need to do to get this authorization? How long will it take?

TIP Leave plenty of time to organize all the paperwork for your family. It can take some time.

- Where will your children go to day-care or school?
- Are there university resources that can help you to settle in with your children and partner?
- Will you be living in a safe neighbourhood for children? What might the concerns be? How can you prepare them for this?
- Do they have particular needs that must be considered when choosing a school? Will these be able to be met?
- Are there day-care facilities on campus? (Remember that costs can be high, and waiting lists long.)

Heads up

If you do not have confirmed long-term housing for your family, one of you should travel ahead of time to organize accommodation. It can take some time to find appropriate housing, and temporary accommodation can get very expensive, as well as being very stressful for a family.

● If you have children, it will be more important to research the neighbouhood ahead of time. Does it have access to schools? Playgrounds? Libraries? Is it safe? Are there other children around?

TIP Go back through the questions throughout this book, this time answering them from the point-of-view of your children.

● What will be the effect of the time away on their schooling? What is the best time of year to go to allow the children to adjust quickly? How long should you stay so that the children can finish a school term or year? Do they have any special needs?
● What health issues will you need to consider (for example, immunizations prior to leaving)?

Heads up

Bear in mind that your children might be legally required to have certain immunizations in order to be admitted to the country, and to be allowed to go to day-care, or to go to school.

If there are factors in your family situation that may lead to forms of discrimination in your new country, bear in mind that your children will also have to deal with the discrimination. Do they have the maturity to negotiate it? Do they have the language skills they will need? How will you support them?

Heads up

If your family is mixed-race, you may find some additional challenges in some parts of the world. In some places, mixed-race relationships are taboo, and you may suffer discrimination as a result. Find out, ahead of time, how you will be received and how you might negotiate these challenges.

Strategies for negotiating potential issues

Remember that children might not be able to conceptualize or imagine their new life in another country before they leave, and so they might be more subject to culture shock when they arrive. On the other hand, many children adapt very quickly, often better than adults. Bear in mind that a child's experience might be very different from your own, and make sure you take the time to find out what they are experiencing. Bear in mind that if they know that you are stressed, they may be reluctant to talk about their own challenges.

Talk about your own culture shock with your children, and help them to strategize ways they can negotiate it themselves, both before you leave and while abroad.

Heads up

If you are travelling abroad with children in a context where they will be separated from their other parent, prepare for the emotional challenge of this, if they are not used to spending long periods of time away. You might also face challenges if the children are close to other family members, such as grandparents, aunts or uncles. Come up with some practical strategies for how they can keep in contact with your family while you are away. You might organize for close family members to come and visit you in your new home if you are there for long enough, so that they can be included in the experience and get to know your children in their new environment. Give your extended family and friends plenty of time to get used to the idea before you leave.

Make sure you travel with all of the relevant documentation for your children. This may include immigration documents, as well as health records and school records, and proof of parental status.

Talk to your doctor or travel health specialist about the particular challenges of travelling with children abroad to the country you are going to.

Contact the airline you are travelling on for advice on travelling with children, if they are young.

Make sure you have medical insurance for every member of your family. Make sure it includes provisions for repatriation in an emergency, and that all family members are included. If one member of the family needs medical care, it will probably affect the whole family so make sure you plan for this eventuality.

Plan well in advance for child-care and schools. Find out how to enrol, and how far in advance you will need to do this.

Try to get involved in local community events as a family, so that you can have fun and enjoy your new country. Your children might also need some modelling from you about dealing with cultural adjustment and making new friends. Find out if there are any programmes on campus for families – these can be a great way to meet people and to save money.

> **Heads up**
>
> Many campuses will have some kind of family-care office, which will offer resources and information on being a student parent, as well as on looking after elderly parents, if that is a challenge you also face. Take advantage of whatever resources will help you, which may include family housing on campus.

Consider your partner's needs. You may find that you quickly make friends and settle into your university life, and your children may make friends quickly at school. Often, it is partners who become isolated. They may not have the same opportunities to practise the local language as you, and may have difficulties getting a job. Sometimes, they may be working in jobs which are not in their own field, or may find that their credentials are not recognized in your new country. If they do not work, they might easily become isolated. Plan in advance how your partner will be stimulated, how his/her social needs will be met, and make sure that you spend quality time together throughout the time you are studying abroad and discuss problems as they arise. Bear in mind that these issues can be exacerbated if your family is part of a marginalized community, or if there are language difficulties to overcome.

> **Heads up**
>
> Depending on the age of your children, be prepared for the possibility that that may not have a clear memory of your home country after being abroad for a period of time. This means that their new country may feel more like home to them than their old one, making them vulnerable to culture shock when they return. Finding ways of maintaining contact with your new country might be especially important in this case.

● Further resources

- Jane Wilson-Howarth and Matthew Ellis, *Your Child's Health Abroad: A Manual for Traveling Parents* (Bradt Travel Guides, 1998).
  A useful guide to health and safety while travelling with children.
- *A Moveable Marriage: Relocate Your Relationship without Breaking It* and Robin Pascoe, *Raising Global Nomads: Parenting Abroad in an On-Demand World* (Expatriate Press, 2003 and 2006).
  Potentially useful books discussing the challenges of balancing a marriage and raising children while working abroad.
- Karen C. McCluskey, *Notes from a Traveling Childhood: Readings for Internationally Mobile Parents and Children* (Foreign Service Youth Foundation, 1994).
  A guide to parenting children internationally, including interviews and case studies from a diversity of parents.
- Beverly Roman, *Footsteps Around the World: Relocation Tips for Teens* (Anchor Publishing, 2005).
  A useful guide for teenagers who are relocating, including discussion of the educational, emotional and practical components of moving.
- Ben Voegele, *We're Moving Where? An Adolescent's Guide to Overseas Living* (American Book Publishing, 2004).
  Aimed at young teenagers who are relocating abroad.

● Mature students

Mature-age students tend to be of two types. The first are students who have returned to study later in life, after having a career or children. The second are those who may not be mature students in their own country but find themselves older than the average student when they go abroad, owing to differences in education systems.

Everybody on campus was a fair bit younger than me. Sounds like a non-issue, but when you're studying in a small country town, it can become a little tedious at times.

Emma, Denmark to US

Strategies for negotiating potential issues

As a mature student, you might face more criticism before you study abroad from people who think you are 'too old'. Try to make contact with others who face similar challenges and find role models who have done what you want to do.

You may be ineligible for some sources of funding which are for younger students. Look for sources which do not specify age or which are specifically for 'non-traditional students'.

Highlight your strengths as a mature student on your scholarship and admission applications. Your experiences in your career, raising children or travelling might be significant assets to your proposed programme. Your maturity, greater insight and experience also give you the edge over younger applicants, so make sure you draw this to your committee's attention. Many universities have a mandate to support students who have taken an unconventional educational path.

Some challenges that mature-age students sometimes face include being in classes with students who are much younger, and potentially being excluded from social events or not enjoying the same social activities. Make the effort to get involved in activities which appeal to older students, both on campus and off-campus, in order to vary your social life, if this is a concern for you. There may be a social group for mature students on campus, as well.

Many mature students report that living with much younger students can be extremely frustrating. Consider choosing a form of housing which gives you contact with older students, such as a college which has post-graduate students as well as undergraduates, or living off campus.

I think it is VERY important to consider the age and maturity of students when they start university in your host country. If you are from Scandinavia and going, for instance, to the UK, you will find that people are a lot younger than you and have generally not lived away from home before. Unless you are very patient and don't mind being woken up in the middle of the night for the tenth night in a row, I strongly suggest that you find an apartment with one of two other people and stay away from student accommodation. It took me some time to find a way out of my lease with the university – find out what kind of place you will be living in before you accept a housing offer.

Katrine, a Scandinavian student in the UK

You may feel uncomfortable being surrounded by younger students in your classes, or being taught by teachers who are younger than you. Try to choose a programme which has a diverse student population. If there are a variety of ages, cultures, ethnicities, backgrounds and interests in your class, you are less likely to feel awkward. You will often have a perspective on course matter that your younger colleagues don't have, which can be invaluable in class discussions. If you can choose evening classes, this can be helpful – they are more likely to have other mature students in them.

Conclusion

If there is one piece of advice we can leave you with, it's

BE PREPARED TO CHANGE.

This applies to almost everything to do with study abroad. Be prepared to change your plans, your budgets, your goals, your intentions. Be prepared to change your opinions, your views, your outlook. Be prepared to change your perceptions of your new country, of your home country, and of your own capabilities and limitations. Be prepared to change how you see yourself in the world, and how you see others in relation to you.

We cannot guarantee you anything about your study abroad. A lot of it is what you make it, and the rest is a combination of good management and good luck. And that is really the most wonderful thing about studying abroad – your experience will be unique, and what you gain from it will also be as individual as you are. Take on board whatever suggestions in this book you find useful and build a strong team around you.

The rest is up to you. Good luck!

Index